Three Early Sufi Texts

Three Early Sufi Texts

A TREATISE ON THE HEART

Bayān al-Farq bayn al-Ṣadr wa-al-Qalb wa-al-Fu'ād wa-al-Lubb

ATTRIBUTED *to* AL-ḤAKĪM AL-TIRMIDHĪ (D. C. 300/912)
INTRODUCED *and* TRANSLATED *by* NICHOLAS HEER

STATIONS OF THE RIGHTEOUS

Darajāt al-ṣādiqīn

&

THE HUMBLE SUBMISSION OF THOSE ASPIRING

Kitāb bayān tadhallul al-fuqarā'

TWO TEXTS FROM THE PATH OF BLAME
by ABŪ ʿABD AL-RAḤMĀN AL-SULAMĪ AL-NAYSABŪRĪ (D. 412/1021)
INTRODUCED *and* TRANSLATED *by* KENNETH L. HONERKAMP

FONS VITAE

LOUISVILLE 2009

First published in 2003 by
Fons Vitae
49 Mockingbird Valley Drive
Louisville, KY 40207
http://www.fonsvitae.com

New and thoroughly revised edition published in 2009

Library of Congress Control Number: 2009927959

ISBN 9781891785375

This book was typeset by Neville Blakemore, Jr.

Printed in Canada

Other Related Fons Vitae Titles

Early Sufi Women, by Abū 'Abd ar-Raḥmān as-Sulamī, Translated by Rkia E. Cornell.

The Autobiography of a Moroccan Soufi: Aḥmad Ibn 'Ajība, Translated by Jean-Louis Michon and from the French by David Streight.

Al Ghazālī's *Faith in Divine Unity & Trust in Divine Providence*, Translated with an introduction by David B. Burrell.

Letters of Sufi Master: The Shaykh ad-Darqawi, Translated by Titus Burckhardt with a foreword by Martin Lings.

Me and Rumi: Autobiography of Shems of Tabrizi, Translated by William Chittick.

CONTENTS

Gnosis (*ma'rifah*) is a bounty which God gives to His servant when He opens for him the door of blessings and favor, beginning without the servant's being worthy of that and then granting him guidance until he believes that this is all from God, granted to him as a grace and a favor from Him Whom he is unable to thank except by means of His assistance. And this, again, is yet another favor to him from God.

From *A Treatise on the Heart*

Their [the *malāmī*] inner state blames their outward appearance on account of its complaisance in the world and its living according to the customs of the common folk. Their outward appearance blames their inner state for though it resides in proximity to divine Being, it ignores the duality of outer manifestation. Such are the states of the great masters of the Path.

From *Stations of the Righteous*

FOREWORD

The three Sufi texts published in this volume all deal with some aspect of the Sufi path to God. The Sufi path is marked by a number of different stages or stations (*maqām/maqāmāt*) which the Sufi traveller (*sālik*) passes through as he advances on the path. On his way the Sufi also experiences various psychological and emotional states (*ḥāl/aḥwāl*). These states differ from the stations through which the Sufi passes in that the states are transitory experiences granted to him by God and over which he has no control, whereas the stations are permanent stages on the path which he has achieved through his own individual effort.

The enumeration of these states and stations and discussions of the distinction between them may be found in such classical Sufi works as al-Kalābādhī's *Ta'arruf*, al-Sarrāj's *Luma'*, al-Qushayrī's *Risālah* and al-Hujwīrī's *Kashf al-Maḥjūb*. There are, however, considerable differences among these writers with respect to the enumeration and description of these stations and states. The existence of such differences should not be surprising since the descriptions of the stations and states found in these works are based on knowledge gained through interior Sufi experiences rather than on knowledge gained through the external senses.

The Sufi path to God, however, is not an easy one. The Sufi's progress along the path is hindered by the machinations of the self (*nafs*), that is, the ego-self or what is called in the Qur'ān the self that incites or exhorts to evil (*al-nafs al-ammārah bi-al-sū'*). In order to maintain his progress along the path to God the Sufi must be able to control the ego-self by disciplining it, and by continually blaming and abasing it.

Of the three Sufi works included in this volume, the first two, *Bayān al-Farq*, attributed to al-Ḥakīm al-Tirmidhī, and al-Sulamī's *Darajāt al-Ṣādiqīn*, deal primarily with the stations and states of the Sufi traveller on the path to God. The third, al-Sulamī's *Kitāb bayān tadhallul al-fuqarā'*, on the other hand, deals with the disciplining and abasement of the ego-self or self that incites to evil. We hope the publication of these three Sufi texts in English translation will contribute to a greater appreciation of Islam and its mystical aspects.

One who has not died does not see the resurrection except that he die, as the Messenger of God said: "When one dies, one's resurrection has arrived." Whoever dies, and the spirit of his self leaves and he is transported by his spirit from this world to the Hereafter, beholds the Hereafter and what is in it. Similarly one who has died in his [own] being, but is alive in his Protector knows that he himself does not control harm or benefit, or death or life, or resurrection. His heedlessness has been revealed to him, his resurrection has arrived, and he has become alive through his Lord, for God has embraced him, taken him under his protection as a friend, supported his heart, and revived it. He has seen by the light of the truth (*nūr al-ḥaqq*) what no one else has seen.

From *A Treatise on the Heart* (*Bayān al-Farq*)

A TREATISE ON THE HEART

Bayān al-Farq bayn al-Ṣadr wa-al-Qalb
wa-al-Fu'ād wa-al-Lubb

ATTRIBUTED *to* AL-ḤAKĪM AL-TIRMIDHĪ (D. *C.* 300/912)
INTRODUCED *and* TRANSLATED *by* NICHOLAS HEER

INTRODUCTION

This volume contains a revised version of my translation of *Bayān al-Farq bayn al-Ṣadr wa-al-Qalb wa-al-Fu'ād wa-al-Lubb*,[1] a Sufi work attributed to al-Ḥakīm al-Tirmidhī. My original translation of this work appeared in 1961 in four consecutive issues of *The Muslim World*.[2] The original Arabic manuscript of the work is in Dār al-Kutub al-Miṣrīyah in Cairo catalogued under *taṣawwuf* 367.[3] This is the only manuscript of the work known so far to exist and it was the basis of my editon of the Arabic text published in Cairo in 1958.[4] Although the manuscript itself attributes the work to Abū 'Abd Allāh Muḥammad ibn 'Alī [al-Ḥakīm] al-Tirmidhī, its attribution to him has been questioned by several scholars.[5] Regardless of the true identity of its author, the work is nevertheless of considerable interest not only because of its precise and detailed description of the heart and the elements which compose it, but also for its compelling descriptions of the Sufi experience of God.

⋆ ⋆ ⋆

Al-Ḥakīm al-Tirmidhī flourished in Khurasan and Transoxiana during the third Islamic century. He is mentioned in most of the Arabic and Persian biographical sources,[6] but these contain little information concerning his life other than the names of his teachers and disciples and some of his more important works. No date is given for his birth, and various dates ranging from 255/869 to 320/932 are given for his death.[7]

His autobiography, *Bad' Sha'n Abī 'Abd Allāh*,[8] is concerned for the most part with the dreams of his wife and provides only scanty information on al-Tirmidhī himself. From it we learn that he began his studies when he was eight years old and that these studies included the science of traditions (*'ilm al-āthār*) and the science of opinion (*'ilm al-ra'y*).[9] At the age of 27 he made the pilgrimage to Mecca and on the way spent some time in Iraq collecting traditions.

After arriving in Mecca he was able to achieve true repentance and prayed to God that He preserve him from attachment to this world. While still there he was taken with a strong desire to memorize the Qur'ān and was able to make a beginning in it on his way home. Upon his return he sought someone to guide him along the path of righteousness, but was unsuccessful until he heard of the people of gnosis (*ahl al-ma'rifah*) and discovered a book by a certain al-Anṭākī from which he learned something of the disciplining of the self (*riyāḍat al-nafs*). During this period he spent long hours alone in the desert and soon began to experience various visions and revelations.

Al-Tirmidhī next tells of his passing through a period of trial and affliction, during which he was falsely accused of holding heretical doctrines, of claiming prophecy, discoursing about love, and corrupting the people. The accusations were brought before the *walī* of Balkh, who ordered him to cease his talk about love. Al-Tirmidhī maintains, however, that this period of trial served only to purify his heart and to discipline his self. He later relates that, owing to a disturbance which broke out in the land, all of his accusers were forced to flee. He also mentions that he once studied the use of the astrolab. The only date recorded in the autobiography is that of ten days before the end of Dhū al-Qa'dah of the year 269/883, the date of one of his wife's dreams.

Al-Tirmidhī was a prolific writer and some sixty titles are ascribed to him. Most of these have survived as manuscripts and many of them have now been edited and printed.[10]

★ ★ ★

Bayān al-Farq, the work here translated, presents a Sufi psychological system concerned with the interaction of the heart (*qalb*) and the self (*nafs*). As will be noticed, the basic elements of the system and the concepts and terms used are all derived from the Qur'ān and the traditions (*ḥadīth*) of the Prophet. Their arrangement into a fairly coherent system, however, is the result of the author's own creative thought.

In this system the heart is described as consisting of four parts or stations (*maqāmāt*). These are the breast (*ṣadr*), the heart proper (*qalb*), the inner heart (*fu'ād*), and the intellect (*lubb*). They are arranged in concentric spheres, the breast being the outermost sphere followed on the inside by the heart, the inner heart and finally the intellect. Within the intellect are yet other stations which, however, are too subtle to be described by words.[11]

Each of these stations of the heart has its own characteristics and functions. Thus the breast (*ṣadr*) is the abode or seat of the light of Islam (*nūr al-islām*). It is also the repository for that kind of knowledge (*'ilm*) required for the practice of Islam, such as knowledge of the Qur'ān, the Prophetic traditions and the religious law (*sharī'ah*).

The heart proper (*qalb*), which is within the breast, is the abode of the light of faith (*nūr al-īmān*). Faith is the acceptance by the heart of the truth of God's revelation. The heart is also the repository of what the author calls valuable or useful knowledge (*al-'ilm al-nāfi'*). This is an inward knowledge of reality that can only be granted to one by God. It cannot be learned from books or from a teacher as can the type of knowledge associated with the breast.

The inner heart (*fu'ād*) is the abode of the light of gnosis (*nūr al-ma'rifah*). It is associated with the vision (*ru'yah*) of reality. Whereas the heart has mere knowledge of reality, the inner heart actually sees reality.

The intellect (*lubb*), the innermost sphere of the heart, is the abode of the light of unification (*nūr al-tawḥīd*). It is the basis of the three outer spheres and is the recipient of God's grace and bounty.

Each of these four stations of the heart is associated with one of the four spiritual stages of the Sufi path. Thus the breast and the light of Islam within it correspond to the first stage, that of the Muslim. The heart proper and light of faith correspond to the believer (*mu'min*), the inner heart and the light of gnosis to the gnostic (*'ārif*), and the intellect and light of unification to the highest stage, that of the unitarian (*muwaḥḥid*).

The self (*nafs*), on the other hand, is not a part of the heart but a separate entity in the stomach. It is like a hot smoke and is the source of evil desires and passions. When these passions are not kept in check through spiritual disciplines, they escape from the self and enter into the breast filling it with smoke. The light of faith in the heart is obscured by this smoke and can no longer illuminate the breast. The breast, in turn, being deprived of this illumination, is no longer able to perform its proper functions and becomes subject to the authority of the self. The self, however, is powerless to affect the heart, and the light of faith within it remains firm and constant even when obscured by the dark passions which have entered into the breast.

Through discipline (*riyāḍah*), however, the self may be brought under control and made to pass through four stages corresponding to the four stages of the spiritual development of the Sufi. Thus the self which exhorts to evil (*al-nafs al-ammārah bi-al-sū'*) is the yet undisciplined self and is related to the stage of the Muslim. The inspired self (*al-nafs al-mulhamah*) is somewhat less evil and corresponds to the stage of the believer (*mu'min*). The blaming self (*al-nafs al-lawwāmah*) is the self of the gnostic (*'ārif*), and the tranquil self (*al-nafs al-muṭma'innah*) is that of the unitarian (*muwaḥḥid*).

The main elements of the system can be summarized in the following table:

Breast (*ṣadr*)	Heart (*qalb*)	Inner Heart (*fu'ād*)	Intellect (*lubb*)
light of Islam (*nūr al-islām*)	light of faith (*nūr al-īmān*)	light of gnosis (*nūr al-ma'rifah*)	light of unification (*nūr al-tawḥīd*)
Muslim (*muslim*)	believer (*mu'min*)	gnostic (*'ārif*)	unitarian (*muwaḥḥid*)
knowledge of *sharī'ah*	inward knowledge	vision (*ru'yah*)	God's grace and bounty
self which exhorts to evil (*al-nafs al-ammārah*)	inspired self (*al-nafs al-mulhamah*)	blaming self (*al-nafs al-lawwāmah*)	tranquil self (*al-nafs al-muṭma'innah*)

* * *

As in the original translation, I have placed square brackets around all words and phrases which have been added in the translation to clarify the meaning of the Arabic text. The page numbers of the Arabic edition of the text have also been inserted within square brackets.

The Qur'ānic verses have been identified in the notes with the help of Muḥammad Fu'ād 'Abd al-Bāqī's *al-Mu'jam al-Mufahras li-Alfāẓ al-Qur'ān al-Karīm*. The translations of the verses are based primarily on the English version of Mohammed Marmaduke Pickthall,[12] but I have also at times followed the translation of A. J. Arberry[13] and have sometimes made my own translations in order to render a verse consistent with my translation of the author's text. The numbering of the verses in the Qur'ānic references in the footnotes is that of the Egyptian edition of 1342.[14] When this numbering differs from the numbering in the Pickthall translation, Pickthall's numbering has been given in parentheses.

In the footnotes I have attempted to identify all of the Prophetic traditions quoted in the text. Traditions contained in any of the nine canonical collections were identified with Sakhr Software's cdrom *Mawsū'at al-Ḥadīth al-Sharīf*. These traditions can also be searched for and found online at one of Sakhr's web sites, http://hadith.ajeeb.com or http://www.ajeeb.com. I have also made use Wensinck's *Concordance et Indices de la Tradition Musulmane*. The identifying numbers of the individual traditions are those of Sakhr. I have been able to find some of the non-canonical traditions in al-Muttaqī's *Kanz al-'Ummāl fī Sunan al-Aqwāl wa-al-Af'āl*. The identifying numbers of these traditions are those of the Hyderabad edition of 1312-1314.

In revising the original English translation of the text it became evident to me that certain revisions to the Arabic edition were also called for. As I pointed out in the introductions to both the Arabic edition and the original English translation, the Arabic manuscript of the work is carelessly written and full of mistakes. Some of the mistakes are obvious, others not so obvious. I was able to correct many of these mistakes in my edition of the Arabic text, but others have become obvious to me only in the course of preparing this new translation. I have therefore made some additional revisions to the Arabic text and they have been incorporated into this translation. These revisions are listed at the end of the book.

* * *

Many people have contributed in one way or another to the publication of this volume. I am indebted to them all.

Professor A.J. Arberry first introduced me to the Arabic text of *Bayān al-Farq* in 1953 when I was a visiting graduate student at Cambridge University. Over a period of several months he read the entire text with me from a photocopy that Jean Watson, assistant keeper at the India Office Library in London, had allowed me to borrow for use in Cambridge.

The next year when I returned to Princeton and had decided to submit an edition and translation of the work as my doctoral dissertation, 'Abduh 'Abd al-Raḥmān al-Khawlī, a fellow graduate student, helped me to solve a number of problems in deciphering the Arabic manuscript. Professor Farhat Ziadeh, as chairman of my dissertation committee read both the Arabic edition and the translation and made many valuable suggestions for improvement.

Later when I was in Cairo in 1958 Nūr al-Dīn Shuraybah assisted me in preparing the Arabic text for publication, and in 1961 Elmer Douglas kindly offered to publish the English translation in four consecutive issues of *The Muslim World*, of which he was then the editor.

Farhat Ziadeh was again most helpful in the solution of some additional textual problems which arose in the course of revising the translation for the present volume. And Bernd Radtke graciously answered my questions to him in regard to the attribution of *Bayān al-Farq* to al-Tirmidhī. I am, of course, also indebted to Fons Vitae and in particular to Gray Henry and Neville Blakemore for making this work once again available to the general public.

Finally a few words must be said about the chain of events that led ultimately to the publication of this volume. On a trip to Pakistan in 1959 Nūr al-Dīn Shuraybah met Abdul Aziz, a Hindu convert to Islam who was passionately interested in Sufism. Abdul Aziz had either met or was in correspondence with many of the prominent Orientalist scholars of the time, among whom were Louis Massignon, Serge de Beaurecueil, Ahmet Ateş, and Annemarie Schimmel. Shuraybah mentioned to Abdul Aziz that I had recently published an edition of *Bayān al-Farq*, and Abdul Aziz subsequently initiated a correspondence with me.

Abdul Aziz was also much interested in Christian mysticism, and in 1960 at the suggestion of Louis Massignon he wrote to Thomas Merton, the Cistercian monk at the Abbey of Gethsemane in Kentucky. Abdul Aziz and Merton continued to correspond with each other until Merton's death in 1968.[15] In 1962 after the publication of my original translation of *Bayān al-Farq* in *The Muslim World* I sent offprints of the translation to Abdul Aziz. He was so pleased with the work that he wrote to Elmer Douglas asking him to send a copy to Thomas Merton. Merton evidently found the work of great interest because after his death the copy which he had received from Elmer Douglas was found among his effects with many notes written in his own hand in the margins. It was Merton's annotated copy of *Bayān al-Farq* which attracted the attention of Gray Henry and Rob Baker to the work and prompted them not only to include an excerpt from it in their volume *Merton and Sufism: The Untold Story*,[16] but also to republish the whole work in the present volume.

بسم الله الرحمن الرحيم رب يسر واعن

قال ابو عبد الله محمد بن علي الترمذي اما بعد فان بعض
اهل العلم والفقه سألني عن بيان الفرق بين الصدر
والقلب والفؤاد واللب وما وراءها من الشغاف
ومواضع العلوم واحببت ان اشرح له بتوفيق الله تعالى
اذ هو ميسر كل خير وبه استعين اعلم ان ذكر القلب
فيها في الدين ان اسم القلب اسم جامع يقتضي اسماء ومقامات
الباطن كلها وفي الباطن مواضع شتى من خارج القلب ومنها
ما هي داخل القلب فاشبه اسم القلب اسم العين اذ
العين اسم يجمع بين الشفرين من البياض والسواد والحدقة
والنور الذي في الحدقة وكل واحد من هذه الاشياء له حكم
على حدة ومعنى غير معنى صاحبه الا ان بعضها معاونة لبعض
ومنافع بعضها متصلة ببعض وكل ما هو خارج فهو اساس
الذي يليه من الداخل وقوام النور بقوامهن وكذلك
اسم الدار اسم جامع لما يحفظ بحيطانها من الباب والدهليز
وصحنها وفي بيوتها وما فيها من المخدع والخزانة وكل مكان
وموضع فيها له حكم غير حكم صاحبه وكذلك اسم الحرم اسم
جامع للحرم من حوالي مكة والبلد والمسجد والبيت العتيق
وفي كل موضع مناسك غير ما يكون في الموضع الآخر
وكذلك اسم القنديل اسم جامع للزجاجة وفي القنديل موضع
الماء غير موضع الفتيلة وموضع الفتيلة غير موضع الماء

Folio 1b of the MS of *Bayān al-Farq*.

وهو داخل موضع الماء والفتيلة هي التي يكون فيها النور
وهي موضع الفتيلة والدهن ليس فيه ماء ولا يصلح
من الاشياء كلها اذا نقص منها واحد فسد ما سواه و
كذلك اسم اللوز اسم جامع للقشر الخارج الذي فوق
القشر الصلب والقشر الثاني الذي هو مثل العظم والمخ
واللب الذي فيه والدهن الذي في داخل اللب فاعلم
زادك الله فقها في الدين ان لهذا الدين اعلاما ومنار
ولاهله فيه مراتب واهل العلم فيه على درجات قال الله
تعالى ورفعنا بعضهم فوق بعض درجات وقال وفوق
كل ذي علم عليم وكل علم هو ارفع موضعه في القلب
في موضع هو اكن واحص واحرز واخفى واستر وهي
ذكر اسم القلب ينوب عن ذكر ساير المقامات عند عامة
الناس ولكن الصدر في القلب هو المقام من القلب
بمنزلة بياض العين في العين ومثل صحن الدار في الدار
ومثل الذي يحوط بمكة ومثل موضع الماء في القنديل ومثل
القشر الاعلى من اللوز الذي يخرج اللوز منه اذا يبس
في الشجر فهذا الصدر موضع دخول الوسواس والآفات
كما يصيب بياض العين آفة البثور وهيجان العرق
وساير علل الرمد وكما يوضع في صحن الدار من الحطب
والقماشات ويدخل فيها كل احد من الاجانب احيانا
وكما يدخل السباع والبهايم في ساحة الحوم وكما يقع

Folio 2a of the MS of *Bayān al-Farq*.

A TREATISE ON THE HEART

[33] In the Name of God, the Merciful, the Compassionate. My Lord, facilitate [this task for me] and assist [me in it].

Abū ʻAbd Allāh Muḥammad ibn ʻAlī al-Tirmidhī said: One of the people of learning (*ʻilm*) and understanding (*fiqh*) has asked me to explain the difference between the breast (*ṣadr*), the heart (*qalb*), the inner heart (*fu'ād*), and the intellect (*lubb*), and what is beyond them within the pericardium (*shaghāf*), as well as the places of knowledge (*mawāḍiʻ al-ʻulūm*). I should like to explain [this difference] to him with the help of God, for He is the facilitator of all that is difficult, and it is from Him that I seek help.

[Part One: The Stations of the Heart]

Know, may God increase your understanding in religion, that the term "heart" (*qalb*) is a comprehensive term and necessarily includes [in its meaning] all the interior stations (*maqāmāt al-bāṭin*), for in the interior [of man] there are places that are outside the heart and others that are within it. The word "heart" is similar to the word "eye" (*ʻayn*), since "eye" includes [in its meaning] that which lies between the two eyelashes, such as the white and black [parts] of the eye, the pupil, and the light within the pupil. Each of these entities has a separate nature (*ḥukm*) and a meaning different from that of the others. Nevertheless, some of them assist some of the others, and the benefits of some are connected with some of the others. Moreover, each one on the outside is the basis of that which follows it on the inside. Thus the subsistence of the light [of the pupil] depends on the subsistence of the other [entities of the eye].

Similarly the word "homestead" (*dār*) is a comprehensive term for what is contained within its walls, such as the gate, the corridor, the courtyard in the midst of its buildings, as well as what is within these buildings such as the closet and storeroom. [34] Every place and position in it has its own nature different from that of its neighbor.

Likewise, the word "*ḥaram*" is a term which includes the sacred area around Mecca,[1] as well as the city, the mosque, and the Ancient House (*al-bayt al-ʻatīq*);[2] and in each of these places there are stations (*manāsik*) [of the pilgrimage] different from those in the others.

Again, the word "lamp" (*qindīl*) is a term which includes the lamp-glass [and the other parts of the lamp]. In the lamp the position of the water is different from that of the wick, and the position of the wick is different from that of the water, since the position of the wick is within the position of the water. Moreover, it is the wick which contains the light, and in the position of the wick there is oil, which has no water in it. Thus the soundness of the lamp depends on the soundness of all of these things, and if one of them is missing, the others become unsound.

Similarly the word "almond" (*lawz*) is a term which includes the outer shell, which is above the hard shell, and this second shell itself, which is like bone, as well as the nut or kernel within this shell, and the oil which is within the kernel.

Know, may God increase your understanding in religion, that this religion possesses guideposts and way stations, that its people are in [various] ranks, and that the people of learning (*ahl al-ʿilm*) in it are in [various] grades. God said: *And we have raised some of them above others in grades.*[3] He also said: *And over every lord of knowledge there is one more knowing.*[4] Thus, as a science is more elevated, its position in the heart is more secret, more special, more guarded, more concealed, and more veiled. Nevertheless, among the common people, mention of the word "heart" takes the place of the mention of all of its other stations (*maqāmāt*).

[35] The breast (*ṣadr*), in the heart, is that station (*maqām*) of the heart that corresponds to the white of the eye in the eye, to the courtyard in the homestead, to [the sacred area] that surrounds Mecca, to the position of the water in the lamp, and to the upper shell of the almond out of which the almond itself emerges if it dries on the tree.

The breast is the place of entry for evil whispering (*waswās*) and afflictions (*āfāt*), just as the white of the eye can be blemished by the affliction of pustules, inflammation of the vein, and all the other illnesses of ophthalmia (*ʿilal al-ramad*). In like manner, firewood and refuse are put in the courtyard of the homestead, and all sorts of strangers enter it from time to time. Likewise predatory animals and beasts enter into the open space of the *ḥaram*, and moths and other [insects] fall into the water of the lamp, for although there is oil above the water, the lowest position [in the lamp] is that of the water. Similarly insects, gnats, and flies crawl into the outer covering of the almond if it splits open until even small vermin enter into it.

That which enters into the breast is seldom felt at the time. The breast is the place of entry for rancor (*ghill*), passions (*shahawāt*), desires (*munā*), and wants (*ḥājāt*). At times it contracts and at other times it expands. It is also the place in which the self which exhorts to evil (*al-nafs al-ammārah bi-al-sū'*) exerts its authority, for the self has an entry into the breast where it burdens itself with matters, becomes proud and manifests power on its own. The breast is also the seat of the light of Islam (*nūr al-islām*), as well as the place for the retention of knowledge that is heard (*al-'ilm al-masmū'*) and must be learned, such as the legal rulings (*aḥkām*) and [Prophetic] traditions (*akhbār*) and all [36] that which can be expressed with the tongue, for the first cause of attaining to it is study and listening [to a teacher].

The breast was so named because it is the first part (*ṣadr*) of the heart and its first station (*maqām*), just as the *ṣadr* of the day is its beginning, or as the courtyard of the homestead is the first place in it. From it emerge tempting desires (*wasāwis al-ḥawā'ij*); and distracting thoughts (*fikar al-ashghāl*) emerge from it into the heart also if they become established over a long period.

The heart proper (*qalb*) is the second station. It is within the breast and is like the black of the eye within the eye, whereas the breast is like the white. The heart is also like the city of Mecca inside the sacred area [which surrounds it], like the place of the wick in the lamp, or the house within the homestead, or the almond inside the outer covering.

The heart is the abode (*ma'din*) of the light of faith (*nūr al-īmān*) and the lights of submission (*khushū'*), piety (*taqwā*), love (*maḥabbah*), contentment (*riḍā'*), certainty (*yaqīn*), fear (*khawf*), hope (*rajā'*), patience (*ṣabr*), and satisfaction (*qanā'ah*). It is the abode of the principles of knowledge (*uṣūl al-'ilm*), for it is like a spring of water, and the breast is like its pool, and just as the water flows out of the spring into the pool, so also knowledge emerges from the heart into the breast. Knowledge, however, also enters the breast through [the sense of] hearing (*sam'*). From the heart arise certainty (*yaqīn*), knowledge (*'ilm*), and intention (*nīyah*), which then enter into the breast, for the heart is the root (*aṣl*) and the breast is the branch (*far'*). And the branch becomes firm only through the root.

The Messenger of God said: [37] "Deeds are only according to intentions,"[5] and explained that the value of a deed performed by the self (*nafs*) increases according to the intention of the heart. Thus a good deed is compounded [in value] commensurate with the intention. Action pertains to the self; and the limit of the authority of the self is only as far as the breast in accord with the intention of the heart and its authority. The heart, however, owing to God's mercy, is not in the hand of the self, for the heart is the king and the self is [his] kingdom. The Messenger of God said: "The two hands are two wings [of an army], the two feet are couriers, the two eyes are an armed band of scouts, the two ears are punishment, the liver is mercy, the spleen is laughter, the two kidneys are cunning and the lung is subterfuge. Thus if the king is virtuous, his troops are also virtuous, and if the king is corrupt, so also are his troops corrupt."[6] The Messenger of God thus explained that the heart is a king, and that the breast is to the heart as the field is to the horseman.

He pointed out that the soundness of the organs [of the body] depends on the soundness of the heart and that their corruption results from the corruption of the heart. The heart is like a wick, and the soundness of the wick [is determined by] its light, and that light, [with respect to the heart], is the light of piety (*tuqā*) and certainty (*yaqīn*), for if the heart lacked this light it would be as a lamp the light of whose wick has gone out. No act which comes from the self, without [the participation] of the heart, is taken into account in the judgment of the Hereafter, nor is the doer of such an act taken to task should it be an act of disobedience, or rewarded should it be an act of obedience. God said: *But He will take you to task for that which your hearts have garnered.*[7]

[38] The likeness of the inner heart (*fu'ād*), which is the third station within the heart, is as the likeness of the pupil in the black part of the eye, of the Sacred Mosque (*al-masjid al-ḥarām*) in Mecca, of the closet or store-room in the house, of the wick in its position in the middle of the lamp, and of the kernel within the almond. This inner heart is the seat of gnosis (*ma'rifah*), passing thoughts (*khawāṭir*), and vision (*ru'yah*). Whenever a man benefits, his inner heart benefits first, then the heart. The inner heart is in the middle of the heart proper (*qalb*), which, in turn, is in the middle of the breast, just as the pearl is within the oyster shell.

The likeness of the intellect (*lubb*) within the inner heart (*fu'ād*) is as the likeness of the light of vision in the eye, of the light of the lamp in the light's wick, and of the fat hidden within the kernel of the almond. Each one of these outer entities is a shield and covering for that which follows it on the inside. Each resembles the others, for they are similar entities working together and close in meaning one to the other. They are in agreement rather than in conflict, since they are the lights of religion (*anwār al-dīn*), and religion is one, even though the ranks of its people are different and varied. The intellect is the seat of the light of unification (*nūr al-tawḥīd*) as well as the light of uniqueness (*nūr al-tafrīd*), and this is the most perfect light and the greatest power.

Beyond this there are other subtle stations (*maqāmāt laṭīfah*), noble places (*amkinah sharīfah*), and elegant subtleties (*laṭā'if ẓarīfah*). The root of them all, however, is the light of unification (*nūr al-tawḥīd*), for unification is a secret (*sirr*) and gnosis is a bounty (*birr*). Faith (*īmān*) is the safeguarding of [39] the secret and the contemplation (*mushāhadah*)[8] of the bounty. Islam is thanksgiving (*shukr*) for the bounty and surrendering the heart to the secret, for unification is a secret [to which] God guides and directs His servant, for he could not comprehend it with his faculty of reason (*'aql*) were it not for God's support and guidance of him.

Gnosis (*ma'rifah*) is a bounty which God gives to His servant when He opens for him the door of blessings and favor, beginning without the servant's being worthy of that and then granting him guidance until he believes that this is all from God, granted to him as a grace and a favor from Him Whom he is unable to thank except by means of His assistance. And this, again, is yet another favor to him from God.

Thus he contemplates the bounty of God and guards His secret (*sirr*), for He is the grantor of assistance. The servant does not comprehend the modality (*kayfīyah*) of His lordship (*rubūbīyah*). However, he knows that He is one and avoids assimilation (*tashbīh*),[9] nullification (*ta'ṭīl*),[10] attributing to Him a modality (*takyīf*), and making Him unjust (*tajnīf*). This, then, is faith, which contemplates [God's] bounty and guards [His] secret.

Islam, however, is the employment of the self (*nafs*) in devotion to God through obedience to Him with thanksgiving and uprightness and the surrender of lordship (*rubūbīyah*) to Him. It is turning away from the comprehension of the secret and turning toward servanthood (*'ubūdīyah*) and persevering in that which brings one closer to Him. This is because Islam is practised only through the self, and the self is blind to the comprehension of the truth (*ḥaqq*) and the contemplation of it.

Moreover, the self is not obligated to comprehend realities (*ḥaqā'iq*). Do you not see that the servant of God was commanded to have faith in the heart but was not obligated to comprehend what he believes in with respect to modality (*kayfīyah*)? His duty is only to follow and to flee from innovation (*ibtidā'*). Surrender alone is sufficient for the self.

[40] The ineffable stations (*al-maqāmāt al-maskūt 'anhā*), which lie beyond those stations of which [we] have mentioned some, are discerned only by the servant of God who has been assisted [by God] to understand those stations [which we have] described with these well-known likenesses, for God helps His servant and assists him in understanding them. These stations, which are beyond those already mentioned, are like the increased purity of water should it remain [for a period] in the jar. By such likenesses is the way of the ineffable secret (*al-sirr al-maskūt 'anhu*) comprehended.

[Part Two: The Breast]

Indeed, the believer has been put to the test by the self (*nafs*) and its desires, for the self has been granted the power (*wilāyah*) and the task (*takalluf*) of entering into the breast. The abode of the self is in the stomach and the area of the waist. It becomes excited by the blood and by the power of impurity (*najāsah*), and the stomach thus becomes filled with the darkness of its smoke and the heat of its fire. The self thereupon enters into the breast with its evil whispering (*waswasah*) and base desires as a test by God of His servant, so that he seeks help of his Lord in his true destitution and lasting humility, and God answers him and averts from him its evil.

In the same way Satan (*al-Shayṭān*) also enters with his evil whispering (*waswasah*) into the breast of the servant of God, for he assumes authority [within the] limits of [the authority of] the self, for the self which exhorts to evil (*al-nafs al-ammārah bi-al-sū'*) is like Satan, and thus both [Satan and the self] are satans. God said: *Satans of humankind and jinn who inspire in one another plausible discourse through guile.*[1]

God had mercy on his believing servant in that He did not place his heart in the hand of his self. God through His mercy protects as a friend His servant and tests him [41] [by allowing] Satan's whispering to enter into his breast in order that He may teach him a little of the insignificance of his worth and show him his complete need [for God]. The verification of this is God's saying: *In order that He might test what is in your breasts,*[2] meaning that God is quite aware of the whisperings of Satan and the self,[3] *and purify what is in your hearts,*[4] which [means] the purity (*ṭahārah*) of the heart through the light of faith (*nūr al-īmān*). God also said: *Who whispereth in the breasts of mankind.*[5]

Know that expansion (*inshirāḥ*) and contraction (*ḍīq*) are attributed to the breast alone and are not attributed to the heart. God said: *So let there be no heaviness in thy breast therefrom,*[6] and: *A likely thing that thou wouldst forsake aught of that which hath been revealed unto thee, and that thy breast should be contracted for it,*[7] and: *Well know We that thy breast is at times contracted by what they say.*[8] God related of his interlocutor Moses that he said: *My Lord! Lo! I fear that they will deny me and that my breast will contract.*[9] Thus God attributed contraction to the breast.

Nevertheless, the contraction of the breast of the Prophet and the breast of Moses (*al-Kalīm*) was not due to the evil whispering which occurs to the generality of Muslims, because God has protected the prophets from the whispering of Satan and the contentions of selves (*munāza'āt al-nufūs*). However, [42] their breasts used to contract if they heard the unbelievers (*kuffār*) allude to an associate (*sharīk*) of God or [if the unbelievers] gave the lie to them when they mentioned God's oneness (*waḥdānīyah*).

Moreover, there is no limit to the contraction of the breast, should it contract, for everyone's breast contracts in proportion to his ignorance and anger. Likewise, there is no limit to the capacity of the breast, should it expand under the guidance of God. Thus if it contracts to the truth (*al-ḥaqq*), it expands to falsehood (*al-bāṭil*), and if it contracts to falsehood, it expands to the truth. Do you not heed what God mentioned to his Prophet: *Have We not caused thy breast to expand*?[10] God granted [him] the expansion of his breast through the lights of the truth of Islam (*anwār ḥaqq al-islām*) until it contracted to any capacity for falsehood.

The breast of the believer contracts sometimes from the abundance of evil whispering, or from sorrow, distraction, the succession of wants, and the occurence of accidents and calamities. The breast also contracts if the believer hears a falsehood which his heart cannot endure, for God has expanded his breast with the light of Islam *so that he followeth a light from his Lord.*[11]

As for the breast of the unbeliever (*kāfir*) and the hypocrite (*munāfiq*), it is filled with the darkness of unbelief (*kufr*), association (*shirk*),[12] and doubt (*shakk*), and has expanded to them, so that no place remains in it for the light of Islam. It has contracted to any capacity for the light of the truth (*nūr al-ḥaqq*) within it. God said: *But those whose breasts expand to unbelief, on them is wrath from God.*[13] He also said: *And whomsoever it is God's will to guide, He expandeth his breast to Islam and whomsoever it is His will to send astray* [43] *He maketh his breast contracted and narrow.*[14] Thus God made clear that the breast, if it becomes filled with the darkness of unbelief, contracts to any capacity for its opposites from among the lights.

The breast of the believer is also the abode of the light of Islam (*nūr al-islām*). Like the comprehensive words "eye," "*ḥaram*," "homestead," "lamp" and "almond," "Islam" is a comprehensive term for the religion of God, although He attributes it also to His servant, for the Prophet said: "Islam is declaration with the tongue, and action with the limbs, with acceptance of it as true through faith, and the contemplation (*mushāhadah*) of some of the works of the Merciful."[15]

Islam is thus a general term comprising faith (*īmān*), the declaration of it with the tongue, and action with the limbs. Moreover, Islam has both an outward (*ẓāhir*) and an inward (*bāṭin*) [aspect]. As for the outward [aspect], it is sometimes assumed by the hypocrite, who appears outwardly as one of the people of Islam although inwardly he is an unbeliever. God said: *The wandering Arabs say: We believe. Say: Ye believe not, but rather say: We have become Muslims.*[16] Thus God made clear that they did not yet believe, but that they had only become Muslims with their mouths, for their hearts did not believe.

As for the inward aspect of Islam, it is obedience to the Lord of mankind and the surrender of the self and the heart to those decrees (*aḥkām*) [of God] which befall one. God said: *Nay, but whosoever surrendereth his purpose to God while excelling* [in worship], *his reward is with his Lord.*[17] This is the Muslim truly, whose light of Islam resembles [44] the light of faith and the light of excellence (*nūr al-iḥsān*), so that all three act in concert, are interconnected, and resemble one another.

God said in the story of the prophets: *Lo! We did reveal the Torah, wherein is guidance and a light by which the prophets who surrendered unto God judged;*[18] and in the story of Abraham: *Then when they had both surrendered to God and he had flung him down upon his face.*[19] These are the elite of God (*khāṣṣat Allāh*), of whom He has demanded uprightness in accordance with the reality of Islam. They have freed themselves of their own power and strength and have surrendered unto God both their outward and inward [aspects].

The proof that Islam and faith are similar in meaning, even though their names are different, is God's saying: *And Moses said: O my people! If ye have faith in God then put trust in Him, if ye are indeed Muslims,*[20] and: *And when it is recited unto them, they say: We have faith in it. Lo! it is the truth from our Lord. Lo! even before it we were Muslims,*[21] and: *Then we brought forth such faithful as were there. But we found there but one house of Muslims.*[22]

Faith, both in the understanding of the common people and from the standpoint of the Sharīʿah,[23] is belief in the truth, acceptance of it with the heart, and the declaration with the tongue that it is true. Islam, on the other hand, is obedience of the heart and the self to the truth, advancement towards it, uprightness with respect to it, and avoidance of what is contrary to it.

[45] The breast is also the place of rancor (*ghill*) and transgression (*jināyah*), for the self, which is characterized by rancor and transgression, has authority to enter into the breast for the purpose of testing [the servant], as has been mentioned before. God said in describing the people of Paradise (*ahl al-jannah*): *And We remove whatever rancor may be in their breasts,*[24] so that they may enter Paradise without rancor.

The heart of the believer, however, is protected from rancor because it is the place of faith. Nevertheless, God ordered His servants to beseech Him and ask Him that He not put rancor into their hearts saying: *And place not in our hearts rancor toward those who believe.*[25] He desired that they beseech Him and fear Him, so that He might purify their hearts. He has not, however, guaranteed to protect their breasts from evil whispering, that they might recognize the grace of God upon them. He does, however, protect their hearts, so that they may seek of Him deliverance from the evil whisperings in their breasts and that they may increase in honor and nobility through God, should He purify and refine their hearts, and increase in humbleness in their selves.

God said: *And He will cure the breasts of folk who are believers. And He will remove the anger of their hearts.*[26] Thus God made clear that the cure is for the breasts, which are the place of rancor. He also said: *There hath come unto you an exhortation from your Lord, a cure for that which is in the breasts.*[27]

[46] The heart of the believer is sound and his breast is sound, but the heart of the unbeliever and the hypocrite is dead and sick, and in his breast is a great wrong. God said: *In their hearts is a sickness,*[28] and: *Lo! to ascribe associates [to God] is a great wrong,*[29] and: *There is naught else in their breasts save pride.*[30]

Know that the breast is the place of all knowledge which is acquired only through study (*ta'allum*), memorization (*taḥaffuẓ*), effort (*ijtihād*), and burdening oneself (*takalluf*), by means of listening and relating, whether it be the Qur'ān or the tradition (*ḥadīth*) [of the Prophet] or something else, and that such knowledge can be characterized by forgetfulness. God said: *But it is clear revelations in the breasts of those who have been given knowledge.*[31] This is that knowledge whose expression, reading, transmission or explanation is possible. The possessor of such knowledge, however, may forget it, since it is the self that carries it and preserves it, and the self is by nature forgetful. He may forget it [even] after memorization and expending much effort [to acquire it]. The breast in this respect is like the back of the heart (*ẓahr al-qalb*). One says: so and so recites from the back of his heart.[32] Nevertheless, in spite of this effort, he sometimes makes mistakes, forgets and has doubts about what he has memorized.

The breast is also to the heart what the shell is to the pearl. Sometimes something other than the pearl, such as water or something similar to it, enters into the shell [47] and then leaves it, for within the shell there is no place other than that of the pearl into which anything can enter unless the pearl is first removed. Its place then becomes vacant and it can hold something else in its stead.[33]

[Part Three: The Difference between the Breast and the Heart]

Blindness and sight, however, are attributes of the heart and not of the breast. God said: *For indeed it is not the eyes that grow blind, but it is the hearts, which are within the breasts, that grow blind.*[1] This is the literal way [of using the words "heart" and "breast"]. Metaphorically, however, and in the understanding of the people, the "heart" is sometimes signified by the word "breast." God said: *Say: Whether ye hide that which is in your breasts or reveal it, God knoweth it,*[2] and: *But that which their breasts hide is greater,*[3] and: *And thy Lord knoweth what their breasts conceal and what they publish.*[4] God meant by that the heart. However, He meant in all [these verses] the hearts of the unbelievers, because their breasts and hearts are obstructive and closed, being empty of the light of guidance (*nūr al-hudā*).

[48] This type of knowledge (*'ilm*)[5] does not become permanent in the breast or become firmly established in it except after repetition, deep reflection and perseverance, for the breast is like a passageway, especially for that knowledge which is heard and which enters it from the outside. As for that which enters [the breast] from inside the heart, such as the subtleties of wisdom (*laṭā'if al-ḥikmah*) and attestations of grace (*shawāhid al-minnah*), its permanence in the breast is firmly established. These [other] states (*aḥwāl*), however, do not remain firm in the breast, because it is the place of entry for distractions (*ashghāl*) and desires (*ḥawā'ij*). The breast is like the courtyard of the house within the homestead. Servants, attendants, neighbors, strangers and others sometimes enter the homestead, but no one enters the house its owner enters except a blood relative (*dhū raḥim*) or a relative unlawful to marry (*maḥram*),[6] or a close relative or friend.

Sometimes the [word] "self" (*nafs*) is used metaphorically to signify the heart (*qalb*). God said in the story of Jesus: *Thou knowest what is in my self.*[7] That is, Thou knowest what is in my heart. He also said: *Know that God knoweth what is in your selves, so beware of Him,*[8] and what He meant [by the word "self"] was the heart.

The Messenger of God said: "Verily, God overlooked in regard to my community (*ummah*) what they told their selves, [as long as they did not act on it or speak about it].[9] It should be clear to you that what is intended in this tradition are the evil whisperings of the breasts, which do not become permanent. [49] One is questioned and held accountable, however, for that which has become permanent in the heart. God said: *Lo! The hearing and the sight and the heart—of each of these it will be asked.*[10]

With every science (*'ilm*) which the self carries and the breast holds the self increases in pride (*takabbur*) and arrogance (*taraffu'*) and refuses to accept the truth. Thus the self, as it increases in knowledge, increases in hatred (*ḥiqd*) towards its brothers and in persistence in vanity (*bāṭil*) and insolence (*ṭughyān*). The Messenger of God said: "Verily, this knowledge possesses an insolence like the insolence of wealth."[11]

Know that if knowledge is of little use, its possessor can buy with it something of only little value, and turns away from obedience to God. Such knowledge is acquired only for the purpose of carrying out the Sharī'ah, disciplining the self, improving it, and protecting it from ignorance (*jahl*), acquainting [it] with the prescribed penalties (*ḥudūd*) of the legal rulings (*aḥkām*) of the religion, and maintaining the outward [aspect] of the religion (*ẓāhir al-dīn*). This knowledge increases in value only if God reveals to one the knowledge of [its] inward [aspect] (*'ilm al-bāṭin*), the knowledge of the heart (*'ilm al-qalb*), which is the [truly] useful knowledge (*al-'ilm al-nāfi'*).

Do you not heed what the Messenger of God said: "Knowledge is of two kinds: knowledge on the tongue (*'ilm bi-al-lisān*), which is the argument of God (*ḥujjat Allāh*)[12] to His creation, and knowledge in the heart (*'ilm bi-al-qalb*), which is the useful knowledge (*al-'ilm al-nāfi'*)."[13] The Messenger of God once sought refuge in God saying: "O my God! Verily I seek refuge in Thee from [50] knowledge that is of no use."[14] He also said: "We take refuge in God from the hypocrite who is learned of tongue (*'alīm al-lisān*) but ignorant of heart (*jahūl al-qalb*)."[15] All this is proof that the [knowledge] such a person possesses through [the sense of] hearing is merely the argument of God (*ḥujjat Allāh*) for the self. With it he buys this world and dispenses with religion, which would be of greater use to him. Nor does he act in accordance with such knowledge until God reveals to him something of that useful knowledge. The Messenger of God is reported to have said: "Whoever acts in accordance with what he knows, God bequeaths to him the knowledge of what he does not know."[16]

Know that there is no limit to the depth of the heart's seas, nor any enumeration of the multitude of its rivers. The likeness of wise men (*ḥukamā'*) in these seas is as divers, and their likeness in these rivers is as the likeness of water drawers and fishermen. Each one of them finds and brings forth from them to the extent to which God provides him. Thus to one of them is revealed some of the gems of the knowledge of the faults of this world, of the rapidity of its transformation, the abundance of its delusion, its lack of stability, and the hastening of its extinction. To him also is revealed some knowledge of the wiles of Satan and the varieties of his evil whisperings.

To another is granted revelation by way of knowledge of the ranks of the people of piety (*ahl al-taqwā*), the grades of the people of learning (*ahl al-'ilm*), [and such virtues as] nobility of character, kind treatment of people during their misfortunes, endurance of pain, generosity in this world, preferring all other beings to oneself, [51] fear of Hellfire (*al-nār*), waging war against Satan, striving against the self and resisting its passion, following [the path of] the Messenger and his companions, and holding fast to the Sunnah.[17]

To another is given revelation by way of conversation about the favors of God, about the recollection of His bounties, the averting of His affliction, and the abundance of His giving, about His gracious protection, His prolonged forbearance, His sublime forgiveness, His ample mercy, and similar [attributes] of this kind.

To another is granted revelation by way of the contemplation of what has been preordained for him (*mā sabaqa lahu*) from God in His eternity (*azalīyah*) and timelessness (*qidam*), such as His remembrance of him, His favorable regard for him, His electing, preferring and choosing him, as well as His preordained bounties (*laṭā'if sābiqah*) to him. To yet another is given revelation by way of the contemplation of the realities (*ḥaqā'iq*) of some of [God's] acts of Lordship (*rubūbīyah*), so that he beholds the effects of God's power in all things, the beauty of His workmanship, and similar things of this kind.

To another is given revelation by way of contemplation of the greatness of God, His majesty and grandeur, and the magnitude of His power along with the insignificant worth of His creatures in contrast to His greatness. [He is granted] vision of the poverty of created beings, their disadvantage, destitution, and [utter] need for God in contrast to His power and independence of them, the amplitude of His treasuries, His sufficiency and His benevolent concern for their affairs.

To yet another is given revelation by way of the vision of [God's] assistance, the sweetness of gnosis (*ma'rifah*) and love (*maḥabbah*), and the vision of God's safeguarding him from error, unbelief and passions.

To another is granted revelation by way of contemplation of God's uniqueness (*fardānīyah*) and oneness (*waḥdānīyah*) only, so that he sees within his inner secret nothing else but God. Thus, as he beholds God, the worth of anyone other than God is reduced to nothing [52] within his inner secret, and he sees His eternity (*qidam*), perfection and everlastingness (*baqā'*), and, [in contrast], the origination [in time] (*ḥudūth*) of mankind and their passing away (*fanā'*).

There is no end to the seas of any of these aspects nor any limit to their gems, for God said: *He giveth wisdom unto whom He will, and he unto whom wisdom is given, he truly hath received abundant good. But none remember except men of intellect.*[18]

Of all these aspects [of wisdom] those which flow from the tongue of the wise man (*ḥakīm*) are like the foam which surges from the sea and which the sea then casts off, so that mankind can put it to use.[19] Thus, the wisdom of the wise man which flows from the tongue and can be expressed to mankind in clear language is like a foam which wells up from the sea of the heart. And just as one who has a disease of the eye uses the foam of the sea [as a remedy], so also one whose heart is sick with the love of this world, and the two eyes of whose heart have become diseased, benefits from the speech of the wise man. [In this way] God cures his breast from the diseases which are in it, such as attachment to passions and similar afflictions.

This, then, is the path of both inward (*bāṭin*) and outward (*ẓāhir*) knowledge, and neither can dispense with the other, for one of the two [forms of] knowledge is the explication of the Sharī'ah, which is the argument of God (*ḥujjat Allāh*) to His creation, and the other is the explication of reality (*bayān al-ḥaqīqah*), some of which I have [already] described. The life of the heart and that of the self [depend] on both of these. Moreover, the soundness of the outward aspect of religion [53] and its sustenance is through the knowledge of the Sharī'ah, whereas the soundness of the inward aspect of religion and its sustenance is through that other knowledge, the knowledge of reality (*'ilm al-ḥaqīqah*).

The proof of this is that the soundness of religion depends upon the genuineness of piety (*taqwā*). The Messenger of God said: "'Piety is here,' and pointed with his hand to his heart."[20] Thus he who is pious through outward knowledge (*al-'ilm al-ẓāhir*) but denies the inward knowledge (*al-'ilm al-bāṭin*) is a hypocrite (*munāfiq*), whereas he who is pious through inward knowledge but has not studied outward knowledge in order to carry out the Sharī'ah and even denies it, is a heretic (*zindīq*). Indeed, this inward knowledge of his is in reality no knowledge at all, but merely [evil] whisperings which Satan inspires in him. God said: *Lo! the satans do inspire their minions.*[21]

As for one who is a faithful Muslim, is righteous and a gnostic (*'ārif*), he believes in the Book of God and the Sunnah of His Messenger. He holds fast to the Shari'ah, acts in accordance with it, and imitates and follows the Messenger of God and the leaders from among his companions. With his heart he beholds the bounties of God by way of [feelings] of destitution (*iftiqār*) and exultation (*iftikhār*). He sees his own poverty (*iḍṭirār*) and abandons [his own free] choice (*ikhtiyār*), seeking the companionship of the Forgiving King (*al-malik al-ghaffār*).

God has so assisted me with His favor that I have greatly expanded the explanation and elucidation [of the difference] between the breast (*ṣadr*) and the heart (*qalb*).

[Part Four: The Heart]

The heart is the abode of the light of faith (*nūr al-īmān*). God said: *He hath written faith upon their hearts,*[1] and: *But God hath endeared the faith to you and hath beautified it in your hearts,*[2] and: *Whose heart is tranquil in the faith.*[3]

The heart is also the abode [54] of piety (*taqwā*), calmness (*sakīnah*), fear (*wajal*), humility (*ikhbāt*), softness (*līn*), tranquility (*iṭma'nīnah*), submission (*khushū'*), refinement (*tamḥīs*), and purity (*ṭahārah*). God said: *And imposed on them is the word of piety for they were worthy of it,*[4] and indicated that this imposition was upon their hearts. He also said: *He it is who sent down calmness into the hearts of the believers,*[5] and: *And He knew what was in their hearts and sent down calmness on them,*[6] and in the story of Abraham (*al-Khalīl*): *But in order that my heart may be tranquil,*[7] and: *That our hearts may be tranquil,*[8] and: *Those are they whose hearts God hath proven unto piety,*[9] and the Messenger of God pointed out piety in his heart.[10] God also said: *God accepteth only from those who are pious.*[11] The root of piety is in the heart and it [means] guarding against doubt (*shakk*), association (*shirk*), unbelief (*kufr*), hypocrisy (*nifāq*) and ostentation (*ri'ā'*).

God said concerning purity (*ṭahārah*): *That is purer for your hearts,*[12] and: [55] *Those are they for whom the will of God is that He purify not their hearts,*[13] and [concerning refinement]: *And to refine what is in your hearts.*[14] Concerning fear (*wajal*) He said: *Their hearts are afraid,*[15] and: *Their hearts feel fear.*[16] He said concerning humility (*ikhbāt*): *And their hearts may be humble before Him,*[17] and concerning softness (*līn*): *Then their flesh and hearts soften to God's reminder.*[18] Concerning lack of understanding (*'adam al-fiqh*) He said: *They have hearts wherewith they understand not,*[19] and concerning submission (*khushū'*) He said: *Is not the time ripe for the hearts and those who believe to submit to God's reminder?*[20] The Messenger of God saw a man play with his beard while praying and said: "If the heart of this man submitted, his limbs would submit also."[21] Those versed in exegesis (*ahl al-tafsīr*) have said that the meaning of submission is continual fear (*khawf dā'im*) in the heart.[22]

Know, may God have mercy on you, that of all God's creation there is nothing better than a heart which has become virtuous through the light of unification (*tawḥīd*), gnosis (*ma'rifah*), and faith (*īmān*), nor is there anything purer, cleaner, more pious, more sincere, nor anything [56] more encompassing [than a heart] if God has cleansed it of impurities and undertaken its revival with the light of the truth (*nūr al-ḥaqq*), and cared for and guarded it, and provided it with benefits. Such is the heart of the believer, and its lights are without limit.

On the other hand, there is nothing more wicked, more putrid, or more impure than the heart of one whom God has forsaken, and whose care He has not assumed, but has entrusted to Satan. Such is the heart of the hypocrite (*munāfiq*) and the unbeliever (*kāfir*), for it is the abode of association (*shirk*), doubt (*shakk*), hypocrisy (*nifāq*), uncertainty (*rayb*) and sickness (*maraḍ*). God said: *The associationists only are impure*,[23] and He said concerning the hypocrites: *For lo! they are unclean*,[24] and concerning uncertainty: *Their hearts are uncertain*,[25] and concerning denial (*inkār*): *Their hearts are given to denial*,[26] and concerning sickness: *In their hearts is a sickness*.[27] The root of all sins is hardness of the heart (*qasāwat al-qalb*). The wise man (*al-ḥakīm*)[28] said: "The heart, should it harden, is not concerned if it does harm."

If, however, the heart is illumined with the light of God and the light of faith, God assumes its care, and fills it with love and fear. He closes it with the lock of power and places the key of will (*mashī'ah*) in the treasury of His unseen [world] (*ghayb*), of which no one becomes cognizant save during the agony of death, for at that time is revealed to one what is in His unseen [world].

On the other hand, if the heart [57] becomes filled with the darkness of unbelief (*kufr*), doubt (*shakk*), and hypocrisy (*nifāq*), God appoints for its owner a satan, who assumes his care and closes [his heart] with the lock of abandonment (*khidhlān*), for God knows his final state (*'āqibah*) and what his end will be. This, however, is not apparent to anyone until he gurgles [in death], for it is the secret (*sirr*) of God, of which no one else is cognizant. How many an unbeliever far [from God] is granted faith and dies in bliss, and how many a believer close [to God] is abandoned by his Lord and dies in misery!

Know, may God have mercy on you, that the power of God is effective and that no one is cognizant of His intention (*murād*) and will (*mashī'ah*) with respect to His creation or the consequences (*khawātim*) of His acts except a number of the prophets, for that is His sign of the truth of their prophethood. The Messenger of God related that ten of his companions were among the people of Paradise (*ahl al-jannah*) as a favor and grace from God to him.[29]

Know that the pivot on which the assurance of the necessity of reward (*thawāb*) and punishment (*ʿiqāb*) [turns] is in the heart, but that the execution [of reward or punishment] falls upon the self (*nafs*) as a consequence. God said: *He will take you to task for that which your hearts have garnered.*[30] This, however, has to do with the judgments (*aḥkām*) of the Hereafter, since as regards the judgment of this world, it is the self which is taken to task for its deeds. As for that which is between the servant and his Lord, judgment is made according to what is in the heart. God said concerning the matter of ʿAmmār ibn Yāsir:[31] *Save him who is forced thereto and whose heart is still tranquil in the faith.*[32] God thus made clear that ʿAmmār's excuse [58] was that [his apostacy] did him no harm because of his heart's tranquility (*ṭuma'nīnah*) through sincerity of faith.

The servant of God is rewarded for the action of his limbs if the intention (*nīyah*) of his heart is genuine through the light of faith (*nūr al-īmān*). The Messenger of God said: "People are rewarded according to their intentions,"[33] and: "Deeds are only according to intentions,"[34] and: "No deed is attributed to one who has no intention."[35]

The breast (*ṣadr*) is the place into which enters expressible knowledge (*ʿilm al-ʿibārah*). The heart (*qalb*), on the other hand, is the abode of that knowledge [lying] beneath expressible knowledge which is the knowledge of wisdom and allusion (*ʿilm al-ḥikmah wa-al-ishārah*). Expressible knowledge is the argument of God (*ḥujjat Allāh*) to his creatures. God says to them: What have you accomplished with what you have learned? The knowledge of allusion, however, is the path of the servant to God by means of God's guidance of him, for God grants to him the uncovering of his heart to contemplate His unseen [world] (*ghayb*) and to view what is behind His veils as if he were seeing all that with his own eyes, so that even if the covering were removed for him,[36] he would not increase [in knowledge] within himself. The heart, then, is the seat of the knowledge of allusion (*ʿilm al-ishārah*). The meaning of expressible knowledge (*ʿilm al-ʿibārah*) is [that knowledge] which the servant expresses with the tongue, whereas the meaning of the knowledge of allusion is that he alludes with his heart to God's lordship, His oneness, grandeur, majesty, power, and all His attributes, as well as the realities of His creation and action.

The abode of the light of faith (*nūr al-īmān*) and of the light of the Qur'ān (*nūr al-Qur'ān*) is the same, and it is the heart, for both of these lights are similar. God said: *Thou knewest not what the Qur'ān was nor what the faith, but* [59] *we have made it a light.*[37] Thus God combined the two lights by using the pronoun "it" as a metonym (*kināyah*) for "one." The meaning of allusion (*ishārah*) is that from the time the servant alluded to the lordship of his Lord, he has not disbelieved in Him, nor has he given thanks to anyone else nor called upon anyone but Him.

Know, then, that the light of the heart, [when considered] as a whole, cannot be divided or partitioned, for it is a fundamental [entity] all of which comes if it comes and all of which goes if it goes. The darkness of unbelief is similar, for it is the root of every misfortune until it goes. Sometimes, however, the authority [of the light of the heart] weakens or wears out or is divided. It is similar to a lamp, which remains a single lamp even though the power of its light increases or decreases.

On the other hand, the light of the breast (*nūr al-ṣadr*), as well as its darkness, increases and decreases, since it is a derivative [entity] and subsists through the self (*nafs*). Moreover, Islam is assigned to the light of the breast, and deficiency therefore enters into this aspect of religion. But sometimes this light increases in the breast. The proof of this is what the Messenger of God said concerning women: "They are deficient in intellect (*'aql*) and religion (*dīn*)."[38] What he meant by this was that aspect of religion [that applies] during the days of menstruation and childbirth.

It should thus be clear to you that the lights of breasts have [various] aspects, and that action in accordance with them depends on [particular] times and amounts. Thus when one desires knowledge of an action, the light of that knowledge increases in one's breast in the [required] amount. Its light also decreases through failure to use it, for the bearer of this type of knowledge is the self, and just as the self increases and decreases, so also do its deeds and attributes.

[60] The lights of the heart, on the other hand, are fundamentally whole. Their likeness is as the likeness of the sun, which is also whole. However, if there is any defect in the atmosphere, such as clouds, fog, or extreme heat or cold, these things veil the sun's light, and the power of its rays decreases and the strength of its heat diminishes. If these defects are removed, however, the power of its light breaks through, its rays extend far, and its strength intensifies. The sun is never deficient in itself, but its benefits are blocked

because of these defects which I have described.

Similarly, if the light of faith (*nūr al-īmān*), the light of gnosis (*nūr al-ma'rifah*), and the light of unification (*nūr al-tawḥīd*) are overtaken by the darkness of heedlessness (*ghaflah*), the clouds of forgetfulness (*nisyān*), or the veils of disobedience (*'iṣyān*), and the breast becomes filled with the dust of passions (*shahawāt*), the fog of the evils of the self, and despair of the spirit of God, (*al-ya's min rūḥ Allāh*)[39] then the authority of these lights over the self decreases and it remains by itself under these veils and behind these curtains. However, if these defects are removed from the breast through God's grace and assistance, and if the servant's repentance to God is genuine, then the covering is removed, the veils are pierced, the benefits of these lights become apparent to the self, and their authority spreads.

If one meditates upon this point with God's assistance and holds fast [61] to the Sunnah [of the Prophet], God will eliminate many of the doubts of his heart and pluck out from his breast the roots of his uncertainty. God will then guide him to the contemplation (*mushāhadah*) of the realities (*ḥaqā'iq*) of His unseen [world] (*ghayb*). This is a matter clear to one for whom God has facilitated the way of understanding and comprehension.

As for the the light of legal rulings (*nūr al-aḥkām*), which is the light of Islam (*nūr al-islām*) in the breast, it increases through correctness of conduct and sincerity of endeavor. Its light decreases, however, through turning away from the application of its laws (*sharā'i'*) and through failure to make use of it. Its likeness is as the likeness of the moon, for it increases and decreases.

Islam is a comprehensive term for both the root of religion and its branches. God completed this religion with its branches and legal rulings (*aḥkām*) in twenty and some years. However, He abrogated some of its rulings and substituted some for others. As regards faith (*īmān*), gnosis (*ma'rifah*), and unification (*tawḥīd*), however, there can be no abrogation in them nor substitution of any of them. It suffices for one who is rational (*'āqil*) and assisted [by God], should he meditate upon these, to know the difference between what is carried by the self (*nafs*) and what is carried by the heart (*qalb*).

The believer, however, every moment and every hour, is in an excess of kindness from God. Moreover, his observation points (*marātib*) with respect to the contemplation (*mushāhadah*) of God's bounties become ever higher, and from hour to hour are lifted for him some of the veils of the unseen [world] (*ghayb*) which had not been lifted before. In like manner, the states of the servant of God weaken at times, and the observation points of his heart are occupied by [other concerns] because of heedlessness (*ghaflah*), [62] although the fundamentals remain as they were.

The likeness of the lights of the heart is also as the likeness of a lamp which is within something that has been draped with curtains. Inside [the curtains] it remains unchanged, but both its light and its usefulness have been concealed, and its power to spread [its light] has been curtailed. Its likeness is also as the likeness of a mirror which has been wrapped in a cloth. It remains in principle as it was, although the usefulness of its surface has been curtailed.

Understand, may God have mercy upon you, that although Gabriel took charge of sending down the Revealed Book with God's knowledge, its abode is in the heart of the Prophet. God said: *Say: Who is an enemy to Gabriel! For he it is who hath revealed it to thy heart by God's leave,*[40] and: *The True Spirit hath brought it down upon thy heart.*[41]

[Part Five: The Inner Heart]

Know that since the inner heart (*fu'ād*) is the seat of seeing (*ru'yah*), it is only the inner heart that sees whereas the heart (*qalb*) knows. If knowledge and seeing are combined in someone, the unseen [world] (*ghayb*) becomes [the object of] seeing, and the servant gains certainty through knowledge, contemplation, and the reality of seeing faith. *So whoso seeth, it is for his own good,*[1] and God shows favor to him by way of guidance and assistance because of his belief; *and whoso is blind is blind to his own hurt,*[2] and God has an argument (*ḥujjah*) against him because of his disbelief. [63] God said concerning the knowledge of certainty (*'ilm al-yaqīn*) and the eye of certainty (*'ayn al-yaqīn*): *Nay, would that ye knew with the knowledge of certainty, for ye will behold Hellfire. Aye, ye will behold it with the eye of certainty.*[3]

God informed his prophet Moses that his people had taken a calf [to worship]. Moses's anger became great, and he returned to his people angry and saddened at what he had become sure of through God's informing [him] about them.[4] He was carrying [with him] the tablets and when he saw them worshipping the calf, he threw down the tablets and seized the head of his brother pulling him to him.[5] Likewise the Messenger of God said: "God had mercy on my brother Moses, for a report (*khabar*) is not like seeing [with the eyes] (*al-mu'āyanah*)."[6] Moses was told by his Lord: *Lo! we have tried thy folk in thine absence, and the Samaritan hath misled them.*[7] Then when he saw them with his own eyes, his anger and fury increased.

Sight (*ru'yah*) is also attributed to the heart (*qalb*), although the heart sees only with the light that is within it. This is indicated by what Abū Ja'far Muḥammad ibn 'Alī[8] said to the Bedouin who had asked him: "Have you seen your Lord?" He answered: "I never worshiped anything I had not seen." He said: "How did you see Him?" He answered: "Verily, the eyes (*abṣār*) did not see Him through [64] the vision of eyesight, but the hearts (*qulūb*) saw Him through the realities of faith."[9] He thus indicated that sight was through the heart, although by means of the realities of the light of faith.

The heart (*qalb*) and the inner heart (*fu'ād*) can also be signified by the word "eyesight" (*baṣar*) since both of them are places for eyesight. God said: *God causeth the revolution of the night and the day. Lo! herein is indeed a lesson to those possessed of eyes*,[10] and: *So learn a lesson, O ye who have eyes*![11] Thus the people who have eyes learn a lesson by seeing in things the subtleties (*laṭā'if*) of the workmanship of God. They are the people of the hearts (*ahl al-qulūb*).

The people of contemplation (*ahl al-mushāhadah*) through the light of faith are in ranks. To one of them, through his true striving, is revealed the misfortunes of heedlessness as well as the vision of the Hereafter through the sight of his heart's two eyes as if he were gazing at it.

[This is] just as Ḥārithah said [to the Messenger of God]: "I have become a true believer." [The Messenger of God] said: "Verily, to every truth (*ḥaqq*) there is a reality (*ḥaqīqah*), so what is the reality of your faith?" He answered: "I turned my self away from this world and passed my night without sleep and my day without water, and it was as if I were gazing at the throne of my Lord appearing [before me], and as if I were gazing at the people of Paradise (*ahl al-jannah*) and how they visited each other and the people of Hellfire (*ahl al-nār*) in the fire and how they howled at one another." The Prophet said to him: "You have learned, so persevere."[12]

Thus, as a result of his turning his self away from this world, God revealed to him the Hereafter, so that he saw it [65] with the light of his heart. He did not speak about the station (*maqām*) of the contemplation (*mushāhadah*) of God, or the contemplation of His attributes, grace, kindness or majesty, and such things, but he spoke only about his own striving (*mujāhadah*), which imparted to him the contemplation of the Throne, of Paradise and its people and of Hellfire and its people. It is clear, then, that from the standpoint of the servant the lights and power of vision (*ru'yah*) and contemplation (*mushāhadah*) increase through God.

Another difference between the heart (*qalb*) and the breast (*ṣadr*) is that the light of the breast is finite, whereas the light of the heart is infinite and limitless. It is not extinguished even when the servant of God dies, for if he dies in a state of belief, his light [remains] with him, leaving him neither in the grave nor on the day of resurrection, but remaining with him always. God said: *God confirmeth those who believe by a firm saying in the life of the world and in the Hereafter.*[13]

As for the legal rulings of Islam (*aḥkām sharāʾiʿ al-islām*) and that which is established for the purpose of legal obligation (*taklīf*), these come to an end with death. This is sufficient proof for one who professes the wholeness of faith, and that faith does not increase or decrease. It is, however, an argument against one who professes the increase and decrease of faith, who likens faith to all other acts and professes that all acts are faith and that faith is [merely an act] with the tongue, or who says that faith is really an act of the servant, or who distinguishes between the reality (*ḥaqīqah*) of the concept of faith and that of Islam.

[66] Among us one is not correct who busies himself with what he is not legally obligated to do. Silence is security for the ignorant; speech is an honor from God for the learned. Do you not see that the questioning of the servant in the grave is about principles only and not about derivatives? He is asked: Who is your Lord? What is your religion? and Who is your prophet? He is not asked: What were your deeds? or How did you pray? On the Day of Resurrection he is asked first about his faith and then about his deeds, one after the other. He is rewarded for his deeds commensurate with the strength of the principles, namely, his intentions.

The heart is called *qalb* only because of the rapidity of its turning over.[14] The Messenger of God said: "The likeness of the heart is as the likeness of a feather in an open space of the earth which is hanging from the trunk of a tree and is being turned back and forth by the wind."[15] The Messenger of God thus related an aspect of God's power and something of His kindness towards his powerless servant by confirming his heart in the faith and by anchoring it in the truth (*ḥaqq*) by means of the rapidity of its turning over, so that through God's power and might it will not stray from [God's] guidance.

The intelligent man is one who does not attribute the action of the heart to his self except [67] to the extent that is appropriate for servanthood (*ʿubūdīyah*), and who is silent about that which does not concern him. He has, moreover, beyond that what diverts him from being curious about what does not concern him. If the structure of one's unification (*tawḥīd*) [of God], along with the foundation of one's faith, and the ground of one's gnosis (*ma'rifah*), collapses, who else but he can rebuild it?

I have explained that Islam has combined knowledge and action. The proof of this is what the Messenger of God answered when Gabriel asked him: "What is Islam?" The Messenger of God said: "Islam is that you bear witness that there is no god but God and that Muḥammad is the Messenger of God, that you perform prayer, give alms, fast in Ramaḍān, and make the pilgrimage to the House[16] if you can find a way thereto." He (Gabriel) said, "You have spoken the truth," and we were amazed that he should ask him and confirm his [answer]. Then he said, "Tell me about faith (*īmān*)." The Messenger of God said, "[Faith] is that you believe in God, His angels, His books, His messengers, the Last Day, and that you believe in destiny (*qadar*),[17] both its good and its evil." He (Gabriel) said, "You have spoken the truth. Now tell me about excellence (*iḥsān*)." He said, "Excellence is that you worship God as if you see Him, for if you do not see Him, He nevertheless sees you."[18]

Thus the two of them [Gabriel and the Messenger of God] agreed that Islam is both knowledge and action. He answered his question about faith, and they both agreed that it is knowledge and that its resting place is in the heart. As for the elite of the people of faith (*khāṣṣat ahl al-īmān*), they derive from the traditions of the Messenger of God subtle benefits which the common people are not aware of, for they are veiled by their own selves from the subtleties of the truth because of their contemplation of their own deeds. God commanded that people be addressed commensurate with with their intellects (*'uqūl*) and said: *Address them in plain terms about their selves.*[19]

[68] As for his answer concerning excellence (*iḥsān*) it is confined to the contemplation (*mushāhadah*) of God only. Either the servant of God beholds his Lord with his heart or else he beholds with his heart that his Lord sees him. In this tradition there are many benefits which the common people do not comprehend. However, this is not the place for their elucidation.

The Messenger of God explained that the stations (*maqāmāt*) of the faithful are commensurate with their ranks (*marātib*), for he tied excellence (*iḥsān*) to vision (*ru'yah*). The abode of vision is the inner heart (*fu'ād*). God said: *The inner heart lied not in what it saw.*[20] The [word] *fu'ād* is derived from *fā'idah*, benefit, because the inner heart sees the benefits of God's love. The inner heart benefits from vision, whereas the heart delights in knowledge. However, as long as the inner heart does not see, the heart cannot benefit from its knowledge.

Do you not see that the knowledge of the blind man is useless at the time of testimony, should he need to give it, because he is deprived of sight? Although his knowledge is truly knowledge, its authority is nevertheless not certain, because of the judge's invalidation (*jarḥ*) of his testimony on account of blindness, even though he is trustworthy (*'adl*). In this there is an allusion (*ishārah*) for one to whom God has given understanding in religion.

God said: *That ye may be witnesses against mankind.*[21] How can someone testify concerning something he knows but has not seen? God mentioned in the story of Joseph and his brothers that they said: *We testify only to that which we know; we are not guardians of the* [69] *unseen,*[22] for they had not seen the drinking-cup in the saddle-bag of their brother, nor had they seen it placed there by the friend of Joseph at the latter's command that [they might know] it had not been stolen.

God has indeed honored us with the Qur'ān, which is His most glorious sea. He has filled it with the gem of [His] bounties, and made it one of the treasuries of [His] graces. Blessed is he whom God honors, in secret and openly, with some of the wisdom and eloquence which is in it.

One of the gnostics said: "The inner heart is called *al-fu'ād* only because there are a thousand valleys (*alfu wād*) in it. Should an inner heart be that of a gnostic, then its valleys flow with the lights of God's beneficence, bounty, and kindness."

The expression "inner heart" (*fu'ād*) has a more precise meaning than the word "heart" (*qalb*). However, their meanings are close, just as are the meanings of the words "merciful" (*raḥmān*) and "compassionate" (*raḥīm*). The guardian of the heart is the Merciful, for the heart is the abode of faith, and the believer has put his trust in the Merciful through the soundness of his faith. God said: *Say: He is the Merciful. In Him we believe and in Him we put our trust.*[23]

The guardian of the inner heart, on the other hand, is the Compassionate. God said: *My compassion embraceth all things, therefore I shall ordain it for those who are pious,*[24] and: *Thus that We may strengthen thy inner heart therewith.*[25]

[70] God described His binding (*rabṭ*) of His servant's heart in the story of the People of the Cave (*aṣḥāb al-kahf*) when He said: *We bound their hearts when they stood forth,*[26] and in the story of the mother of Moses: *If we had not bound her heart.*[27] Those versed in exegesis (*ahl al-tafsīr*) have said that the binding of the heart is by means of the light of unification (*nūr al-tawḥīd*). That is because the heart knows and as a knower requires the binding of support, so that it may become tranquil in the recollection of God.

The inner heart (*fu'ād*), on the other hand, sees and beholds and therefore [a state of] emptiness (*farāghah*) befalls it. It has no need of binding but requires instead supportive help through [God's] guidance. God said: *The inner heart of the mother of Moses became empty and she would have betrayed him.*[28] God thus ascribed emptiness to the inner heart and favored it over the [outer] heart (*qalb*), since the latter requires binding. Moreover, the inner heart sees and beholds, whereas the [outer] heart merely knows, and as the Messenger of God said: "A report (*khabar*) is not like seeing [with the eyes] (*al-mu'āyanah*)."[29]

[Part Six: The Intellect]

The intellect (*lubb*) is the greatest mountain and the purest station of the heart. It is like an axis, which is permanent and does not move. It is through the intellect that religion is sustained, for all the lights depend upon it and encircle it. These lights are not perfected nor is their power effective save through the soundness of the intellect and its support, nor are they made firm except by its firmness, nor [71] do they exist except by its existence. The intellect is the abode of the light of unification (*nūr al-tawḥīd*) and the light of the contemplation of the uniqueness [of God] (*nūr mushāhadat al-tafrīd*), for through the intellect the reality of detachment [from this world], as well as the light of glorification [of God] become proper for the servant of God.

The intellect (*lubb*) is a balanced light, a planted field, and an imprinted intelligence. It is unlike the compounds which enter into the self, for it is a simple light, like elemental things.

This intellect, which is the same as the faculty of reason (*'aql*), is planted in the ground of unification (*tawḥīd*), and its soil is the light of uniqueness (*nūr al-tafrīd*). It has been irrigated with the water of [God's] kindness from the sea of glorification until its roots have been filled with the lights of certainty (*anwār al-yaqīn*), for God undertook its cultivation and with His power attended to that directly without any intermediary. He planted it in the garden of contentment and then protected [it] with the wall of preservation. He anchored it in His eternity (*azalīyah*), in His everlastingness (*abadīyah*) and in His primordiality (*awwalīyah*), so that the beast of the self with its passions and ignorance could hardly approach it, nor the predatory animals of the deserts of error, nor any of the animals which are the characteristics of the self, such as its arrogance, foolishness, or faults.

The Lord is the owner and protector (*walī*) of this garden, which is the most beautiful of all gardens, for it is the garden of faith. God has undertaken its planting, watering and cultivation, so that with the help of the Merciful [72] and the bounties of the fruits of beneficence its trees have brought forth the light of faith (*nūr al-īmān*). God said: *But God hath endeared the faith to you and hath beautified it in your hearts.*[1]

This is the explanation of the word *lubb* (intellect): It is made up of the [Arabic] letters *lām* and *bā'*. It begins with *lām*, like the *lām* in the word *luṭf* (kindness). The *bā'* is doubled, for, although it is written as one, it is one of the letters of a doubled root (*al-muḍā'af*)[2] and is in reality two. These are the *bā'* of *birr* (bounty) in the beginning (*bidāyah*) and the *bā'* of *baqā'*(remaining) with blessing (*barakah*) upon it. This light[3] does not exist for any reason except by the grace of the Opener of Doors, for the root of all that God has granted to His servant from among the principles of religion (*uṣūl al-dīn*) is His grace, [which He gives] without any purpose. Then He created the derivatives of religion (*furū' al-dīn*) for the purpose of servanthood (*'ubūdīyah*).

The striving (*mujāhadah*) of the servant of God is linked to the support of Lordship (*rubūbīyah*) and the guidance of Divinity (*ulūhīyah*), for the servant's striving cannot succeed except through God's assistance at that time and [His] favorable regard beforehand through [His] benign arrangement and favorable determination. Thus the intellect was the first thing God favored in eternity in order that good works might become easy for God's servant.

Know that the intellect is possessed only by the people of faith (*ahl al-īmān*), who are the elite servants of the Merciful, and who have turned towards obedience to the Protector (*al-mawlā*) and turned away from the self and this world. God has clothed them [73] in the dress of piety and has averted from them all manner of affliction. He has called them the possessors of intellects (*ulū al-albāb*), and has favored them with [His] address (*khiṭāb*). He has admonished them in various ways and praised them in much of the Book. Thus He said: *So fear God, O possessors of intellects;*[4] *Therefore fear me, O possessors of intellects;*[5] *Those are they whom God guideth, so follow their guidance;*[6] *And he unto whom wisdom is given, he truly hath received abundant good. But none remember except the possessors of intellects;*[7] *And that they may know that He is only one God, and that the possessors of intellects may take heed;*[8] *And that they may ponder its revelations, and that the possessors of intellects may reflect.*[9]

Thus God praised those possessing intellects and made clear their ranks (*marātib*), their secret states (*sarā'ir*) with their Lord, and their merits with respect to their understanding, comprehension, and insight, until He rendered the likes of us incapable of comprehending their states (*aḥwāl*), for He has favored them with the light of the intellect (*nūr al-lubb*), to an extent He has not done with others.

Among people of letters (*ahl al-adab*) generally and those who have some knowledge of the [Arabic] language, the intellect (*lubb*) is [the same as] the faculty of reason (*'aql*). There is, however, a difference between the two just as there is between the light of the sun and the light of a lamp, [74] although both of them are lights. This is quite apparent, since one rarely sees two rational beings the power of whose light and reason are equal. On the contrary, one of the two will be superior to the other because of a certain increment by which one is favored to an extent not apparent in the other. What do you think, then, of one whom God has favored with knowledge of Himself, of one whom He has honored with the bounties of His kindness and upon whom He has poured forth from the seas of His goodness what he has not poured forth upon anyone else?

Reason (*'aql*) is one in name, and its authority decreases and increases. It is [both] fundamental and [at the same time] derivative, since it becomes stronger through the strength of its fundamentals and increases with the increase of its authority.

The first stage (*maqām*) of reason is innate reason (*'aql al-fiṭrah*). This is [the stage] attained by a boy, or by a man recovering from insanity. [At this stage] he can understand what is said to him, since he can be forbidden and commanded, and with his faculty of reason he distinguishes between good and evil, and knows respect from contempt, profit from loss, neighbors from those who are distant, and relatives from strangers.

Another [kind] is the reason of argumentation (*'aql al-ḥujjah*). It is [the stage] in which the servant becomes worthy of being addressed by God.[10] When he reaches puberty, the light of reason (*nūr al-'aql*), which has been described, becomes firm through the light of support (*nūr al-ta'yīd*), for this [latter light] supports the reason, so that the servant attains to God's address (*khiṭāb*).

A [third kind] is the reason of experience (*'aql al-tajribah*). It is the most useful and the most excellent of the three, for by experience the servant becomes wise (*ḥakīm*), and can know what has not yet come to be by the evidence of what has already been. The Messenger of God said: [75] "No one is wise unless he has experience, and no one is insightful unless he has taken a false step."[11]

Still another [kind] is inherited reason (*'aql mawrūth*), which may be described in the following way. A rational, wise, learned, insightful, and dignified old man is afflicted with a foolish boy or pupil who does not benefit from his company. This rational man dies, and God, through His blessing, bequeathes to the foolish boy the man's reason, his light and illumination, his usefulness, his dignity, serenity, and character. The boy's condition changes immediately, and he becomes dignified and rational in the manner of his predecessor. One sees this only at the time of the death of the rational old man and the change in the condition of the foolish and ignorant boy. The boy is bequeathed only the reason of the old man, but the blessing of his prayer and the light of his learning reach the boy also. God is kind enough to accomplish this through His benevolence and magnanimity.

The benefits of each of these aspects [of reason] are commensurate [with the aspect]. Moreover, it is by means of these aspects of reason that one becomes fit to associate with other people, and that they in turn can benefit from one. It is possible, however, for all these aspects [of reason] to be found in people who do not believe in God or the Last Day, such as the philosophers (*falāsifah*) and the wise men (*ḥukamā'*) of India and Byzantium and others, for these varieties of reason are only for the support of the self and for dealing with people in this world in an ostentatious manner.

However, from among [all] these [aspects], that which is most beneficial is balanced reason (*al-'aql al-mawzūn*), which is imprinted with the light of God's guidance. [76] It is [the same as] the intellect (*lubb*), which I have just described. It is also called reason (*'aql*), and the word "reason" is used metaphorically, but within the capacity of the language, to signify knowledge. However, those who possess intellects (*ulū al-albāb*) are the knowers of God (*al-'ulamā' bi-Allāh*), and not every rational man is a knower of God (*'ālim bi-Allāh*), although every knower of God is rational. God said: *But none will grasp their meaning save the knowers.*[12]

Reason has other names also. It is called *ḥilm*, *nuhā*, *ḥijr*, and *ḥijā*. God said: *Lo! herein verily are portents for men of reason (ulū al-nuhā),*[13] and: *There surely is an oath for reasoning man (dhū ḥijr).*[14] The Messenger of God said: "Let those among you of reason (*ulū al-aḥlām wa-al-nuhā*) follow me, then those who follow them."[15]

It has been said that reason (*'aql*) binds (*ya'qilu*) the self from pursuing passions, just as the hobble (*'iqāl*) keeps a riding animal from its pasture and grazing land. The word "reason" is a general term and is interchangeable [with these other terms], but it is the only one of them which can be used with inflection. One says: I reason (*a'qilu*), he reasons (*ya'qilu*), a reasoning (*'aqlan*), he is a reasoner (*'āqil*), and that is reasonable (*ma'qūl*).

[77] God said: *Lo! therein is indeed a portent for people who reason.*[16] This means that [the servant of God] should reason concerning God's commandments and His prohibitions, His exhortations, His promise (*wa'd*) and His threat (*wa'īd*), and that he should understand His purpose (*murād*) in affairs to the extent to which He helps him and reveals to him the way to honor His commandments and to avoid what He has prohibited.

None of these [acts of reasoning] can exist [in him] without God's kindness and His favorable regard towards him. Thus He favors him over others through the intellect described [above] and [its] well-known light. Such a one is learned both in the fundamentals of religion and in its derivatives. However, not everyone who is learned in the derivatives is learned in the fundamentals, for learning in the science of legal rulings (*al-fiqh fī 'ilm al-aḥkām*) is abundant. Such a one is learned only through study and is a mere bearer of learning and knowledge. Moreover, learning (*fiqh*) is another word for knowledge (*'ilm*) and is used as an expression for it. One says that so and so learns [using either] *yata'allamu* or *yatafaqqahu*.

Real learning, however, is the learning of the heart. The Messenger of God said: "Many a bearer of learning possesses no learning [himself] and many a man bears learning to one who is more learned than he."[17] The wise man (*al-ḥakīm*)[18] said: "He is not learned who does not consider affliction a blessing and contentment a calamity." Al-Ḥasan said: "The learned man is only he who is abstemious in this world and desirous of the next world, conscious of his sin and steadfast in obedience to his Lord."[19]

I indicated at the beginning of this book that the seat of learning (*fiqh*) in the student is in the interior of the breast and that its light increases with study and practise. The lights of learning (*fiqh*) and understanding (*fahm*) branch out for him [78] and with the light of his learning he can interpret questions and then infer what he does not know from what resembles these questions, is similar to them and comes close to their meaning.

Understanding in religion (*al-fiqh fī al-dīn*),[20] on the other hand, is that light which God casts into the heart of His believing servant. It is like a lamp by which he sees. This light is not possessed by the unbeliever or the hypocrite, for God said: *But the hypocrites understand not.*[21]

As for the man of understanding (*faqīh*) whose heart God has illumined with the light of sight (*nūr al-baṣar*), he is the one to whom the Messenger of God alluded when he said: "If God wishes good for His servant, He gives him understanding in religion and shows him the faults of his self and the sickness of this world and its remedy."[22] He in whom God combines both of these types of knowledge[23] is known as the red sulphur (*al-kibrīt al-aḥmar*),[24] the most learned man (*al-'ālim al-akbar*), and the most able intellectual (*al-labīb al-awfar*).

As regards the interpretation (*istinbāṭ*)[25] of the learned man (*faqīh*) with respect to legal rulings (*aḥkām*), it is the interpretation of questions in accordance with the Sunnah [for the purpose of] putting into practice the Sharī'ah. The interpretation of the man who understands inward knowledge (*bāṭin al-'ilm*), however, is the interpretation of passing thoughts (*khawāṭir*) [in the heart] in accordance with Reality (*al-ḥaqīqah*) and the contemplation of Lordship (*al-rubūbīyah*).

The difference in merit between these two is evident only in the interpretation of the inward (*bāṭin*) and outward (*ẓāhir*) meaning of a verse revealed by God, a verse whose outward meaning necessitates a legal ruling (*ḥukm*) but under whose outward expression, j39

in its inward meaning, there is [symbolic] allusion (*ishārah*) [79] and knowledge (*'ilm*). The learned man (*faqīh*) gives an interpretion that is in accordance with the argument of God (*ḥujjat Allāh*),[26] whereas the wise man (*ḥakīm*) gives an interpretion that is in accordance with the intended meaning of God and points to His way by means of what has become clear from subtle allusions (*laṭā'if al-ishārat*). [His interpretation] is in accord with unification (*tawḥīd*) and reveals a meaning to which God agrees.

[Part Seven: The Lights of the Heart]

Although their names differ, the lights which I have described in the beginning of the book, such as the light of Islam (*nūr al-islām*), the light of faith (*nūr al-īmān*), the light of gnosis (*nūr al-ma'rifah*), and the light of unification (*nūr al-tawḥīd*), are all similar and not opposites. From each of these lights individually, and commensurate with their ranks, are generated benefits unlike the benefits that are generated from any of the others.

Thus, from the light of Islam are generated fear (*khawf*) and hope (*rajā'*), from the light of unification are generated fear and hope, from the light of faith are generated fear and hope, and from the light of gnosis are generated fear and hope. Similarly all the other states (*aḥwāl*) which spring up from the heart, such as thanksgiving (*shukr*), patience (*ṣabr*), love (*maḥabbah*), modesty (*ḥayā'*), truthfulness (*ṣidq*), and fidelity (*wafā'*), are generated from these interior lights (*anwār al-bāṭin*). I shall, however, with God's help, explain only this one section.[1]

Know, then, that from the light of Islam are generated fear of the final end (*khawf al-khātimah*) and hope for a good conclusion [to life] (*rajā' ḥusn al-'āqibah*). God said: *Therefore* [80] *die not save as men who have surrendered unto Him.*[2] He also said in the story of Joseph: *Make me to die submissive unto Thee and join me to the righteous.*[3] From the light of faith is generated the fear of evil events (*ṭawāriq al-sū'*) as well as the hope of good events (*ṭawāriq al-khayr*) at all times.

From the light of gnosis is generated the fear of the antecedent (*al-sābiqah*)[4] and the hope of the antecedent. From the light of unification is generated the fear of the realities (*al-ḥaqā'iq*) and the hope of the realities. Fear of this type originates in the contemplation of Lordship. [This means] that one fears God and no one but Him, and that one puts one's hope in Him and in no one but Him. All the other states which I have mentioned can be explained in this manner as I have described to you.

The likeness of these lights is as the likeness of mountains. Islam is a mountain whose land is the breast (*ṣadr*); faith is a mountain whose place is the heart (*qalb*); gnosis is a mountain whose abode is the inner heart (*fu'ād*); unification is a mountain and its resting place is the intellect (*lubb*).

On the summit of each of these mountains is a bird. The bird of the mountain of the breast is the self which exhorts to evil (*al-nafs al-ammārah bi-al-sū'*); the bird of the mountain of the heart is the inspired self (*al-nafs al-mulhamah*); the bird of the mountain of the inner heart is the blaming self (*al-nafs al-lawwāmah*); and the bird of the mountain of the intellect is the tranquil self (*al-nafs al-muṭma'innah*).

The self which exhorts to evil [81] flies in the valleys of association (*shirk*), doubt (*shakk*), hypocrisy (*nifāq*), and what resembles them. God, however, has had mercy on His friends (*awliyā'*) and has protected them from its evil. He said: *Lo! The self exhorteth unto evil, save that whereon thy Lord hath mercy.*[5] The inspired self flies in the valleys of piety at times and in the valleys of wickedness at other times. God said: *And inspired it to wickedness and piety.*[6]

The bird of the mountain of gnosis is the blaming self (*al-nafs al-lawwāmah*) and it flies at times in the valleys of pride, might, contemplation of God's blessings, and exultation and joy in the favors of God. At other times [it flies] in the valleys of destitution, humility, scorn of itself, and the vision of humbleness, misery, and poverty. Nevertheless, it [remains] a blamer (*lawwāmah*) of its owner in [all] its [various] states. God said: *Nay, I swear by the blaming self.*[7]

The bird of the mountain of the intellect is the tranquil self (*al-nafs al-muṭma'innah*), and it flies in the valleys of contentment, modesty, steadfastness in unification, and discovery of the sweetness of recollecting God. It is similar to the spirit (*rūḥ*), for God has purified it from the evil of contention. He said: [82] *But ah! thou tranquil self! Return unto thy Lord, content in His good pleasure*;[8] and also: *Then spirit and plenty and a garden of delight.*[9]

The term "self," includes these [different] meanings just as we mentioned with respect to the meaning of the term "heart."[10] It is like God's saying: *Ask the town*,[11] the meaning being the people of the town, or His saying: *If only there had been a town that believed*,[12] meaning by that the people of the town. Likewise the heart is a piece of flesh, but what is meant is what is within it. The self is similar; what is meant is what is inside the body in the way of fire and light.

The [word] "self" is a generic term, some of its substance being better than the rest, and some of it more evil, more iniquitous, and more wicked than the rest. This is the self which exhorts (*al-nafs al-ammārah*) [to evil]. The self, however, which through the light of outward Islam (*ẓāhir al-islām*) has become free of the wickedness of the outward self (*ẓāhir al-nafs*) increases in goodness through sincerity of striving (*mujāhadah*) if accompanied by God's assistance. The Messenger of God said in his prayers: "We take refuge in God from the evils of our selves."[13] The Messenger thus took refuge in God in spite of the varieties of blessings and purity of self and intention with which God had favored him. He said: "I had a satan (*shayṭān*), but God helped me against it and so he surrendered."[14]

[83] The substance (*jawhar*) of the self is a hot wind like smoke, dark (*ẓulmānīyah*) and evil in behavior, although its spirit (*rūḥ*) is in principle luminous (*nūrānīyah*). It increases in righteousness through God's assistance, and through good behavior and true humility. It does not, however, increase in righteousness except through the servant's opposition to its passions, and his renunciation and conquest of it through hunger and hardships. The blaming self (*al-nafs al-lawwāmah*) is closer to the truth (*ḥaqq*) but is nevertheless deceitful and beguiling. Only the gnostics from among the sagacious (*akyās*) are acquainted with it.

The tranquil self (*al-nafs al-muṭma'innah*) is the self which God has purified from the evil of darkness, so that it has become luminous (*nūrānīyah*) and resembles the spirit (*rūḥ*), for it walks in obedience to God, being led without resistance on its part. Through submission to God it has become obedient. This is the self of the veracious one (*ṣiddīq*) whose inner secret (*sirr*) and outward aspect (*'alanīyah*) God has filled.

I have likened these lights to mountains only because the light of Islam in the breast of the Muslim is too certain and too strong for anyone to extinguish it as long as God preserves it. Thus no one is able to extinguish the light of Islam in the breast. Perhaps the Muslim is not faultless in obedience, but he nevertheless clings to the firmest hold (*al-'urwah al-wuthqā*),[15] although he does not in this way escape from the evil whispering of the self.

The mountain [84] of the light of faith (*nūr al-īmān*) is greater, more firmly anchored, more deeply rooted and more stable than [the mountain of] the light of Islam (*nūr al-islām*). This is because the self has the power (*wilāyah*) and the burden (*takalluf*) of safeguarding Islam and putting into practise its laws (*sharā'i'*), but does not have the burden of safeguarding the heart. What confirms [the heart] is the light of the Lord (*nūr al-rabb*). God said: *God confirmeth those who believe by a firm saying in the life of the world and in the Hereafter.*[16] The Messenger of God said in praise of this community: "The faith in their hearts is like firm mountains,"[17] for the heart is the place of useful knowledge (*'ilm al-naf'*).

The light of gnosis (*nūr al-ma'rifah*) is more extensive and its illumination is more exalted since it is the abode of vision (*ru'yah*) and vision is more certain than a report, for "a report is not like seeing [with the eyes]."[18] The light of unification (*nūr al-tawḥīd*) is the greatest of these mountains, and it is like Mount Qāf[19] with respect to all the other mountains [of the Earth].

The boundaries of the mountain of the light of Islam terminate with striving against the self (*mujāhadat al-nafs*) and the improvement of its actions. However, the people of Islam are in ranks, some of them being more excellent than others.

The boundaries of the mountain of the light of faith terminate with trust [in God] and commitment [to Him], as well as contemplation (*mushāhadah*), [which is] more sublime than what the self sees, reflection on what one has seen, and consideration by means of the light of faith of what is not present to the eyes. The people of faith are equal with respect to the root of faith, but some are better than others with respect to their contemplations (*mushāhadāt*), and in the fruits and branches of faith which are generated in its lights.

[85] The boundaries of the mountain of the light of gnosis (*nūr al-ma'rifah*) terminate with the understanding of the science of abiding (*baqā'*)

and passing away (*fanā'*), weakness and strength, and the contemplation of the bounty of God and His favors. By this light is known that which passes away and perishes along with its lowness and baseness, and by it is also known He who abides as well as His power and glory, and the impotence and weakness of created beings.

The gnostic (*'ārif*) in this similitude is as if he were the mountain of God. His gnosis (*ma'rifah*) has become firm through the vision of God's majesty, glory, and power, and his Lord has taken hold of him, so that he does not withdraw when struck by a mishap, nor does he move away when subjected to a tribulation, for God has taken hold of him through His power and mercy.

The meaning of the letter *'ayn* in [the verb] *'arafa* is that [the gnostic] has learned of (*'alima*) and come to know (*'arafa*) God's might (*'izzah*), majesty (*'aẓamah*), sublimity (*'ulū*) and omniscience (*'ilm*), so that his self has become humble at the vision of His might, become small at the vision of His majesty and become nothing at the vision of His sublimity.

The meaning of the letter *rā'* in [the word] *'arafa* is that he has seen (*ra'ā*) the lordship (*rubūbīyah*) of God and His compassion (*ra'fah*), mercy (*raḥmah*), and sustenance (*rizq*); that he has put his trust and faith in Him and has come to rely on His compassion, to have hope for His mercy, and to accept God as lord and director.

The meaning of the letter *fā'* is that he has gained understanding (*faquha*) in religion for God's sake, has understood (*fahima*) His purpose, has abandoned (*fāraqa*) all that is perishing (*fānī*), and has fled (*farra*) from all temptation (*fitnah*) to the Omniscient Opener (*al-Fattāḥ al-'Alīm*). It means, moreover, that the abiding light of his heart has transcended (*fāqa*) all that is perishing (*fānī*).

From another aspect the *'ayn* means that [the gnostic's] heart has become free (*'ariya*) from [86] regard for anything save his Lord, and that God has clothed him in the dress of piety so that [his] heart has become accustomed (*'āwada*) to remaining close by the door of his Protector. The meaning of the *rā'* is that his heart has seen (*ra'ā*) everything just as God created it. The meaning of the *fā'* is that he has seen that which is perishable (*fānī*) as if it had already perished (*faniya*), so that he has become alone (*infarada*) with that Individual (*fard*) Who is his Protector.

From yet another aspect the *'ayn* means that his self has become patient (*'azat*) through faith; the *rā'*, that his spirit (*rūḥ*) has rejoiced (*rāḥat*) in the joy (*irtiyāḥ*) of the recollection of the Merciful (*al-Raḥmān*); and the *fā'*, that

God has opened (*fataḥa*) his heart to understanding (*fiqh*) of the sciences of the Qur'ān.

And from another aspect: his self has become pure (*'affat*), his heart has become refined (*raqqa*), and his spirit has become elevated (*fāqat*).

Another aspect is a servant whose Lord has helped him, so that he has seen, with His help, what was concealed from his eyes. The meanings of things were revealed to him, so that with his heart he has abandoned the self and created beings. He subsists through his Lord, rather than through his own power, with his inner secret (*sirr*) exposed, preoccupied with his Lord, having preferred Him above all else. Indeed, he has come to know that He is greater, more exalted, more majestic, mightier, more generous, more sublime, more knowing, richer and more kindly [than he had imagined]. The light of his inner heart (*fu'ād*) has drowned in the contemplation (*mushāhadah*) of His majesty, for he is in the sea of God's bounties, which are limitless in their succour, and to the depths of which sea no one reaches.

This is the least of the marks of the gnostic (*'ārif*), for the gnostic is not overtaken in his various states (*aḥwāl*) by violent wind, nor is he touched by flashing lightning, nor is he characterized by any description. Around his inner secret (*sirr*) there circulates from God at all times some of His bounty, favors, mercy, blessing, majesty, [87] benefits and graces. [The gnostic] is not cut off from these favors from God for the least twinkling of an eye, for he is a knower of God and his self is with God. He knows nothing, however, of that which is blameworthy in his self, such as its evil habits and its faults, but in his words and deeds he exhibits wisdom (*ḥikmah*). All of this becomes clear to him only from the sea of His grace.

The mountain of the light of unification (*nūr al-tawḥīd*), which is the fourth mountain, confirms him in this high rank. This mountain resides in the abode of the intellect (*lubb*) and is limitless in elevation and endless in magnificence. It is the source of all good things as well as the sea from which emerges all good and to which all good returns. It is impossible for any creature to describe its light with a verbal expression except to the extent that he is helped and assisted thereto [by God].

[Part Eight: The Unitarian]

Know, may God support you, that this is a servant whom the light of unification (*nūr al-tawḥīd*) has taken hold of. It has embraced him until it has drowned him in its sea. The light of unification has become, to use a similitude, like the sun, for in the summer it [shines] longer and is hotter. [It is as if] it has risen up above [the servant] until it has reached its position at midday, for that is the highest point to which the sun rises during the days of summer. There are no clouds in the sky [88] nor anything to block the sun's light, nor is there anything to protect against its heat and brightness such as a sunshade. Nothing is between this servant and the sun, so that the sun has encompassed his head, has burned it with its heat, and has changed his state both in habit and in nature. He sees no shadow for his person, because of the height of the sun and the elevation of its position, except at his feet, and his feet, because of the extreme heat, remain firmly on the ground only through necessity.

What, then, is [the plight of] this unitarian (*muwaḥḥid*) whom God has elevated to the station of unification (*maqām al-tawḥīd*) with His power and might? It is the plight of someone who has been sensed by a lion which is about to kill him and devour him. He has become certain of his destruction and has no support, no [way of] deterence, and no one to call for help. How close is the state of the man in this similitude to that of the unitarian, for he [appears] a living person to [other] people, yet within himself he is already dead because of his proximity to his Lord, for he has remained in the darkness of the confines of [sense] perception and does not yet perceive the modality of unification (*kayfīyat al-tawḥīd*) . . . .[1] the light of unification and encompassed him both secretly and openly.

This servant has strayed from the path of assuming burdens (*takalluf*) and has no burdens to bear in affairs [of this world]. He has abandoned choice and his servanthood (*'ubūdīyah*) has become a captive in the grasp of the majesty of the Lord. He fears hidden association (*al-shirk al-khafī*) [89] in his inner secret (*sirr*) for even a moment. He gazes with his heart from his Lord to His creation, so as not to turn towards any other save Him from among His creation, or towards his own self, or his own movements, or towards the extreme of nullification (*ta'ṭīl*),[2] so that he sees himself unable to perceive His lordship, or towards the extreme of assimilation (*tashbīh*),[3] so that he sees himself drowning in the sea of unification, a great, deep sea whose shore is invisible and whose depth has no limit.

He is [at once both] sated with drink and thirsty, hungry and well-fed, naked and clothed, seeing and blind, learned and ignorant, intelligent and foolish, poised and clumsy, rich and poor, capable and impotent, healthy and sick, living and dead, remaining and perishing, far and near, strong and weak, and desirous and without desires. This, then, is the character of the divine knower (*al-ʿālim al-rabbānī*), the spiritual gnostic (*al-ʿārif al-rūḥānī*), and the luminous forerunner (*al-sābiq al-nūrānī*).[4] He is not like the tenebrous fool (*al-jāhil al-ẓulmānī*), nor is his knowledge related to the self (*nafsānī*).

I fear, however, that should I add [anything] to this explanation of the state of the unitarian (*muwaḥḥid*), it would cause distress to someone whom God has excused from this affliction, who has drowned in the darkness of sins and passions and love of this world to the exclusion of the contemplation of God's favors, for these latter deliver one from doubt (*shakk*) and association (*shirk*), and who has failed before [attaining to] the Protector.

[90] [The unitarian] is in the worst affliction, as I have to a certain extent described to you. The Messenger of God said: "The people in the worst affliction in the world are the prophets, then those most like them, and then those most like them."[5] The Messenger of God also said: "If you knew what I know you would laugh but little, would weep much, and pour dust upon your heads,"[6] and: "He who sees God and His glory is in the worst affliction,"[7] and: "If you see the people of affliction, ask God for [their] deliverance [from it]."[8]

So meditate, may God have mercy on you, upon the state of him on whom this affliction has fallen and from whom the cloak of deliverance has been stripped. What manner of life is his? Have you not heard what was the condition of the Messenger of God in every state and time? When he began his prayer a boiling sound like that from a kettle was heard [to come] from him,[9] and if a wind arose or an accident occurred, the color of his face would change.

But the heedlessness (*ghaflah*) in us has veiled us from beholding what the people of gnosis (*ahl al-maʿrifah*) have beheld and has filled the thoughts (*khawāṭir*) of our hearts to the exclusion of such states as these. God blamed certain communities, saying: *They know only some appearance of the life of this world, and are heedless of the Hereafter.*[10]

This servant of God who has drowned in the light of unification (*nūr al-tawḥīd*) and whose affliction has become intense, enjoys, nevertheless, a life of ease, for his life with his Lord has become good. [91] God said: *We shall quicken him with good life.*[11] This servant of God has forgotten all other kinds of sweetness at the sweetness of recollecting God, of obeying Him, and knowing and loving Him. The Messenger of God said: "He has tasted the flavor of faith who has accepted God as his Lord, Islam as his religion, and Muhammad as His messenger."[12] He also said: "He discovers the sweetness of faith who has the [characteristics of these] three: the man to whom God and His Messenger are dearer than anyone else, the man who hates to return to unbelief after God has saved him from it just as much as he would hate to be thrown into a fire, and the man who loves a servant of God merely for the sake of God."[13] This, however, is not the place to explain these [characteristics].

This, then, is a servant whom God has given to drink from the sea of guidance (*baḥr al-hudā*). He has discovered its sweetness and is like a mad man (*majnūn*) in the judgment of the people. God has adorned him in the finest of garments, has protected him from the evil of the Whisperer (*al-waswās*)[14] and has favored him over many of the people.

The states of this unitarian cannot be understood by reason (*naẓar*) or logic (*qiyās*), for God has favored him in all his states with a power from Himself which cannot be perceived either by faculties of reason (*'uqūl*) or by the senses (*ḥawāss*). God said: *God is the protector of those who believe,*[15] and: *That is because God is the protector of those who believe, and because the disbelievers have no protector,*[16] and: *He protects the righteous.*[17]

[92] What, then, is your opinion of one to whom God is a protector (*walī*), helper, assistant, and supporter? Can the reality of his states be known through the rational sense (*ḥāssat al-'aql*)? Have you not seen those who have strayed deny the miracles (*karāmāt*) of the friends [of God] (*awliyā'*) and the ascent (*mi'rāj*) of the Prophet because they viewed them with their passions (*ahwā'*), which they call faculties of reason (*'uqūl*), and claimed that their reason cannot accept these things, that such things cannot be true from a rational standpoint (*min ṭarīq al-ma'qūl*), and that everything that their reason cannot accept must be false (*bāṭil*)?

But how, O my brother, can you perceive with a compound instrument (*ālah murakkabah*) created in time (*makhlūqah muḥdathah*) the lordship of an omnipotent Creator and an omniscient Lord, who does what He wills and judges as He wishes? When can a thing which increases and decreases, which [sometimes] falls short and [sometimes] excels perceive the lordship of a Lord who is beyond increase and decrease and whose state never changes? Indeed, the faculty of reason is an argument from God addressed to His servant. It is a compound instrument for performing service [to God] not for the perception of [His] lordship.

One who is incapable of perceiving things created within himself such as sleep, the states of the heart, or the characteristics of the self or the spirit, who does not know their reality except through conjecture (*ẓann*) or imagination (*khayāl*), who does not know what the reality of the self is, or even the reality of the faculty of reason, by which he claims to know everything, how can such a one have a way of perceiving that which is superior to him? Indeed, what is proper is surrender to the judgment [of God], submission to the Lord, and return to the Truth (*al-ḥaqq*).

This unitarian, whom God has described by saying: *Lo! therein verily is a reminder for him who hath a heart, or giveth ear* [93] *with a present mind*,[18] is truly the possessor of a heart, for the guardian of his heart is his Lord. The heart of one whom God has entrusted with the care of his heart strays [from the truth], whereas one whose heart is cared for by his Lord falls from engagement [in the world] into freedom [from it].

People exalt this man, for he is of high status. He has humbled his self and reviled it, and it has become to the light of his heart as a mirror to his eye. He looks at his self with the light of his heart and thus knows it and, by knowing it, arrives at the knowledge of his Lord. God said: *And do ye not look into your selves*?[19] The Messenger of God said: "He who knows his self knows his Lord."[20]

This, however, applies only to the beginner in the initial [stages] of his career and of his journey along his way, for when he attains to the light of the truth (*nūr al-ḥaqq*) and becomes strong through the strength of the truth, the worth of those who are beneath Him in His creation disappears before the power of His majesty, and at the appearance of His truth the status of all His creation is reduced to naught.

God offered an example of the light of the heart of the believer by way of a similitude. He said: *God is the light of the heavens and the earth. The likeness of His light is as a niche wherein is a lamp. The lamp is in a glass. The glass is as it were a shining star. This lamp is kindled from a blessed tree, an olive neither of the East nor of the West, whose oil would almost glow forth of itself though no fire touched it. Light upon light, God guideth unto His light whom He will. And God speaketh to mankind in similitudes, for God is the knower of all things.*[21] One who reflects, with the help of God, in order to comprehend something [94] of the meaning of the eloquence of this verse will find, from the beginning of the Book[22] to its end, what will guide him to an explanation of its meaning. God, however, is most knowing. After that God said: *And he for whom God hath not appointed light, for him there is no light.*[23]

The names of the stations of the interior (*maqāmāt al-sirr*), such as the breast (*ṣadr*) and the heart (*qalb*), are [merely] expressions of the tongue. In their reality, however, they are allusions (*ishārāt*) to the lights [of these stations], which God has brought forth from the treasuries of His light. Do you not observe what the Messenger of God said: "The insight (*firāsah*) of the believer does not err, and the believer sees by the light of God,"[24] and: "Let your heart pronounce for you,"[25] and: "The admonisher of God is in the heart of every believer and His exhorter is in the heart of every believer."[26]

Know, O my brother, that the subsistence of all creation is through God. What then is your opinion of one whom God has specially taken under His protection as a friend, whom He has embraced with His sponsorship, and made one of His elite (*khāṣṣah*) and one of the people of His protection (*walāyah*)?

One who has not died does not see the resurrection except that he die, as the Messenger of God said: "When one dies, one's resurrection has arrived."[27] Whoever dies, and the spirit of his self leaves and he is transported by his spirit from this world to the Hereafter, beholds the Hereafter and what is in it. Similarly one who has died in his [own] being, but is alive in his Protector knows that he himself does not control harm or benefit, or death or life, or resurrection. His heedlessness has been revealed to him, his resurrection has arrived, and he has become alive through his Lord, for God has embraced him, taken him under his protection as a friend, supported his heart, [95] and revived it. He has seen by the light of the truth (*nūr al-ḥaqq*) what no one else has seen.

God said: *Think not of those who are slain in the way of God as dead. Nay, they are living,*[28] and: *And call not those who are slain in the way of God dead. Nay, they are living.*[29] Thus God through His beneficence restores to life as a martyr (*shahīd*) whoever is slain by an unbeliever in the way of God. What, then, is your opinion of one who has been slain by the light of love, the fire of the fear of separation, the fire of resistence to passion, the light of conformity with the truth, and the fire of longing; of one who has slain his self with the sword of unification so that he has become alive to God?

Life as understood by the common people has many aspects. One of them is the life of the self (*nafs*) through the spirit (*rūḥ*). This is the life of animals and beasts. Another is the life of the heart (*qalb*) [revived] from the darkness of unbelief by the light of faith. Another is the life of the self through knowledge (*'ilm*), for the learned man is alive but the ignorant man is dead. Still other aspects are the life of a servant of God [revived] from the darkness of transgression through the light of obedience, and the life of the repentent [revived] from the darkness of misfortunes through the light of repentance and from the darkness of the vision of [his own] striving (*mujāhadah*) through the light of God's assistance. Finally, there is the life of the servant [revived] from the darkness of regarding [his own] action through the vision of God's favor and His favorable regard for him. There are, however, [still other aspects] the mention of which cannot be endured by the hearts of the common people.

[96] God said: *Say: the spirit is by command of my Lord, and of knowledge ye have been vouchsafed but little,*[30] and: *He has strengthened them with a spirit from Him,*[31] and: *He casteth the spirit of His command upon whom He will of His servants,*[32] and: *And thus have we inspired in thee a spirit of Our command.*[33] Every living being from among those created by God is called living only because of the spirit (*rūḥ*). The spirit is an expression for that light by which God gave life to creatures, for, as God mentioned, the spirit is from His command, its subsistence is through God, and through it the self subsists.

One whom God has caused to understand this much can understand, through His support, and His strengthening and assistance, what is beyond that concerning the life of the heart by means of the spirit of wisdom (*ḥikmah*), the spirit of truthfulness (*ṣidq*), the spirit of love (*maḥabbah*), the spirit of [God's] protection (*walāyah*), the spirit of bearing witness (*shahādah*), the spirit of the message (*risālah*), the spirit of speech (*kalām*), and the spirit of amity (*khullah*). The life of the breast (*ṣadr*) is through the spirit of Islam; the life of the heart (*qalb*) is through the spirit of faith (*īmān*); the life of the inner heart (*fu'ād*) is through the spirit of gnosis (*ma'rifah*) and contemplation (*mushāhadah*); and the life of the intellect (*lubb*) is through the spirit of unification (*tawḥīd*) and through detachment (*infiṣāl*) from [one's own] strength and power and connection (*ittiṣāl*) to the truth.

[97] The likeness of the traveller along this way in the beginning of his journey is as the likeness of a man whom the darkness of the night has encompassed and surrounded within a dark house. He is then given a lamp from which he gains some light. Later the window and the door of his house is opened, so that the light of the moon enters and he takes delight in it and rejoices until he goes out into the desert and is able to do without the light of the lamp because of the light of the moon and its illumination. Then, as he is rejoicing [in the light of the moon], the break of dawn comes, and the light of day and its power overwhelm the light of the moon. While he is thus rejoicing [in the dawn's light], the sun itself rises, and its light and illumination begin to increase until it reaches its highest points.

The likeness of the dark house is the self (*nafs*), ignorant because of its darkness, and the light of the lamp is the light of reason (*nūr al-'aql*) in the self. This reason then increases, like the rising of the moon, by means of the lights of the Sharī'ah and the knowledge of the Sunnah. It then increases again through the light of the purity of gnosis (*ma'rifah*), and this is like the break of dawn. Then it increases still further through its vision in "time" (*fī al-waqt*)[34] of God's graces, as well as the [vision of] the good outcome forordained for it[35] from God outwardly and inwardly, and the subtleties of His workmanship and decree. It increases again through the light of unification (*nūr al-tawḥīd*), and this is [like] the rising of the sun. Then the sun's illumination grows and increases as does also its light, power and benefits [and this is like the increase of reason] through the vision of the realities of the effects of God's power and the subleties of His lordship.

If these lights reach perfection and join together, the servant of God fears [98] their extinction and is afraid of their passing away, for he does not feel safe from a change in their condition. One who has attained to this station fears the departure of this light and the passing of this happiness even more than one who is enjoying the light of the sun fears its passing and its setting. A poet has said:

> The sun of His light has risen in the hearts (*qulūb*).
> It shines, and for it there is no setting (*ghurūb*).
> They delight in the Beloved, and each
> takes from His Beloved a portion (*nasīb*).

The likeness of a servant of God who directs his attention to his own deeds, acts and states is as the likeness of a man who, having lighted a lamp, as we stated before, is then overtaken by these lights, which I have described. Does this man, then, after these other lights have appeared to him, continue to pay attention to the lamp? On the contrary, he thanks Him who has given him success in these deeds. The unitarian (*muwaḥḥid*) is similar, for his inner secret (*sirr*) has seen with eyesight, by means of the realities of faith, and with contemplation, by means of the light of the guidance of the Merciful, the effects of God's magnificence, power, majesty, grandeur, and uniqueness.

Thus he has not turned towards his own activity nor has he relied on it, but has relied instead on God, for he has drowned in the lights of the contemplation of His grace, the bounties of His mercy, and the attestations to His compassion. He has freed himself from regarding the movements of his self (*nafs*), and has blamed it for what he sees in it of evil character and vile intention.

Another likeness is that of the planets, whose power [of casting light] is restricted to a dark night, for if the moon rises on a night in which it is full, its light overpowers the light of the planets and conceals most [99] of the stars. Then if dawn breaks and the sun rises, the traces of the remaining planets are effaced and the light of the moon vanishes.

What, then, is your opinion of the activity of the self at the appearance of Lordship with [His] assistance, support and guidance? Does the unitarian rely on the activity [of the self] as long as he sees the bounties of His lordship and the breadth of His mercy? The servant subsists through his Lord, unable to do without Him outwardly or inwardly for a moment either in respect of his religion or his world. When guidance, the lights of [God's] protection, and the bounties of [His] benevolent care have been collected and assembled and have become numerous, the movements and deeds of the self are no longer seen in the same way in which are seen in every moment and instant the bounties of the Lord.

I shall explain to you something of the attributes of these hearts which are protected as friends by their Lord. Know, then, may God have mercy upon you, that the hearts of the friends of God (*awliyā' Allāh*)[36] are storehouses of wisdom, seats of mercy, sources of contemplation, treasuries of gnosis (*ma'rifah*) and houses of generosity. They are the places of God's merciful regard, the gardens of His compassion, the vessels of His knowledge, the tents of His wisdom, the reservoirs of His unification, the sites of His benefits, the dwellings of His favors, and the shelters of lights from His light. God looks upon these hearts with His mercy every moment, increases their lights, and restores their inner secrets. He has embellished them with the light of faith and founded them upon reliance on the Merciful. He has filled them with the bounties of munificence, built their walls from the favors of beneficence, and made good their ground with the light of truth and guidance, so that its soil has become cleansed from the wickedness of association (*shirk*), doubt (*shakk*), hypocrisy (*nifāq*) and all other abominations.

This is the ground of gnosis (*ma'rifah*), which God watered from the sea of contentment until some of the lights of the self sprouted in it, [100] and which He supported through the good management of the gardeners, who are the foremost from among the pious. He opened their buds with the wind of obedience to the Foremost of the Messengers (*sayyid al-mursalīn*)[37] and nurtured them with divine winds such as the wind of mercy, the wind of compassion, the wind of triumph, and similar winds of Lordship. He ripened their fruits with the warmth of the sun of gnosis and provided them with the passage of the night of destitution (*iftiqār*) and the day of exultation (*iftikhār*). He perfected the color of their fruits with the dye of God (*ṣibghat Allāh*),[38] which is the exposition of the legal rulings (*aḥkām*) of the Sharīʻah and the servant's grasping of the firmest hold (*al-ʻurwah al-wuthqā*).[39] He enhanced their flavor with adherence to the Sunnah of His prophet.

Then He placed the throne of love upon the ground of the truth, whose soil had been made good by the light of the intellect (*lubb*), the throne being supported by the light of [God's] assistance, nourished through the nourishment of belief, founded on the basis of realization (*taḥqīq*), and strengthened by His firm support. Then He spread upon this throne the soft covering of strength and of power and placed on them the pillows of humility and submission. He made uprightnessness its cushion and made it dependent upon God, that He might make it firm in the truth and in adherence to the community [of Muslims].

Then He seated upon this throne His servant and friend (*walī*) in a state of happiness, being supported and aided [by God]. He clothed him in the dress of piety and removed from him the garment of affectation and pretension. He bestowed upon him His blessing from the treasuries of His grace and supported him with His favor and assistance. He crowned him with the crown of His protection (*walāyah*), and washed him with the water of His bounty and care. He increased him in purity from the sea of guidance and fed him from the sweetness of His recollection and love. Into the cup of unification (*tawḥīd*) from the sea of uniqueness (*tafrīd*) He poured for him a pure drink mixed with the sweetness of his bond [with God], until [101] he came to subsist through God alone, his inner secret (*sirr*) far removed from all else but God. Indeed, his self (*nafs*) has become humbled at the appearance of His majesty, and at the sight of His assistance has become as nothing with regard to pretension. His self has risen to His service like a guarded slave, like one compelled and subdued, or like a shackled prisoner.

Then His Lord looked upon him with the gaze of His mercy, and from the treasuries of Lordship sprinkled upon him the powder of the blessings of privilege, until he reached the station of the reality of servanthood (*ʻubūdīyah*), and with that God enriched him. Then He caused him to come near, and called to him, and honored him. He mentioned him by name, and was kind to him, summoned him and came to him when He heard his prayer. God supported him and strengthened him, embraced him and sheltered him until he answered Him and responded to Him, called out to

Him in his inner secret (*sirr*), and conversed secretly with Him at all times, and cried out to his Protector not acknowledging any lord save Him.

[God] granted him his request and his wishes, and chose him for His service. He guided him and accepted him for His love, and chose him for knowledge of Himself. He caused to flow before him rivers of truthfulness (*ṣidq*) and purity (*ṣafā'*), realization (*taḥqīq*), modesty (*ḥayā'*), love (*maḥabbah*), contentment (*riḍā'*), fear (*khawf*), hope (*rajā'*), patience (*ṣabr*), fidelity (*wafā'*), thanksgiving (*shukr*), compliance (*qaḍā'*), continuance (*baqā'*), encounter (*liqā'*), exultation (*iftikhār*), destitution (*iftiqār*), glorification (*ta'ẓīm*), abandonment of choice (*tark al-ikhtiyār*), consideration of [God's] decrees (*aqdār*), and the contemplation (*mushāhadah*) of [God] the Almighty and Omnipotent.

Every moment God gives him more bounties to an indescribable extent. He is close to his Protector estranged from his world, preoccupied with God, with no concern for his [final] end. He enjoys the most luxurious life with his Protector and fears the passing of this state as he fears any event [102] which might cause [his] removal from the station (*maqām*) of the contemplation (*mushāhadah*) of Grandeur and Majesty.

In this state he is as one both sociable and estranged, or calm and excited, or tranquil and disturbed. He has drowned in a sea whose shore he cannot see. It is the sea of unification, and he has no desire to be rescued from this drowning. This unitarian takes pleasure [in it] just as one takes pleasure in the delights of this world. However, he also suffers from the pain of his separation [from God], a pain worse than that suffered by people with aches, illnesses or misfortunes or by those struck with whips or those pierced by sharp [weapons]. But then God delivers him from the pain of separation and gathers together for him every type of deliverance. He puts him in His presence and makes him secure.

Glory be to Him Who has bestowed such great bounties upon the elect of His friends (*awliyā'*) and upon those drawn close to Him from among the pure (*aṣfiyā'*); Who has granted them an immense grace, has protected them from unwholesome passions, granted them pure hearts, and directed their travel along the straight path. To Him belongs praise for the removal of affliction, the bestowal of gifts, the increase of grace, the blessing of guidance, and the elimination of ruin.

[God's] assistance is [gained] by following His chosen Prophet, the community of His elect Friend, and the Sunnah of the sanctioned Messenger of God, the Seal of the prophets and messengers, along the clearest of paths. With him God sealed His prophecy and through obedience to him He initiated the practice of manliness (*murūwah*) and the revival of magnanimity (*futūwah*). [103] With him He brought to an end His argument (*ḥujjah*), and as a mercy He sent him to the worlds. Through him He drove away all affliction, and through him fulfilled His blessing, for he is His chosen messenger.

May God bless him and his family, the people of truth and purity, and his companions, the people of love and loyalty, and his wives, the people of chastity and piety. May God give them all peace, for there is no refuge or deliverance from Him. He is the protector (*walī*) of every believer and a most excellent protector (*mawlā*) *is He. May God bless our master, Muhammad, his family and companions and give them peace.*

[The End]

Know that the pivot on which the assurance of the necessity of reward (*thawāb*) and punishment (*'iqāb*) [turns] is in the heart, but that the execution [of reward or punishment] falls upon the self (*nafs*) as a consequence. God said: *He will take you to task for that which your hearts have garnered.*[30] This, however, has to do with the judgments (*aḥkām*) of the Hereafter, since as regards the judgment of this world, it is the self which is taken to task for its deeds. As for that which is between the servant and his Lord, judgment is made according to what is in the heart.

NOTES

INTRODUCTION

1. The Elucidation of the Difference between the Breast, the Heart, the Inner Heart, and the Intellect.

2. See "A Sufi Psychological Treatise" in *The Muslim World*, Vol. LI (1961), Nos. 1-4.

3. See *Fihris al-Kutub al-'Arabīyah al-Mawjūdah bi-al-Dār*, Cairo 1924, I, 345.

4. Abū 'Abd Allāh Muḥammad ibn 'Alī al-Ḥakīm al-Tirmidhī, *Bayān al-Farq bayn al-Ṣadr wa-al-Qalb wa-al-Fu'ād wa-al-Lubb*. Edited by Nicholas Heer. Cairo 1958.

5. See 'Abd al-Fattāḥ 'Abd Allāh Barakah, *Al-Ḥakīm al-Tirmidhī wa-Naẓarīyatuhu fī al-Wilāyah*, Cairo 1971, p. 10; and the following references in the works of Bernd Radtke: *Al-Ḥakīm at-Tirmidī: Ein islamischer Theosoph des 3./9. Jahrhunderts*, Freiburg 1980, pp. 70-71; "Theologen und Mystiker in Ḫurāsān und Transoxanien" in *Zeitschrift der deutschen morgenländischen Gesellschaft*, Vol. 136 (1986), pp. 555-556; and *The Concept of Sainthood in Early Islamic Mysticism: Two Works by al-Ḥakīm al-Tirmidhī*, Richmond, Surrey 1996, p. 5.

The strongest argument against the attribution of *Bayān al-Farq* to al-Tirmidhī is that the psychological system described in the work, with its division of the heart into four stations, is not repeated or even referred to in any of al-Tirmidhi's other works. A four-part division of the heart similar to the one found in *Bayān al-Farq* is given by Abū al-Ḥasan al-Nūrī (d. 295/907) in his *Risālat Maqāmāt al-Qulūb*. (See Paul Nwiya's edition of this work in *Mélanges de l'Université Saint-Joseph*, Vol. XLIV (1968), pp. 117-154 and specifically pp. 130-131; see also Annemarie Schimmel, *Mystical Dimensions of Islam*, p. 192). Perhaps al-Nūrī, then, is the author of *Bayān al-Farq*. Another strong argument against the attribution of *Bayān al-Farq* to al-Tirmidhī, conveyed to me in an e-mail message by Bernd Radtke, is the extensive use of *saj'* or rhymed prose especially towards the end of the work. Rhymed prose was not a characteristic of al-Tirmidhī'°s style. The strongest argument in favor of the attribution to al-Tirmidhī is simply the fact that the only manuscript that exists of the work attributes it to him. Perhaps in the future other manuscripts will be discovered that attribute the work to its true author.

6. See my "Some Biographical and Bibliographical Notes on al-Ḥakīm al-Tirmidhi," in *The World of Islam*, pp. 121-127.

7. Bernd Radtke puts the date of his death somewhere between 295/907 and 310/922. See his work *Al-Ḥakīm at-Tirmidī*, pp. 16-38.

8. A facsimile of the manuscript of this work (Ismā'īl Ṣā'ib 1571, 9, fols. 217b-218a) along with a German translation will be found in Bernd Radtke, "Tirmidiana Minora" in *Oriens*, Vol. 34 (1994), pp. 242-277. An English translation can be found in Bernd Radtke and John O'Kane, *The Concept of Sainthood in Early Islamic Mysticism: Two Works by al-Ḥakīm al-Tirmidhī*, Richmond, Surrey 1996.

9. That is, opinion in questions of Islamic law.

10. For a list of his works see Bernd Radtke, *Al-Ḥakīm at-Tirmidī*, pp. 39-58; Fuat Sezgin, *Geschichte des arabischen Schriftums*, I, 653-659; Nicholas Heer, "Some Biographical

and Bibliographical Notes on al-Ḥakīm al-Tirmidhi" in *The World of Islam*, pp. 121-134; Othman Yahya, "L'Oeuvre de Tirmidī" in *Mélanges Louis Massignon*, III, 411-479.

11. Similar descriptions of the heart can be found in Abū al-Ḥasan al-Nūrī's *Risālat Maqāmat al-Qulūb*, pp. 130-131 and in Abū Manṣūr al-Māturīdī's *Sharḥ al-Fiqh al-Akbar*, p. 7.

12. Mohammed Marmaduke Pickthall, *The Meaning of the Glorious Koran*. New York: New American Library, 1953.

13. A.J. Arberry, *The Koran Interpreted*. Two volumes. London: George Allen and Unwin, 1955.

14. *Al-Qur'ān al-Karīm*. Edited by Muḥammad 'Alī Khalaf al-Ḥusaynī, Ḥifnī Nāṣif, Naṣr al-'Ādilī, Muṣṭafā 'Inānī, and Aḥmad al-Iskandarī. Būlāq: al-Maṭba'ah al-Amīrīyah, 1342.

15. On the correspondence between Merton and Abdul Aziz see Sydney H. Griffith, "As One Spiritual Man to Another: The Merton-Abdul Aziz Correspondence" in *Merton and Sufism: The Untold Story*, pp. 101-129.

16. See pp. 79-88.

[Part One: The Stations of the Heart]

1. For a map of the sacred area around Mecca see R. Bayly Winder's section of the article "Makka" in *The Encyclopaedia of Islam*, VI, 165.

2. That is, the Ka'bah. See Qur'ān, XXII, 29 and 33.

3. Qur'ān, XLIII, 32.

4. Qur'ān, XII, 76.

5. A tradition reported by al-Bukhārī (*bad' al-waḥy* 1, *al-īmān* 52, *al-'itq* 2344, *al-manāqib* 3609, *al-nikāḥ* 4682, *al-aymān wa-al-nudhūr* 6195, *al-ḥiyal* 6439), Muslim (*al-imārah* 3530), al-Tirmidhī (*faḍā'il al-jihād* 1571), al-Nasā'ī (*al-ṭahārah* 74, *al-ṭalāq* 3383, *al-aymān wa-al-nudhūr* 3734), Abū Dāwūd (*al-ṭalāq* 1882), Ibn Mājah (*al-zuhd* 4217), and Aḥmad ibn Ḥanbal (*musnad al-'asharah al-mubashsharīn bi-al-jannah* 163, 283). See also Wensinck, *Concordance*, VII, 55.

6. See al-Muttaqī, *Kanz al-'Ummāl*, I, Nos. 1206-1207.

7. Qur'ān, II, 225.

8. Contemplation (*mushāhadah*) is a state in which the Sufi is able to behold God, His attributes and acts, and His unseen world including Paradise and Hellfire. Al-Hujwīrī has a short chapter on comtemplation in his *Kashf al-Maḥjūb*. See pp. 329-333 of Nicholson's translation. See also Nicholson's edition of al-Sarrāj's *Kitāb al-Luma'*, pp. 68-69.

9. That is, likening God to what is other than He.

10. That is, the denial of God's attributes.

[Part Two: The Breast]

1. Qur'ān, VI, 113 (114).

2. Qur'ān, III, 154.

3. This is a reference to another section of Qur'ān, III, 154: *God is aware of what is hidden in the breasts.*

4. Qur'ān, III, 154.

5. Qur'ān, CXIV, 5.
6. Qur'ān, VII, 2.
7. Qur'ān, XI, 12.
8. Qur'ān, XV, 97.
9. Qur'ān, XXVI, 12-13.
10. Qur'ān, XCIV, 1.
11. Qur'ān, XXXIX, 22.
12. That is, the sin of ascribing associates or partners to God. *Shirk* is often loosely translated as "polytheism." James W. Redhouse gives "syntheism" as a translation for *shirk*. See his *A Turkish and English Lexicon*, Constantinople 1921, p. 1123.
13. Qur'ān, XVI, 106.
14. Qur'ān, VI, 125 (126).
15. A tradition reported by Ibn Mājah (*al-muqaddimah* 64). See also Wensinck, *Concordance*, II, 303.
16. Qur'ān, XLIX, 14.
17. Qur'ān, II, 112.
18. Qur'ān, V, 44.
19. Qur'ān, XXXVII, 103. The verse is about Abraham's sacrifice of his son, which he had begun to carry out in obedience to God's command.
20. Qur'ān, X, 84.
21. Qur'ān, XXVIII, 53.
22. Qur'ān, LI, 35-36.
23. That is, Islamic law, which is based on the Qur'ān and the Sunnah or sayings and actions of the Prophet.
24. Qur'ān, VII, 43; XV, 47.
25. Qur'ān, LIX, 10.
26. Qur'ān, IX, 14-15.
27. Qur'ān, X, 57.
28. Qur'ān, II, 10; V, 52.
29. Qur'ān, XXXI, 13.
30. Qur'ān, XL, 56.
31. Qur'ān, XXIX, 49.
32. That is, from memory.
33. The text of this paragraph in the Arabic manuscript is not at all clear. The translation represents what I believe the author may have wished to say. The point of the analogy seems to be that human memory is limited in its capacity and that one can put more knowledge into it only at the expense of the knowledge already there.

[Part Three: The Difference between the Breast and the Heart]

1. Qur'ān, XXII, 46
2. Qur'ān, III, 29.
3. Qur'ān, III, 118.
4. Qur'ān, XXVIII, 69.
5. That is, knowledge of such things as the Prophetic traditions and the law.
6. Such as one's mother, daughter, sister, etc.

7. Qur'ān, V, 116.

8. Qur'ān, II, 235.

9. A tradition reported by al-Bukhārī (*al-'itq* 2343, *al-ṭalāq* 4864, *al-aymān wa-al-nudhūr* 6171), Muslim (*al-īmān* 181, 182), al-Tirmidhī (*al-ṭalāq wa-al-li'ān* 1103), al-Nasā'ī (*al-ṭalāq* 3379, 3380, 3381), Abū Dāwūd (*al-ṭalāq* 1888), Ibn Mājah (*al-ṭalāq* 2030, 2034), and Aḥmad ibn Ḥanbal (*bāqī musnad al-mukthirīn* 8745, 9134, 9752, 9848, 9968). See also Wensinck, *Concordance*, I, 401.

10. Qur'ān, XVII, 36.

11. A tradition not found in the canonical collections.

12. As revealed by God to his prophets. See Qur'ān VI, 83, 149.

13. A tradition reported by al-Dārimī (*al-muqaddimah* 367). See also al-Muttaqī, *Kanz al-'Ummāl*, V, Nos. 4050, 4338-4339; and al-Sulamī, *Kitāb al-Arba'īn fī al-Taṣawwuf*, p. 5.

14. Part of a tradition reported by Muslim (*al-dhikr wa-al-du'ā'* 4899), al-Nasā'ī (*al-isti'ādhah* 5347, 5363, 5375, 5443), Abū Dāwūd (*al-ṣalāh* 1324), Ibn Mājah (*al-muqaddimah* 246), Aḥmad ibn Ḥanbal (*musnad al-kūfīyīn* 18503, 18590). See also al-Muttaqī, *Kanz al-'Ummāl*, I, No. 3633.

15. A somewhat similar tradition is reported by Aḥmad ibn Ḥanbal (*musnad al-'asharah al-mubashsharīn bi-al-jannah* 137, 293). See also al-Muttaqī, *Kanz al-'Ummāl*, V, Nos. 4440-4441, 4793, 4801.

16. A tradition not found in the canonical collections.

17. That is, the way of the Prophet as known through his recorded sayings and actions.

18. Qur'ān, II, 269.

19. This is a reference to *zabad al-baḥr*, or foam of the sea, perhaps to be identified as meerschaum or sepiolite, a whitish clay sometimes found floating on the sea as if it were sea-foam. See the article "Meerschaum" in *The Encyclopaedia Britannica*, Eleventh edition, New York, 1911, XVIII, 72. *Zabad al-baḥr* has also been identified as the bone of the cuttlefish, which, when ground up, was used as a remedy for diseases of the eye. See *The Medical Formulary or Aqrābādhīn of al-Kindī*, translated with a study on its materia medica by Martin Levey, Madison: University of Wisconsin Press, 1966, pp. 172, 272.

20. Part of a tradition reported by Muslim (*al-birr wa-al-ṣilah wa-al-ādāb* 465) and Aḥmad ibn Ḥanbal (*musnad al-baṣrīyīn* 19397, 19405, 19767, 19768; *musnad al-madanīyīn* 16029, 16047; *musnad al-makkīyīn* 15444; *bāqī musnad al-mukthirīn* 7402, 8365, 11933; *bāqī musnad al-anṣār* 22129, 22145). See also Wensinck, *Concordance*, VII, 300.

21. Qur'ān, VI, 121.

[Part Four: The Heart]

1. Qur'ān, LVIII, 22.

2. Qur'ān, XLIX, 7.

3. Qur'ān, XVI, 106.

4. Qur'ān, XLVIII, 26.

5. Qur'ān, XLVIII, 4.

6. Qur'ān, XLVIII, 18

7. Qur'ān, II, 260.
8. Qur'ān, V, 113.
9. Qur'ān, XLIX, 3.
10. A tradition reported by Muslim (*al-birr wa-al-ṣilah wa-al-ādāb* 465) and Aḥmad ibn Ḥanbal (*musnad al-baṣrīyīn* 19397, 19405, 19767, 19768; *musnad al-madanīyīn* 16029, 16047; *musnad al-makkīyīn* 15444; *bāqī musnad al-mukthirīn* 7402, 8365, 11933; *bāqī musnad al-anṣār* 22129, 22145). See also Wensinck, *Concordance*, VII, 300.
11. Qur'ān, V, 27.
12. Qur'ān, XXXIII, 53.
13. Qur'ān, V, 41.
14. Qur'ān, III, 154.
15. Qur'ān, XXIII, 60.
16. Qur'ān, VIII, 2.
17. Qur'ān, XXII, 54.
18. Qur'ān, XXXIX, 23.
19. Qur'ān, XXVII, 179.
20. Qur'ān, LVII, 16.
21. See al-Muttaqī, *Kanz al-'Ummāl*, II, No. 766.
22. See, for example, al-Ṭabarī, *Jāmi' al-Bayān*, XVIII, 2, and XXVIII, 8.
23. Qur'ān, IX, 28.
24. Qur'ān, IX, 95.
25. Qur'ān, IX, 45.
26. Qur'ān, XVI, 22.
27. Qur'ān, II, 10.
28. Perhaps this is Luqmān al-Ḥakīm, who is mentioned in Qur'ān XXXI, 12-13, and is known for the many proverbs attibuted to him. See the article "Luḳmān" by B. Heller and N.A. Stillman in *The Encyclopaedia of Islam*, V, 811-813.
29. See the traditions reported by Sa'īd ibn Zayd and found in al-Tirmidhī (*al-manāqib* 3681, 3690), Abū Dāwūd (*al-sunnah* 4030, 4031), Ibn Mājah (*al-muqaddimah* 130, 131), and Aḥmad ibn Ḥanbal (*musnad al-'asharah al-mubashsharīn bi-al-jannah* 1543, 1544, 1545, 1551). In all of these traditions except No. 3681 of al-Tirmidhī those who are in Paradise are the Prophet himself and nine of his companions, all of whom were early converts to Islam: Abū Bakr, 'Umar, 'Uthmān, 'Alī, Ṭalḥah, al-Zubayr, Sa'd ibn Abī Waqqāṣ, 'Abd al-Raḥmān ibn 'Awf, and Sa'īd ibn Zayd. In No. 3681 a tenth companion, Abū 'Ubaydah ['Āmir ibn 'Abd Allāh], is added to the list but the Prophet himself is not mentioned. See also al-Muttaqī, *Kanz al-'Ummāl*, VI, Nos. 2724-2725, 6371-6378.
30. Qur'ān, II, 225.
31. 'Ammār ibn Yāsir was one of the companions of the Prophet. He was captured by infidels and forced to speak well of their gods and blaspheme the Prophet. See Abū Nu'aym al-Isbahānī, *Ḥilyat al-Awliyā'*, I, 140; Ibn al-Jawzī, *Ṣifat al-Ṣafwah*, I, 175; and al-Ṭabarī, *Jāmi' al-Bayān*, XIV, 122.
32. Qur'ān, XVI, 106.
33. A tradition not found in the canonical collections.
34. A tradition reported by al-Bukhārī (*bad' al-waḥy* 1, *al-īmān* 52, *al-'itq* 2344, *al-manāqib* 3609, *al-nikāḥ* 4682, *al-aymān wa-al-nudhūr* 6195, *al-ḥiyal* 6439), Muslim (*al-*

imārah 3530), al-Tirmidhī (*faḍā'il al-jihād* 1571), al-Nasā'ī (*al-ṭahārah* 74, *al-ṭalāq* 3383, *al-aymān wa-al-nudhūr* 3734), Abū Dāwūd (*al-ṭalāq* 1882), Ibn Mājah (*al-zuhd* 4217), and Aḥmad ibn Ḥanbal (*musnad al-'asharah al-mubashsharīn bi-al-jannah* 163, 283). See also Wensinck, *Concordance*, VII, 55.

35. A tradition not found in the canonical collections.

36. That is, on the day of judgment. This is a reference to Qur'ān, L, 19-22: *And the agony of death cometh in truth. This is that which thou wast wont to shun. And the trumpet is blown. This is the threatened Day. And every soul cometh, along with it a driver and a witness. Thou wast in heedlessness of this. Now we have removed from thee thy covering, and piercing is thy sight this day.*

37. Qur'ān, XLII, 52.

38. A tradition reported by al-Bukhārī (*al-ḥayḍ* 293, *al-zakāh* 1369), Muslim (*al-īmān* 114), al-Tirmidhī (*al-īmān* 2538), Abū Dāwūd (*al-sunnah* 4059), Ibn Mājah (*al-fitan* 3993), and Aḥmad ibn Ḥanbal (*musnad al-mukthirīn min al-ṣaḥābah* 5091). See also Wensinck, *Concordance*, VI, 538-539.

39. This is a reference to Qur'ān, XII, 87: *Go, O my sons, and ascertain concerning Joseph and his brother, and despair not of the spirit of God. Lo! none despaireth of the spirit of God save disbelieving folk.* According to al-Ṭabarī, *Jāmi' al-Bayān*, Vol. 13, 32-33, to despair of the spirit of God means to despair of God's power to release one from suffering and sadness.

40. Qur'ān, II, 97.

41. Qur'ān, XXVI, 193-4.

[Part Five: The Inner Heart]

1. Qur'ān, VI, 104 (105).

2. Qur'ān, VI, 104 (105).

3. Qur'ān, CII, 5-7.

4. See Qur'ān, XX, 86.

5. The story of Moses and the calf is mentioned a number of times in the Qur'ān. See for example II, 51-54, 92-93 and XX, 85-98. The story is given in more detail by al-Tha'labī in his *Qiṣaṣ al-Anbiyā'*, Cairo, al-Maṭba'ah wa-al-Maktabah al-Sa'īdīyah, no date, p. 199.

6. A tradition similar to one reported by Aḥmad ibn Ḥanbal (*musnad banī hāshim* 1745, 2320) See also Wensinck, *Concordance*, II, 5; IV, 451, and al-Haythamī, *Majma' al-Zawā'id*, I, 153.

7. Qur'ān, XX, 85.

8. This is apparently Abū Ja'far Muḥammad (al-Bāqir) ibn 'Alī ibn al-Ḥusayn ibn 'Alī ibn Abī Ṭālib, the great grandson of 'Alī ibn Abī Ṭālib and the fifth imam of the Shi'ites.

9. In al-Sarrāj's *Kitāb al-Luma'* this saying is attributed to 'Alī ibn Abī Ṭālib himself rather than to his great grandson. See p. 350.

10. Qur'ān, XXIV, 44.

11. Qur'ān, LIX, 2.

12. The Arabic manuscript does not include the complete text of the tradition, nor is the tradition to be found in any of the canonical collections. Several versions of it,

however, may be found in al-Haythamī, *Majma' al-Zawā'id*, I, 57; and in many of the early Sufi works such as al-Sarrāj, *Kitāb al-Luma'*, pp. 12-13; al-Sulamī, *Kitāb al-Arba'īn*, pp. 5-6; al-Tirmidhī, *Kitab al-Riyāḍah*, p. 69 and *Adab al-Nafs*, p. 127; al-Kalābādhī, *al-Ta'arruf*, pp. 7, 73, 78, 90-91, 94, 107 (Arberry translation, p. 7); al-Hujwīrī, *Kashf al-Maḥjūb*, pp. 38-39 (Nicholson translation, pp. 33-34). I have used the version in al-Sarrāj's *Kitāb al-Luma'* to complete the translation.

13. Qur'ān, XIV, 27.

14. Part of a tradition reported by Aḥmad ibn Ḥanbal (*musnad al-kūfīyīn* 18830). See also Wensinck, *Concordance*, V, 453.

15. A tradition reported by Ibn Mājah (*al-muqaddimah* 85) and Aḥmad ibn Ḥanbal (*musnad al-kūfīyīn* 18830, 18922). See also Wensinck, *Concordance*, II, 323; V, 453.

16. That is, the Sacred Mosque in Mecca.

17. That is, destiny as determined by God's eternal decree.

18. A tradition reported by al-Bukhārī (*al-īmān* 48, *tafsīr al-qur'ān* 4404), Muslim (*al-īmān* 9, 10, 11), al-Tirmidhī (*al-īmān* 2535), al-Nasā'ī (*al-īmān* 4904, 4905), Abū Dāwūd (*al-sunnah* 4075), Ibn Mājah (*al-muqaddimah* 62, 63), and Aḥmad ibn Ḥanbal (*musnad al-'asharah al-mubashsharīn bi-al-jannah* 179, 346, *bāqī musnad al-mukthirīn* 9137). See also Noah Ha Mim Keller, *The Reliance of the Traveller*, pp. 807-815, and Wensinck, *Concordance*, I, 467. The Arabic manuscript contains only the first few words of the tradition. The translation of the rest of the tradition is based on the version reported by Muslim (*al-īmān* 9).

19. Qur'ān, IV, 63.

20. Qur'ān, LIII, 11.

21. Qur'ān, XXII, 78.

22. Qur'ān, XII, 81.

23. Qur'ān, LXVIII, 29.

24. Qur'ān, VII, 156.

25. Qur'ān, XXV, 32.

26. Qur'ān, XVIII, 14.

27. Qur'ān, XXVIII, 10.

28. Qur'ān, XXVIII, 10.

29. See note 6 above.

[Part Six: The Intellect]

1. Qur'ān, XLIX, 7.

2. In an Arabic doubled root the last two of the three root letters are the same.

3. That is, the intellect.

4. Qur'ān, V, 100.

5. Qur'ān, II, 197.

6. Qur'ān, VI, 90 (91).

7. Qur'ān, II, 269.

8. Qur'ān, XIV, 52.

9. Qur'ān, XXXVIII, 29 (30).

10. That is, he becomes capable of understanding God's argument addressed to him in the Qur'ān.

11. A tradition reported by al-Tirmidhī (*al-birr wa-al-ṣilah*, 1956) and Aḥmad ibn Ḥanbal (*bāqī musnad al-mukthirīn*, 10634, 11234). See also Winsinck, *Concordance*, I, 504.

12. Qur'ān, XXIX, 43. The full verse is: *As for these similitudes, we coin them for mankind, but none will grasp their meaning save the knowers.*

13. Qur'an, XX, 54, 128.

14. Qur'ān, LXXXIX, 5.

15. A tradition reported by Muslim (*al-ṣalāh* 654), al-Nasā'ī (*al-imāmah* 798, 803), Ibn Mājah (*iqāmat al-ṣalāh wa-al-sunnah fīhā* 966), Aḥmad ibn Ḥanbal (*musnad al-shāmīyīn* 16482) and al-Dārimī (*al-ṣalāh* 1238). See also Wensinck, *Concordance*, I, 504.

16. Qur'ān, XVI, 67.

17. A tradition reported by al-Tirmidhī (*al-'ilm* 2582), Ibn Mājah (*al-muqaddimah* 226), Abū Dāwūd (*al-'ilm* 3175), Aḥmad ibn Ḥanbal (*musnad al-anṣār* 20608) and al-Dārimī (*al-muqaddimah* 229, 231). See also Wensinck, *Concordance*, I, 516.

18. Perhaps this is Luqmān al-Ḥakīm. See note 28 to Part Six above.

19. al-Ḥasan ibn 'Alī ibn Abī Ṭālib, grandson of the Prophet.

20. As opposed to "learning in the science of legal rulings" mentioned previously. The word *fiqh* is applied to both scholarly learning attained through study and a to deeper understanding of religion attained through illumination from God.

21. Qur'ān, LXIII, 7.

22. See al-Muttaqī, *Kanz al-'Ummāl*, V, Nos. 4072, 4098.

23. That is, scholarly learning and understanding in religion.

24. That is, the philosopher's stone or elixir believed to possess the power of turning base metals into gold or silver. See the article "Al-Kibrīt" by M. Ullmann in *The Encyclopaedia of Islam*, V, 88-90.

25. A discussion of the science of interpretation (*istinbāṭ*) may be found in al-Sarrāj, *Kitāb al-Luma'*, pp. 30-35 of the English abstract and pp. 105-119 of the Arabic text.

26. That is, God's argument to mankind as revealed to His prophets. See Qur'ān, VI, 83, 149.

[Part Seven: The Lights of the Heart]

1. That is, what pertains to fear and hope.

2. Qur'ān, II, 132.

3. Qur'ān, XII, 101.

4. That is, fear of the antecedent judgment of God, of what God has preordained in His eternity. See al-Bustānī, *Muḥīṭ al-Muḥīṭ*, I, 918 where *al-sābiqah* is defined as *al-'ināyah al-azalīyah* or eternal providence. See also al-Sarrāj, *Kitāb al-Luma'*, p. 24 of the English abstract and p. 84 of the Arabic text.

5. Qur'ān, XII, 53.

6. Qur'ān, XCI, 8.

7. Qur'ān, LXXV, 2.

8. Qur'ān, LXXXIX, 27-28.

9. Qur'ān, LVI, 89. In this verse (as in XII, 87) the word *rūḥ* (spirit) can also be read as *rawḥ* (joy or happiness; rest or ease). See al-Tabarī, *Jāmi' al-Bayān*, XXVII, 121-122; al-Tirmidhī, *Nawādir al-Uṣūl*, p. 81; Radtke, *The Concept of Sainthood*, p. 147.

10. A reference to the author's description of the heart as consisting of four stations: breast (*ṣadr*), heart (*qalb*), inner heart (*fu'ād*) and intellect (*lubb*) at the beginning of the work.

11. Qur'ān, XII, 82.

12. Qur'ān, X, 98 (99).

13. Part of a tradition reported by al-Tirmidhī (*al-nikāḥ* 1023), al-Nasā'ī (*al-jum'ah* 1387), Abū Dāwūd (*al-nikāḥ* 1809, 1883), Aḥmad ibn Ḥanbal (*musnad banī hāshim* 2613, *musnad al-mukthirīn min al-ṣaḥābah* 3536, 3906) and al-Dārimī (*al-nikāḥ* 2105).

14. Part of several different traditions reported by Muslim (*ṣifat al-qiyāmah* 5034), al-Tirmidhī (*al-raḍā'* 1092), al-Nasā'ī (*'ishrat al-nisā'* 3898), Aḥmad ibn Ḥanbal (*musnad banī hāshim* 2209, *musnad al-mukthirīn min al-ṣaḥābah* 3591, 3611, 4160, 4366, *bāqī musnad al-mukthirīn* 13804, *bāqī musnad al-anṣār* 23701), and al-Dārimī (*al-riqāq* 2618, 2663). In these traditions the last word of the part quoted here is vocalized sometimes as *aslama* and sometimes as *aslamu*. *Aslama* means "he surrendered" [to God], whereas *aslamu* means "I am safe" [from the influence of the satan]. See also Wensinck, *Concordance*, II, 514.

15. That is, the true faith. See Qur'ān, II, 256; XXXI, 22.

16. Qur'ān, XIV, 27.

17. A tradition not found in the canonical collections.

18. See above note 6 to Part Five above.

19. A high mountain range believed to encircle the Earth. See Yāqūt, *Mu'jam al-Buldān*, IV, 298 (under *qāf*) and Mustawfī, *Nuzhat al-Qulūb* (Le Strange translation), p. 188. The name of the 50th sūrah of the Qur'ān, *sūrat Qāf*, is sometimes identified with this mountain. See al-Ṭabarī, *Jāmi' al-Bayān*, XXVI, 93.

[Part Eight: The Unitarian]

1. At the end of the line at this point in the Arabic MS there is a small blank space which is probably meant to indicate that some words or even lines have been left out. As a result the meaning of the analogy between the man about to be devoured by the lion and the unitarian is not very clear. The point of the analogy, however, seems to be that just as the man threatened by the lion sees himself caught in a state between life and death, the unitarian finds himself caught between his normal state in the world of sense perception and the state of unification which he is about to enter.

2. That is, the extreme of denying God's attributes.

3. That is, the extreme of likening God to what is other than He.

4. The forerunners are mentioned in Qur'ān LVI, 10-11; see also al-Sarrāj, *Luma'*, pp. 84-86 of the Arabic text, p. 24 of the English abstract.

5. A tradition reported by al-Tirmidhī (*al-zuhd* 2322), Ibn Mājah (*al-fitan* 4013), Aḥmad ibn Ḥanbal (*musnad al-'asharah al-mubashsharīn bi-al-jannah* 1400, 1412, 1473, 1521), and al-Dārimī (*al-riqāq* 2664). See also Wensinck, *Corcordance*, I, 220.

6. The first part of this tradition is reported in all nine of the canonical collections in Sakhr's *Mawsū'ah*. The latter part, "and pour dust upon your heads," is not reported in any of them. See also Wensinck, *Concordance*, I, 211.

7. A tradition not found in the canonical collections.

8. A tradition not found in the canonical collections.

9. This is reported by al-Nasā'ī (*al-sahw* 1199), Abū Dāwūd (*al-ṣalāh* 769) and Aḥmad ibn Ḥanbal (*musnad al-madanīyīn* 15722, 15727, 15735). See also Wensinck, *Concordance*, I, 58; and Lane, *Arabic-English Lexicon*, I, 52.

10. Qur'ān, XXX, 7.

11. Qur'ān, XVI, 97.

12. A tradition reported by Muslim (*al-īmān* 49), al-Tirmidhī (*al-īmān* 2547) and Aḥmad ibn Ḥanbal (*musnad banī hāshim* 1682, 1683). See also Wensinck, *Concordance*, II, 195. Only the first part of the tradition is quoted in the Arabic manuscript.

13. A tradition found, with various different wordings, in the collections of al-Bukhārī (*al-īmān* 15), Muslim (*al-īmān* 60, 61), al-Tirmidhī (*al-īmān* 2548), al-Nasā'ī (*al-īmān wa-sharā'i 'uhu* 4901, 4902, 4903), and Aḥmad ibn Ḥanbal (*bāqī musnad al-mukthirīn* 11564, 11679, 12304, 12321, 12927, 13102, 13449, 13556). See also Wensinck, *Concordance*, I, 296.

14. That is, Satan. See Qur'ān, CXIV, 4.

15. Qur'ān, II, 257.

16. Qur'ān, XLVII, 11.

17. Qur'ān, VII, 196.

18. Qur'ān, L, 37.

19. Qur'ān, LI, 21.

20. A non-canonical tradition often quoted in Sufi works. See al-Hujwīrī, *Kashf al-Maḥjūb*, pp. 247, 353 (Nicholson translation, pp. 197, 275).

21. Qur'ān, XXIV, 35.

22. That is, the Qur'ān.

23. Qur'ān, XXIV, 40.

24. A somewhat similar tradition is found in al-Tirmidhī (*tafsīr al-qur'ān* 44): "Beware the insight of the believer, for he sees with the light of God." This was reported to have been said by the Prophet in conjunction with the revelation of Qur'ān, XV, 75. See al-Ṭabarī, *Jāmi' al-Bayān*, XIV, 31-32; Lane, *Lexicon*, II, 2368; and al-Muttaqī, *Kanz al-'Ummāl*, I, 825.

25. That is, let your heart pronounce for you the correct course of action. The tradition is not found in the canonical collections.

26. A tradition not found in the canonical collections. See, however, the last sentence of a tradition reported by Aḥmad ibn Ḥanbal (*musnad al-shāmīyīn* 16976).

27. A tradition not found in the canonical collections.

28. Qur'ān, III, 169.

29. Qur'ān, II, 154.

30. Qur'ān, XVII, 85.

31. Qur'ān, LVIII, 22.

32. Qur'ān, XL, 15.

33. Qur'ān, XLII, 52.

34. That is, in a state in which one is no longer aware of the past and future of created time but only of the "present time" of eternity. See al-Hujwīrī, *Kashf al-Maḥjūb*, pp. 480-481; (Nicholson translation pp. 367-370), and Schimmel, *Mystical Dimensions of Islam*, p. 220.

35. See Qur'ān, XXI, 101. See also al-Ṭabarī, *Jāmi' al-Bayān*, XIX, 75; and Lane, *Lexicon*, I, 571.

36. See Qur'ān X, 62.

37. That is, the Prophet Muhammad.

38. That is, Islam or the religion of God. See Qur'ān, II, 138; Lane, *Lexicon*, II, 1648; and al-Ṭabarī, *Jāmi' al-Bayān*, I, 444-445.

39. An allusion to faith in God or to Islam or to the profession of faith (*shahādah*). See Qur'ān, II, 256; XXXI, 22; Lane, *Lexicon*, II, 2028-2029; and al-Ṭabarī, *Jāmi' al-Bayān*, III, 13-14.

The breast of the believer contracts sometimes from the abundance of evil whispering, or from sorrow, distraction, the succession of wants, and the occurence of accidents and calamities. The breast also contracts if the believer hears a falsehood which his heart cannot endure, for God has expanded his breast with the light of Islam *so that he followeth a light from his Lord.*

REVISIONS TO THE ARABIC TEXT

The page and line numbers refer to the Arabic edition, not to the present translation.

p. 35, line 9: *qamlah* should be changed to *qaml*. A collective noun like *ba'ūḍ* and *dhubāb* is called for here.

p. 37, lines 5-7: According to the text of this tradition given by al-Muttaqī in his *Kanz al-'Ummāl*, *al-yad janāḥ* should be *al-yadān janaḥān*; *maṣlaḥah* (with *ṣād*) should be *maslaḥah* (with *sīn*); and *ḍaḥkah* should be *ḍaḥk*.

p. 40, line 7: Perhaps *wilāyat al-takalluf* should be *wilāyah wa-takalluf*. See p. 84, line 2 of the Arabic text.

p. 40, line 10: *ākhir* should probably be *ākhidh*, which is what the Arabic manuscript has.

p. 50, line 10: *makā'id* should be *makāyid*.

p. 53, line 7: *āmana* should be *fa-āmana* to indicate the beginning of the predicate of the sentence.

p. 53, line 9: *ma'a Allāh* makes little sense; *minan Allāh* would be a better reading.

p. 54, line 10: *wa-al-riyā'* should be *wa-al-ri'ā'*.

p. 61, line 4: *mathal* near the beginning of the line seems to be superfluous here.

p. 71, line 2: Perhaps *maqrūn* should be *mawzūn* as in *'aql mawzūn*. See the last line of p. 75 where one type of *'aql* is described as *mawzūn* and *maṭbū'*.

p. 71, line 3: *allatī hiya dākhilah* should probably be *allatī hiya dākhilah fīhā*.

p. 71, lines 7-8: *'aṣama hādhihi al-buḥūr* does not make much sense since only one *baḥr* has been mentioned. Perhaps the correct reading is simply *'asamahu* with the *hu* referring to *lubb.*

p. 72, line 4: *al-ḥurūf al-muḍā'afah* should be *ḥurūf al-muḍā'af.*

p. 76, line 9: I now believe this line makes better sense without the added *ghayr.*

p. 77, line 3: the *hamzah* on *ijtināb* should be removed.

p. 82, line 3: *lafẓat ism al-nafs* should probably be simply *ism al-nafs* or *lafẓat al-nafs.*

p. 82, line 9: *wa-hiya* seems to be superfluous.

p. 84, line 9: *ṣāliḥ a'mālihā* should probably be read *iṣlāḥ a'mālihā.*

p. 84, line 11: The period between *al-tafwīḍ* and *al-mushāhadah* should probably be removed. The meaning of the Arabic text is not clear here. Perhaps it should be emended to read *wa-al-mushāhadah allatī hiya ajallu mimmā yarā al-nafs.*

p. 86, line 6: *'ashiqat* does not make much sense. Perhaps the correct reading is *'affat.*

p. 87, line 3: *min aqwālihi* should probably be *fī aqwālihi.*

p. 88, line 1: Instead of *ẓulmah* the Arabic manuscript has *maẓlimah.* Neither word makes much sense in this context. The correct reading is probably *miẓallah.*

p. 88, line 11: *ṭarīq al-takayyuf* should probably be *ṭarīq al-takalluf.*

p. 89, line 12: Perhaps *mu'āfāh* should be *mu'āfiyah.* The active participle makes better sense here than the passive participle.

p. 92, line 7: *yataqārabu wa-yatafāḍalu* does not make much sense. Perhaps the correct reading should be *yataqāṣaru wa-yatafāḍalu.*

p. 96, line 7: *tawḥīd* should probably be *tawṭīd.*

p. 97, line 7: *yablughu* should be *tablughu* since its subject is *al-shams.*

p. 97, line 11: *wa-hiya ṭulūʻ al-shams* should probably be *wa-huwa ṭulūʻ al-shams*, the antecedent of *huwa* being *nūr al-tawḥīd.*

p. 98, line 4: *ṭalaʻat nūru shamsihi* should be *ṭalaʻat shamsu nūrihi* since *shams* is feminine and *nūr* is masculine. The change does not affect the meter, which is *khafīf.*

p. 100, line 8: *musaddad* should probably be *mushaddad.*

p. 101, line 6: *duʻāhu* should be *duʻā'ahu*, as in the Arabic manuscript.

p. 102, line 5: *mujarramūn* should be *mukharramūn.*

p. 102, line 6: *jamalahu* should be *jaʻalahu* as in the Arabic manuscript.

BIBLIOGRAPY

'Abd al-Bāqī, Muḥammad Fu'ād. *al-Mu'jam al-Mufahras li-Alfāẓ al-Qur'ān al-Karīm*, Cairo: Dār al-Kutub al-Miṣrīyah, 1364.

Arberry, A.J. *The Koran Interpreted*. Two volumes. London: George Allen and Unwin, 1955.

Barakah, 'Abd al-Fattāḥ 'Abd Allāh. *Al-Ḥakīm al-Tirmidhī wa-Naẓarīyatuhu fī al-Wilāyah*. Cairo, 1971.

al-Bustānī, Buṭrus. *Muḥīṭ al-Muḥīṭ*. Two volumes. Beirut 1286/1870.

The Encyclopaedia Britannica. Eleventh edition. New York 1911.

The Encyclopaedia of Islam. New Edition. Leiden: E.J. Brill, 1960-2002.

Fihris al-Kutub al-'Arabīyah al-Mawjūdah bi-al-Dār, Cairo 1924.

Griffith, Sydney H. "As One Spiritual Man to Another: The Merton-Abdul Aziz Correspondence" in *Merton and Sufism: The Untold Story*, pp. 101-129.

al-Haythamī, Nūr al-Dīn 'Alī ibn Abī Bakr. *Majma' al-Zawā'id wa-Manba' al-Fawā'id*. Six volumes. Cairo 1352-1353.

Heer, Nicholas. "A Sufi Psychological Treatise" in *The Muslim World*, Vol. 51 (1961), pp. 25-36, 83-91, 163-172, 244-258. (A translation of *Bayān al-Farq bayn al-Ṣadr wa-al-Qalb wa-al-Fu'ād wa-al-Lubb*.)

———. "Some Biographical and Bibliographical Notes on al-Ḥakīm al-Tirmidhi" in *The World of Islam: Studies in honour of Philip K. Hitti*. London 1959. pp. 121-134.

Heller, B. and Stillman, N.A. "Luḳmān" in *The Encyclopaedia of Islam*, V, 811-813.

al-Hujwīrī, 'Alī ibn 'Uthmān al-Jullābī. *Kashf al-Maḥjūb*. Edited by Valentin A. Zhukovskij. Leningrad 1926. Reprinted, Tehran 1336/1957.

———. *Kashf al-Maḥjūb*. Translated by Reynold A. Nicholson. E.J.W. Gibb Memorial Series, Vol. 17. London 1911.

Ibn al-Jawzī, Abū al-Faraj 'Abd al-Raḥmān ibn 'Alī ibn Muḥammad ibn 'Alī. *Ṣifat al-Ṣafwah*. Four volumes. Hyderabad 1355-1356.

al-Iṣbahānī, Abū Nu'aym Aḥmad ibn 'Abd Allāh. *Ḥilyat al-Awliyā' wa-Ṭabaqāt al-Aṣfiyā'*. Ten volumes. Cairo 1351/1932-1357/1938.

al-Kalābādhī. *Kitāb al-Ta'arruf li-Madhhab Ahl al-Taṣawwuf*. Edited by A.J. Arberry. Cairo 1352/1933.

Keller, Noah Ha Mim. *The Reliance of the Traveller*. Evanston: Sunna Books, 1991 (An edition and translation of *'Umdat al-Sālik wa-'Uddat al-Nāsik* by Aḥmad ibn al-Naqīb al-Miṣrī.)

Lane, E. W. *Arabic-English Lexicon*. London 1863. Reprint. Two volumes. Cambridge: The Islamic Texts Society, 1984.

Levey, Martin. *The Medical Formulary or Aqrābādhīn of al-Kindī*. Madison: University of Wisconsin Press, 1966.

al-Māturīdī, Abū Manṣūr Muḥammad ibn Muḥammad ibn Maḥmūd. *Sharḥ al-Fiqh al-Akbar*. Hyderabad 1321.

Mawsū 'at al-Ḥadīth al-Sharīf. Version 1.2. CD-ROM. Cairo: Sakhr Software Co., 1996. This collection is also available online at hadith.ajeeb.com or www.ajeeb.com.

Mélanges Louis Massignon. Three volumes. Damascus: Institut Français de Damas, 1957.

Merton and Sufism: The Untold Story. A Complete Compendium. Edited by Rob Baker and Gray Henry. Louisville: Fons Vitae, 1999.

Mustawfī, Ḥamd Allāh. *Nuzhat al-Qulūb*. Translated by Guy le Strange. E.J.W. Gibb Memorial Series, Vol. XXIII, No. 2. Leyden and London, 1919.

al-Muttaqī, 'Alī ibn 'Abd al-Malik. *Kanz al-'Ummāl fī Sunan al-Aqwāl wa-al-Af'āl*. Eight volumes. Hyderabad 1312-1314.

———. *Kanz al-'Ummāl fī Sunan al-Aqwāl wa-al-Af'āl*. 16 volumes. Aleppo: Maktabat al-Turāth al-Islāmī, [1969]-1977.

al-Nūrī, Abū al-Ḥasan. "Risālat Maqāmāt al-Qulūb," edited by Paul Nwyia in *Mélanges de l'Université Saint-Joseph*, Vol. XLIV (1968), pp. 129-143.

Nwyia, Paul. "Textes mystiques inédits d'Abū-l-Ḥasan al-Nūrī " in *Mélanges de l'Université Saint-Joseph*, Vol. XLIV (1968), pp. 115-154.

Pickthall, Mohammed Marmaduke. *The Meaning of the Glorious Koran*. New York: New American Library, 1953.

al-Qur'ān al-Karīm. Edited by Muḥammad 'Alī Khalaf al-Ḥusaynī, Ḥifnī Nāṣif, Naṣr al-'Ādilī, Muṣṭafā 'Ināni, and Aḥmad al-Iskandarī. Būlāq: al-Maṭba'ah al-Amīrīyah, 1342. (Published under the auspices of King Fu'ād I of Egypt.)

Radtke, Bernd. *Al-Ḥakīm at-Tirmidī: Ein islamischer Theosoph des 3./9. Jahrhunderts*. Freiburg 1980.

———. "Theologen und Mystiker in Ḫurāsān und Transoxanien" in *Zeitschrift der deutschen morgenländischen Gesellschaft*. Vol. 136 (1986), pp. 536-569.

Radtke, Bernd and O'Kane, John. *The Concept of Sainthood in Early Islamic Mysticism: Two Works by al-Ḥakīm al-Tirmidhī*. Richmond, Surrey 1996. (Contains English translations of *Sīrat al-Awliyā'* and *Bad' Sha'n Abī 'Abd Allāh*.)

Radtke, Bernd. "Tirmidiana Minora" in *Oriens*, Vol. 34 (1994), pp. 242-277.

Redhouse, James W. *A Turkish and English Lexicon*. Constantinople 1921.

al-Sarrāj, Abū Naṣr 'Abd Allāh ibn 'Alī. *Kitāb al-Luma' fī al-Taṣawwuf*. Edited by Reynold Alleyne Nicholson. Leiden: E.J. Brill, 1914. (E.J.W. Gibb Memorial Series, Vol. XXII)

Schimmel, Annemarie. *Mystical Dimensions of Islam*. Chapel Hill: University of North Carolina Press, 1975.

Sezgin, Fuat. *Geschichte des arabischen Schriftums*. Leiden: E.J. Brill. 1967-.

al-Sulamī, Abū 'Abd al-Raḥmān Muḥammad ibn al-Ḥusayn. *Kitāb al-Arba'īn fī al-Taṣawwuf*. Hyderabad 1369/1950.

al-Ṭabarī, Muḥammad ibn Jarīr. *Jāmi' al-Bayān fī Tafsīr al-Qur'ān*. 30 volumes. Būlāq 1323-1329.

al-Tha'labī, Abū Isḥāq Aḥmad ibn Muḥammad. *Qiṣaṣ al-Anbiyā'*, Cairo: al-Maṭba'ah wa-al-Maktabah al-Sa'īdīyah, no date.

al-Tirmidhī, Muḥammad ibn 'Alī al-Ḥakīm. *Bayān al-Farq bayn al-Ṣadr wa-al-Qalb wa-al-Fu'ād wa-al-Lubb*. Edited by Nicholas Heer. Cairo 1958.

———. *Kitāb al-Riyāḍah wa-Adab al-Nafs*. Edited by A.J. Arberry and 'Alī Ḥusayn 'Abd al-Qādir. Cairo 1366/1947.

al-Tirmidhī, Muḥammad ibn 'Alī al-Ḥakīm. *Nawādir al-Uṣūl*. Constantinople 1294.

Ullmann, M.. "Al-Kibrīt" in *The Encyclopaedia of Islam*, V, 88-90.

Wensinck, A. J.. *Concordance et indices de la tradition musulmane*. Seven volumes. Leiden 1936-1969.

Winder, R. Bayly. "Makka" (3. The Modern City), in *The Encyclopaedia of Islam*, VI, 152-180.

The World of Islam: Studies in honour of Philip K. Hitti. Edited by James Kritzeck and R. Bayly Winder. London 1959.

Yahya, Othman. "L'Oeuvre de Tirmidī " in *Mélanges Louis Massignon*, Vol. 3, pp. 411-480.

Yāqūt ibn 'Abd Allāh, Shihāb al-Dīn Abū 'Abd Allāh. *Mu'jam al-Buldān*. Five volumes. Beirut 1374/1955-1376/1957.

BIOGRAPHY

Nicholas Heer was born on 8 February 1928 in Chapel Hill, North Carolina. He received his B.A. from Yale University in 1949 and his Ph.D. from Princeton University in 1955. From 1955 to 1957 he worked as a translation analyst for the Arabian American Oil Company in Saudi Arabia. In 1958 he returned to the United States to become curator of the Middle East collections of the Hoover Institution at Stanford University. The following year he was appointed an assistant professor of Arabic in the Department of Asian Languages at Stanford. During the academic year 1962-63 he was a visiting lecturer at Yale University, and from 1963 to 1965 he was an assistant professor of Arabic at Harvard University.

In 1965 he was appointed associate professor of Arabic at the University of Washington and was subsequently promoted to full professor in 1976. In 1982 he was named chair of the Department of Near Eastern Languages and Civilization and served in that capacity until 1987. He retired from the University of Washington in 1990.

His publications include an Arabic edition of 'Abd al-Raḥmān al-Jāmī's *al-Durrah al-Fākhirah* (Wisdom of Persia Series XIX, Tehran, 1980), and an English translation of the same work published under the title *The Precious Pearl* (Albany: SUNY Press, 1979).

INDEX OF ARABIC WORDS

The Truly Sincere *Faqīr*

The *faqīr* who is truly sincere in his *faqr* prefers the honor of others to his [own] honor, and his [own] abasement to the abasement of others. I heard from Muḥammad ibn ʻAbdallāh al-Rāzī that al-Ḥusayn ibn ʻAlī al-Qirmīsīnī said:

> ʻĀṣim al-Balkhī sent a [gift] to Ḥātim al-Aṣamm (d. 230/851), who accepted it. When he was asked why he had accepted it, he replied, "In accepting it I found my abasement and his honor; while in refusing it, his abasement and my honor. I preferred his honor to mine and my abasement to his."

> When a servant has realised the state of true *faqr*, he dons the raiment of contentment, and in so doing increases his compassion for others, such that he conceals their faults, prays for them, and shows them mercy.
>
> Abū ʻAbdallāh ibn al-Jalā'

STATIONS OF THE RIGHTEOUS

Darajāt al-ṣādiqīn

&

THE HUMBLE SUBMISSION OF THOSE ASPIRING

Kitāb bayān tadhallul al-fuqarā'

TWO TEXTS FROM THE PATH OF BLAME

by ABŪ 'ABD AL-RAḤMĀN AL-SULAMĪ AL-NAYSABŪRĪ (D. 412/1021)
INTRODUCED *and* TRANSLATED *by* KENNETH L. HONERKAMP

Dedicated to Mustafa Naji

A Precious Friendship 1980 - 2000
He taught me the beauty of a manuscript

ACKNOWLEDGEMENTS

I would like to give my heartfelt thanks to everyone who made the appearance of these texts from the Path of Blame a possibility. First I would like to express a great debt of gratitude to my dear friend Mustapha Naji, bookseller of Rabat who was known and loved by scholars of many diverse fields and nationalities. Mustapha first brought the manuscripts translated here to my attention. Mr. Saad M. al-Sheikh helped with a copy of the Sulamiyyat manuscript from the Muhammad Ibn Saad Islamic University in Riyadh, Saudi Arabia. Dr. Nasrollah Pourjavady and Mohammed Soori kindly provided me with an excellent copy of the Baku manuscript of *Kitāb bayān tadhallul al-fuqara'*. Dr. Alan Godlas of the University of Georgia afforded me much valuable advice on the translations. Dr. Laury Silvers of Skidmore College meticulously read and edited the manuscript; her advice has been invaluable, I cannot thank her enough. Ahmad Muttaqi of Marrakesh, Morocco, kindly proofread the critical edition of the Arabic manuscripts. Michael Fitzgerald provided invaluable advice on the translations and spent hours revising the style; his efforts went a long way in making the translations as readable as they are. Dr. Jean-Jaques Thibon of the University of Clermont, France, and I have shared a mutual interest in Sulamī, our collaboration has been a pleasure. I owe much to my parents who have been so supportive during all my years of itinerant scholarship within the Islamic world. In closing I would like to thank my wife and child for being so generous with their time. Their patience and understanding have sustained me and been a constant source of encouragement for me. Without them these texts would never have seen the light of day.

PREFACE

In tenth century Nishapur, in northeastern Iran in a region known as Khurasan, a small circle of teachers and their disciples emerged who stressed the central role of *blame* (*malāma*) in perfecting an aspirant's intimate knowledge of God (*ma'rifa*). They became known as the *Malāmatīya, The People of Blame*. For the *Malāmatīya*, blame comprised sincere self-awareness and self-criticism originating in attitudes that abandoned any outward manifestations of distinctiveness. Their only distinctive characteristic was an unpretentious but strict adherence to the *Sharī'a*. Blame became, for the *Malāmatīya*, a double-edged sword with inner and outer dimensions. On the one hand it affirmed the essentially intimate and ineffable nature of the spiritual path in an epoch searching for definitions and codes of conduct. While on the other it affirmed the essential dependence of conduct on inward attitudes in an era when distinctive modes of conduct and eloquence in doctrinal exposition were becoming the measure of spirituality. The reverberations of the Malāmatī response to the dynamics of life in tenth century Nishapur would resonate in the eras to come as Sufism became "a systematized expression of a way of life intended for all levels of pious citizenry, from the saintly ecstatic to the craftsman or merchant." (Bulliet, *Islam: The View from the Edge*, 161.)

Abū 'Abd al-Raḥmān al-Sulamī was born and educated in Nishapur, home of the Malāmatīya. He was introduced to Sufism at an early age by disciples of the principal teachers among the Malāmatīya of Nishapur. His *Treatise of the People of Blame* (*Risālat al-malāmatīya*) is the most definitive work we have on the doctrine and practices of the Malāmatīya. Sulamī spent his life composing works on all the domains of the spiritual path, to the degree that much of what we know about the formative period of Sufism has reached us either directly through his works or through those of his disciples. The themes that define his works embody the teachings of the Malāmatīya: the necessary reciprocity of inner and outer attitudes to the realization of sincerity, which for Sulamī and the Malāmatīya, was the key to intimate knowledge of God.

Darajāt al-ṣādiqīn and *Tadhallul al-fuqarā'* are textual examples of these teachings: the inner and the outward aspects of aspiration. While *Darajāt al-ṣādiqīn* depicts the states of the aspirant upon the ascendant path, *Tadhallul al-fuqarā'* treats the conduct incumbent upon the aspirant. *Darajāt al-ṣādiqīn* provides the metaphysical tenets upon which the teachings of the

Malāmatīya are based. *Tadhallul al-fuqarā'* illustrates how these tenets are to be implemented. *Darajāt al-ṣādiqīn* is representative of Sulamī's personal teaching style in which he employs a minimum of narrative material from earlier sources. *Tadhallul al-fuqarā'* exemplifies Sulamī's role as a transmitter of spiritual counsel (*naṣīḥa*), counsel richly supported by narratives from both Malāmatī and Sufi sources. In *Darajāt al-ṣādiqīn* Sulamī affirms the theoretical synthesis of *malāma* and Sufism as complimentary aspects of the Islamic mystical tradition. In *Tadhallul al-fuqarā'* he provides us with the thread that unites them, *inherent poverty* (*faqr*).

Darajāt al-ṣādiqīn and *Tadhallul al-fuqarā'* are not only textual examples of the teachings of Sulamī as they bear witness to his fidelity to Malāmatī principles; they also show the profound degree to which he himself participated in the pursuit of intimate knowledge of God. Sulamī himself was a living example of the Malāmatīya way. His teachings, mirrored in his works, demonstrate the principles, attitudes, and conduct of the *path of blame*; while his life exemplifies his spiritual function as a guiding light to those aspiring on the path to intimate knowledge of God.

The present edition of *Darajāt al-ṣādiqīn* and *Tadhallul al-fuqarā'* has been revised and updated based on my recent acquisition of a very early manuscript from Baku, Azerbaijan and microfilm copies of the two Fātiḥ manuscripts that I had previously accessed through the critical editions of Dr. Süleyman Ateş, published in his collection of nine of Sulamī's texts (Ankara, 1401/1981). I have in particular updated the section describing these manuscripts and provided photographic examples of each. I have also slightly revised my introduction in the light of recent scholarship in the field and revised my critical edition of *Tadhallul al-fuqarā'* based on new insights afforded by the Baku and Fātiḥ Library manuscripts.

INTRODUCTION

The Life and Times of ABŪ 'ABD AL-RAḤMĀN AL-SULAMĪ

The works of Abū 'Abd Raḥmān al-Sulamī al-Naysabūrī (d. 412/1021) have long been regarded as an essential source of some of the deepest insights we have into the formative period of Islamic mysticism. During his own time he was highly respected by his contemporaries for his knowledge of hadith and his devotion to the principles of Sufism. He continues to be influential not only through his own works on all aspects of formative Islamic mysticism but also through the works of his students and disciples. Figures such as Abū Qāsim al-Qushayrī (d. 465/1073), Abū Nu'aym al-Iṣbahānī (d. 430/1038), al-Ḥākim Muḥammad ibn 'Abdallāh al-Naysāburī (d. 405/10140 and Aḥmad ibn al-Ḥusayn al-Bayhaqī (d. 458/1066) were students of Sulamī and all played a central role in the transmission of the teachings of that period. Sulamī was however, more than a major figure in the history of Sufism, he was a 'school' in himself, a precursor whose personal example and works set the norms of much of what we know today as Islamic mysticism. *Darajāt al-ṣādiqīn* and *Tadhallul al-fuqarā'* are among the defining works of this school.

Abū 'Abd al-Raḥmān Sulamī is best known to western scholars for his works of Sufi hagiography, Sufi commentary on the Qur'ān, and treatises on Sufi manners and customs. By his contemporaries he was known as "a celebrated mystic,"[1] involved in the initiation and instruction of aspirants. He was well versed in the study of the Traditions of the Prophet (*aḥādīth*), the transmission of these Traditions, and in the lore of the founding fathers of Sufism. He was able to "situate and class this knowledge within a synthetic vision in accordance with the 'grasp' of one that had himself tasted the intense spiritual fervor [of an intimate knowledge of God.]"[2] Affirming Sulamī's stature among the scholars of Sufism, Ahmet Karamsustafa, in his recently published *Sufism: The Formative Period*, notes that, "There can be no doubt whatsoever about Sulamī's standing as a major Sufi figure.[3]

Sulamī – His life and times

Sulamī[4] was born in Nishapur in the northeastern region of Iran called Khurasan in 325/937 and died in the same city in 412/1021.[5] His family was well off and known in Nishapur for their involvement in the intellectual and political life of that city.[6] Among his ancestors had been Aḥmad ibn Yūsuf ibn Khālid al-Naysabūrī, a famous scholar of hadith. Little is known of Sulamī's father, al-Ḥusayn ibn Muḥammad ibn Mūsā al-Azdī (d. 348/958), except that he was counted among those who frequented the early Malāmatīya of Nishapur,[7] and later migrated to Mecca, leaving Sulamī in the care of his maternal grandfather, ibn Nujayd (d. 366/976)[8]. Ibn Nujayd was a well known scholar of hadith. He had had contacts with the most important Sufi shaykhs of his time, Abū 'Uthmān al-Ḥīrī (d. 298/910)[9], his mentor Abū Ḥafṣ (270/880)[10] in Nishapur and Junayd in Baghdad. Ibn Nujayd through Abū 'Uthmān and Abū Ḥafṣ was directly affiliated with the Malāmatīya. Sulamī thus inherited the Malāmatīya tradition at an early age from both his father and grandfather.

Sulamī studied theology, jurisprudence of the Shāfi'ī school and hadith in his youth. He was given a certificate of competence (*ijāza*) to issue religious judgements (*fatwa*) and to teach pupils.[11] Yet like so many of the scholars of his day he also followed the mystical path. Sulamī was initiated into the spiritual path by an heir to the most venerated representatives of Nishapur's Malāmatīya, Abū Sahl al-Ṣu'lūkī (d. 367/977). Ṣu'lūkī, initiated Sulamī into the spiritual path[12] and gave him permission to instruct novices. Ṣu'lūkī's mentor was Abū 'Alī al-Thaqafī (d. 329/940),[13] heir to the Malāmatīya through Abū 'Uthmān al-Ḥīrī, Abū Ḥafṣ and the shaykh of the Malāmatīya, Ḥamdūn al-Qaṣṣār (d. 271/885)[14], who was considered the founder of the Malāmatīya. Sulamī was thus initiated into the spiritual path by the heirs to the most venerated representatives of the Malāmatīya of Nishapur. According to Jāmī, Abū al-Qāsim al-Naṣrābādhī (d. 367/978), a scholar of hadith and an associate of Ṣu'lūkī invested Sulamī with the Sufi mantle (*khirqa*).[15]

Darajāt al-ṣādiqīn and *Tadhallul al-fuqarā'* give the reader access to the spiritual teachings and methods of a time before Sufism as a term had gained general use. They also afford us important insights into the doctrines and discipline of the Malāmatīya of Nishapur as taught by Abū 'Abd al-Raḥmān al-Sulamī himself. The doctrines and discipline that Sulamī taught until the end of his days from the small lodge (*khānqāh*) that he built for Sufis in his native city,[16] Nishapur.

Sulamī's contemporaries and later Sufis held him in high esteem as an author and transmitter of Sufi traditions and as a spiritual authority of great sanctity. Abū Nu'aym al-Iṣbahānī (d. 430/1038), author of the well known work, *Ḥilyat al-awliyā'*, both a contemporary and student of Sulamī, writes that Sulamī was devoted to the precepts and disciplines of Sufism, saying:

> He is one of those we have encountered who have devoted themselves completely to the precepts and disciplines of Sufism in accordance with that upon which the founders based their Path, rightly guided by their examples, steadfast on their Path, following in their footsteps; dissociating himself from all the deranged and confused among the ignorant of these factions; totally disclaiming them.[17]

Sulamī's student, al-Khashshāb (d. 456/1063), praising Sulamī's ability to harmonize with all of those around him, said:

> He was well considered by the elect and the masses, with those in accord (with his views), and with those against, with the sultan and with the subjects, in his own country, and in all the Islamic countries; and thus he passed from this world onto God.[18]

Perhaps a fitting and final testimony to Sulamī's spiritual, even saintly standing among his contemporaries is this quote by al-Ḥākim Muḥammad ibn 'Abdallāh al-Naysāburī (d. 405/1014), a well-known scholar of hadith, "If Abū 'Abd al-Raḥmān is not of the *abdāl*,[19] then God has no saints upon this earth."[20]

Even many years after his death in the tenth century Sulamī was cited and his works praised by Sufis. Ibn 'Abbād al-Rundī (d. 792/1390) of Merinid Fes, Morocco refers in his commentary on *Kitāb al-Ḥikam* (*The Book of Sufi Aphorisms*) by Ibn 'Aṭā'allāh, to Sulamī's work *'Uyūb al-nafs wa-mudāwātuha* (*The Faults of the Ego-self and Their Cures*) encouraging his disciples to read Sulamī saying, "Abū 'Abd al-Raḥmān al-Sulamī wrote a treatise on the faults of the ego-self (*al-nafs*) and the means of effecting their cures, [a work] which though small in size is great in benefits; so let the aspirant seek therein."[21]

Nishapur in the Tenth and Eleventh Centuries

Nishapur in the fourth/tenth century was a city whose social fabric was beginning to unravel. Its religious, political and economic life were facing multiple challenges.[22] The religious diversity that had marked early Islam in

Iran had begun to recede before an increasing tendency towards a uniformity that was presupposed to reflect the nature of the first Islamic community during the times of the Prophet. The need to isolate and label multiple levels of religious experience brought with it a perception of religion as being divided into esoteric and exoteric realms.[23] This vision of religious experience into differing domains led to a tendency to codify religious knowledge into fields of study and establish institutions for the transmission of this knowledge with the intention of preserving the integrity of the Faith. Hadith, Arabic grammar, linguistic forms, jurisprudence, and many other domains of Islamic discourse were being studied, collected, codified and taught in the newly built *madrasas*, institutes of Islamic learning.[24] This coincided with the period of the formation of the four Sunni schools of jurisprudence; the Ḥanafī, the Mālikī, the Shāfi'ī, and the Ḥanbalī schools.[25] This initial pursuit of uniformity in Nishapur however produced quite the opposite effect and many religious sects and parties of a partisan nature arose among the population, each claiming to represent the 'true teachings' of Islam and differentiating themselves from each other by distinctive dogmas, forms of dress and comportment. Asceticism, which had begun long before as a response to the excesses of the caliphate and urban society, had become in certain circles, a sectarian statement of pious renunciation of a world grown too mundane. With this sectarianism came a tendency to compartmentalize religious attitudes, seeing spirituality in either an ascetic or ecstatic light.[26]

Nishapur was the foremost city of Khurasan, intellectually, economically and politically, and susceptible to the vicissitudes that so often threaten these domains. It stood on the caravan route connecting to the west Baghdad, to the south-west to the Persian Gulf, to the north-east to Bukhāra and India, and to the north-east to Samarqand, Central Asia, and China. Nishapur was the center of government and the capital of Khurasan during the Ṭāhirid Dynasty (820-873).[27] It experienced an interval of Shi'ite influence under Buyid rule when Baghdad fell to them in 945. This interval ended with the arrival of the forces of the Seljuk Turks from the east. Under the Seljuks Nishapur became the most important center of Sunni Islam in the empire. Wars and civil strife had been the rule more than the exception in Khurasan from the seventh to the tenth centuries, yet Nishapur had sustained its preeminent role within the province. The middle of the twelfth century witnessed the disintegration of Seljuk power in the face of incursions by nomadic Turkoman tribes.

Eventually, the failing political situation, famine and sectarian violence brought an end to what had been the center of political, intellectual and spiritual life in Khurasan.[28]

Despite Nishapur's solid Sunni base since Seljuk times the city was rocked by violent sectarian conflicts beginning in the fourth/tenth centuries. These conflicts grew out of the fierce struggle that arose between the various schools of religious law (*madhāhib*), especially the Ḥanafites and the Shāfi'ites.[29] There were also violent clashes between Shi'ite and Karrāmīya factions.[30] It was in this atmosphere of political and social dispersion and sectarian violence that a new, yet at the same time old, response appeared to the confusion that reigned. This response entailed a return to spiritual principles that were reflective of a more holistic vision of what constituted religious experience. Those espousing this answer were known as the Malāmatīya of Nishapur.[31]

THE MALĀMTĪYA OF NISHAPUR

Their Origins and Teachings

The Malāmatīya of fourth/tenth century Nishapur were known for their teachings emphasizing blame (*malāma*) in perfecting sincerity.[32] *Malāma,* inspired by Qur'ānic verses and Prophetic example, became the term used to refer to the spiritual attitude of blame. The *Path of Blame* was the name applied to the teachings of the Muslim mystics who considered blame central to spiritual development and who derived a comprehensive mode of conduct which was in accord with this attitude.

Sufis typically perceived a region to be characterized by the spiritual orientation of the most influential shaykhs. Khurasan, home to the Malāmatīya, was reputed for sincerity. Al-Junayd (d. 297/910), known as *the Leader of the Folk*, testified to this trait of the Khurasanian tradition when he said, "Chivalry is in Syria, eloquence is in 'Irāq, and sincerity is in Khurasan."[33] In his work the *Treatise of the People of Blame* (*al-Risālat al-malāmatīya*) Sulamī contrasts the spiritual perspectives and conduct the Malāmatīya of Nishapur to those of the Sufis of Iraq.[34] He attributes to the Sufis of Baghdad all the outward signs of spiritual perfection; detachment from the mundane world, impeccable *ādāb* with their teachers, miracles and lofty aspirations. He attributes the Malāmatīya with the inner attitudes of a permanent intimate knowledge of God and proximity to Him while they reside in anonymity their inner state hidden from the crowd. Understanding the relationship between these two complimentary spiritual tendencies and their eventual 'fusion' into what would constitute the norms and character of subsequent Sufi thought and practice is one of the keys to understanding the nature of Islamic mysticism itself.[35] To a large extent it was Sulamī himself and the rich textual heritage he left us that documented this phenomenon for future generations of scholars and researchers.

Linguistic and Traditional Origins

Malāma (blame) is the term from which Malāmatyīa is derived. The root *LWM* from which *malāma* is derived has linguistic and textual origins that are central to our understanding the implication of blame as a spiritual attitude. The Malāmatīya of Nishapur established a set of criteria or principles founded upon this attitude. Let us look at the term *malāma*, as it appears in the Qur'an and hadith, and then consider linguistic issues derived from these sources.

The origins of the attitudes of the *Path of Blame* are found in the Qur'ān and hadith. A careful consideration of the verses in which the root *LWM* occurs in the Qur'ān[36] will help clarify the double-edged nature of blame, as both an active and a passive principle. The root *LWM* is used on the one hand for the self-blaming soul, the *al-nafs al-lawwāma* [5:59]. This self-blaming soul in its Qur'anic context is a central stage within a framework of ascendant levels to the process of the soul's perfection. At the mundane level the soul incites to evil (*al-nafs ammāra*), then recognizes its fallen nature and blaming itself becomes the Blaming Soul (*nafs lawwāma*), blame awakes the soul to its inherent spiritual nature and it becomes the Inspired Soul (*nafs mulhama*). Realizing its innate nature (*fitra*) this perfected soul, now referred to in the Qur'ān as the Serene Soul (*nafs muṭma'inna*), is called to return to its Lord and reside among His servants in Paradise, this marks the final stage of the soul's perfection.[37] In another verse *LWM* refers to the blame incurred from others. In this context a lack of concern for the blame leveled at one from others, if one is guided rightly, is crucial to striving in the path of God. *They struggle in the path of God and fear not the blame of any blamer, that is the grace of God, which He bestows on whomsoever He pleases; God is bounteous and wise.* [5:54] This verse refers to the Prophet and his companions, whom the Malāmatīya considered to be the first travelers on the *Path of Blame*.[38]

Among the most outstanding allusions to blame as understood in the early Qur'anic context is the testimony of Najm al-Dīn Rāzī (d. 654/1256), in his *Merṣād al-'ebād* (*The Path of God's Bondsman*). Rāzī was a disciple of Najm al-Dīn al-Kubrā (d. 618/1221), the founder of the Kubrāwīya order in Khurasan. This passage is a commentary of verse thirty of the Chapter of the Heifer which treats the accusations the angels brought against God after He had informed them that he was about to create Adam. Najm al-Dīn ascribes the attitude of incurring blame to God and affirms the role played by reproach in the spiritual perfection that is sincere love of God.

> The first seeker of reproach in the world was Adam; or, to tell the truth, it was none other than God the glorious Himself, for the first objection was that made to him: *Wilt Thou make upon earth one who will cause corruption and bloodshed?* [2:30] Here lies a wondrous indication that the foundation of love is the courting of reproach (*malāma*). Better for love to be in the company of blame. Safety is for the ascetic held back by shame. The soul of Adam silently addressed the Majestic Presence, saying: "With the rope of reproach we have lifted the burden of the Trust onto the shoulder of our soul; we have sold safety and bought reproach. We fear the blame of no one; let them say what they will, for it matters not.[39]

Among the best known hadith employing a cognate of LWM is the long *ḥadīth qudsī* narrated by Muslim of which the last part reads:

> O my servants, it is verily according to your deeds that I call you to account and then recompense you. So let them that find good [in the Hereafter] praise God and let them that find other than that blame no one but themselves.[40]

The emphasis in this hadith on self-reproach reflects the manner in which the early Islamic community perceived blame as an inner attitude. The above passages from the Qur'ān and hadith and the manner in which they were understood by early writers illustrate that blame was seen as an intrinsically Islamic perspective which led to the perfection of sincerity on the part of the aspirant of spiritual knowledge.

Although the origins of the root *LWM* indisputably derive from traditional sources, it has been used since early times to denote a spiritual leaning known as the *way of blame*. *Malāmī*, an adjective derived from *malāma* has been used to refer to individuals or Sufi orders that reflect this leaning. The term *Ahl al-Malāma* or the Malāmatīya, as most commonly used, refers to the People of Blame of tenth and eleventh century Nishapur. The term *malāma* expresses a multi-faceted attitude expressible in the terms blame, reproach or censure, yet is by no means exhausted by such terms. In his *Kashf al-Maḥjūb* (*The Revelation of the Veiled*), one of the earliest treatises on Sufism in Persian, Hujwīrī (d. 465/1072) portrays blame as a passive principle, as accepting the reproach of others in a detached manner. He writes, "*Blame* has a great effect in making love sincere. Those who adhere to the Real (*ahl al-Ḥaqq*) are distinguished by being objects of vulgar blame, especially the eminent ones of this community.[41] While Ibn 'Arabī (d. 638/1240) the Andalusian Sufi known as *Shaykh al-Akbār*, "The Greatest of the Masters" portrays blame as an active principle of self-criticism on the part of the *malāmī*. He writes in his *al-Futūḥāt al-Makkīya* (*The Meccan Revelations*), "they cease not blaming themselves for their imperfections for they judge none of their actions sufficiently free of impurity to be pleasing to God."[42] Thus *blaming* one's self or *being blamed* came to be understood as the generic connotation of *malāma* as it was variously interpreted in active or passive modes or principles.[43]

For the Malāmatīya of Nishapur the "double edged sword of blame" was not perceived in terms of a subject-object relationship. They understood the two facets of blame, active and passive, as being necessarily complementary and concurrent with one another. The loss of one or the other, or an exaggerated preoccupation with one or the other was a sign of the degeneration of the attitude of blame. In his *Treatise of Blame* Sulamī elucidates the complementary relationship that exists between *blaming one's self* and *being blamed* as two attitudes which simultaneously manifest themselves in the person of the *malāmī*.

> Their [the *malāmī*] inner state blames their outward appearance on account of its complaisance in the world and its living according to the customs of the common folk. Their outward appearance blames their inner state for though it resides in proximity to divine Being, it ignores the duality of outer manifestation. Such are the states of the great masters of the Path.[44]

This passage accents the transformative power of blame, as a result of the interaction between active and passive modes. It elucidates as well that the Malāmatīya emphasis on blame represents a comprehensive teaching and parallel mode of conduct representative of the earliest ideals of the Islamic mystical tradition.

The Teachings of the Malāmatīya

The teachings of the Malāmatīya were of a twofold nature, they emphasized attitudes and conduct. A unity of inner attitudes and outward conduct perceived as being the only means that could accommodate the *perfect sincerity* that was the goal of these teachings. The "normative" or prescriptive nature of the *path of blame* reflects this striving for inward and outward balance and reciprocity. The foundational principle of their teachings was twofold: the awareness of the inherently defective nature of the self,[45] and a code of conduct that accorded with this awareness. The Malāmatīya were vigilant over their interior states and constant in their awareness of their inner shortcomings. In practice this vigilance led them to deny themselves any outward signs of piety, spirituality, or intrinsic worth that they knew contradicted their inner state. They strongly advocated conformity to social norms and avoided anything that set them apart from the common people, to the point that they were often criticized for being overly passive in the face of forbidding immoral behavior (*nahy 'an al-munkar*). They avoided anything that set them apart from the common people. It was this perception of the self and its states, coupled with correct comportment, that the Malāmatīya saw as essential to attaining intimate knowledge of God. For in *blaming* themselves and manifesting no distinctive signs of piety or spirituality to others they turned others from themselves, and in doing so they preserved their states with God from ostentatious piety (*riyā'*), self-conceit (*'ujb*), and spiritual pretension (*iddi'ā*) that they perceived as inherent traits of the lower-self. This twofold aspect of blame is well portrayed in the following words of Abū Ḥafṣ al-Nayshbūrī[46] (d. 260/874), master of the Malīmatīya[47] of Nishapur:

> They are a people established in God, constant in their vigilance over each of their moments and watchful over their innermost selves, they thus find fault with themselves and all that they manifest of intimacy with God or acts of worship; while exposing to

> others their base natures and secreting from them their virtues. Others blame them for what they see of their outward [appearances] while they blame themselves for what they know of their inward states. God has shown them His generosity by unveiling secrets [to them] and making apparent to them different aspects of the unseen and true intuition (*al-firāsa*) and in miracles performed by them. They have hidden that which is between God and them by making apparent that upon which they began [their traveling of the path], self-blame and self-denial, manifesting to others that which causes aversion; and in turning others from themselves, they preserve their states with God. This is the path of the people of blame (*malāmatīya*).[48]

The fundamental precepts of the Malāmatīya, as depicted in the above quote, stress the practical nature of the attitude of blame, and its role in the perfection of one's sincerity of intention in submission to God. The importance placed on the defective nature of the self and the manner in which this attitude determined one's conduct gave a metaphysical perspective to the teaching of the Malāmatīya on the one hand, while on the other it imbued the conduct of the aspirant with integral meaning.

The concept of the defective nature of the ego-self for the Malāmatīya stemmed from their acute awareness of the defective nature of creation in comparison to God's perfection.[49] In *Darajāt al-ṣādiqīn,*[50] Sulamī, speaking for the aspirant who has attained the divine presence writes, "He perceives that the locus of created being *(maḥal al-ḥawādith)* will never be devoid of defects."[51] This view of the defective nature of manifestation was instrumental to how the Malāmatīya regarded themselves, their states, and their deeds. This is the metaphysical foundation of the Path of Blame. No spiritual state was worthy of praise, no deed free of ostentation. Isma'īl ibn Nujayd, Sulamī's maternal grandfather, expressed this point of view when he said, "No one shall attain to the station of the people of this Path until [they see] all their deeds as ostentation (*riyā'*), and all their spiritual states as vain pretension (*da'āwī*)."[52] For the Malāmatīya constant vigilance over the self and its states was a consequence of their view of the defective nature of manifestation itself. This perspective was essential to realizing *perfect sincerity* and a key element for the attainment of direct knowledge of God.[53]

In their quest for perfect sincerity, the Malāmatīya, never ceasing to blame their *selves*, attained a subtle understanding of the psychological centers of experience. For the Malāmatīya, our individual states are reflected within a hierarchy of subtle centers of consciousness. These centers were referred to as the *rūḥ*, *sirr*, *qalb*, and *nafs*. At the summit of the hierarchy was the Divine made manifest to the *rūḥ* (spirit). The *sirr* (innermost mystery) relates to the spiritual or angelic realm. The *qalb* (heart) relates to the intermediate realm between the worldly and spiritual realms and the *nafs* (ego-self) relates to the worldly or mundane realm. Within this hierarchy the superior centers were cognizant of the inferior realms, not vice versa. The *rūḥ* was cognizant of the multi-leveled nature of spiritual reality, while the *nafs* was cognizant of only its own realm.

This hierarchical comprehension of the psychological levels of the soul led the Malāmatīya to perceive ostentation (*riyā'*), the antithesis of sincerity, in a new light. They believed that the appearance of the spiritual states of the *spirit* within the center of the *sirr* (innermost mystery), was ostentation itself. The descent of the spiritual states of the *sirr* to the level of the *qalb* (heart) was idolatry. Likewise for the awareness of the level of the heart, to find expression in the *nafs* (ego-self) became "chaff blown by the wind."[54] Within this hierarchy, even the most minimal experience emanating from the superior plane upon the inferior was regarded as ostentation, and therefore without value. The Malāmatīya therefore did not seek affirmation of their states in experience, spiritual or otherwise. Their certainty is affirmed by God and in God, as is pointed out by this saying of Ḥamdūn al-Qaṣṣār:[55]

> The *malāmatī* is one who has no interior pretension, nor exterior affectation or ostentation. His inner secret, between him and God is not apparent to his own heart (*ṣadr*) how then could it be to the other creatures?[56]

The Malāmatīya founded their search for *perfect sincerity* upon this hierarchical comprehension of the psychological levels of the soul. This understanding of the nature of the soul is the essence of blame, while at the same time being the basis for the most intimate knowledge of God, for "Whoever knows himself, knows his Lord."[57]

The two aforementioned views, one ontological, concerning the defective nature of manifestation, the other, psychological, concerning the multi-leveled nature of the soul, gave rise to a basic set of practical criteria, or fundamental attitudes, that were considered the keys to the perfection of sincerity in one's submission to God. The criteria, by which the *Malāmatīya* became known, were for them a means of surpassing the defective nature of the soul and attaining to the perfection of the unmanifest in knowledge of the divine. This explains, in part at least, the relevance of these criteria to the more gnostic or intellectually oriented teachings of later masters. In the teachings of Bahā' al-Dīn Naqshband, Abū al-Ḥasan al-Shādhilī, Ibn al-'Arabī, and in later times the Moroccan Sufi Mulay al-'Arabī al-Darqāwī we find the heritage of 10th century Nishapur. These criteria can all be derived from the forty-five tenets of Malāmatī doctrine enumerated by Sulamī in the second part of his *Treatise of the People of Blame*. Stated concisely they are as follows:

1. Compliance to the Qur'ān and Sunna.[58]
2. Submission to correct conduct (*ādāb*).[59]
3. Disdain for the ego-self (*nafs*).[60]
4. Disclaiming all pretensions to piety and spiritual states.[61]
5. Secreting one's spiritual state in God.[62]

The most basic characteristic of the Malāmatīya was compliance with the Qur'ān and the Sunna of the Prophet. These were the foundation of all knowledge and the key to the direct and intimate knowledge of God. The *Sharī'a* itself was more than a source of the legal dictums; it was a means of conformity with divine reality. In *Darajāt al-ṣādiqīn* Sulamī informs his reader that there is no path without the Qur'ān and the *Sunna:*

> There can be no successful completion of the journey through the spiritual stations without a sound beginning (*ṣiḥat al-ibtidā'*). He who has not founded his aspirant's journey upon the Qur'ān and the Traditions of the Prophet (*al-kitāb wa-al-sunna*) will attain nothing of knowledge of God.[63]

Perfect servanthood, the necessary condition for the realization *of perfect sincerity*, meant in practice strict adherence to the Sunna, for it left the ego-self no respite. Sulamī reports in the above mentioned treatise:

> Among their tenets is that the state of servanthood is founded upon two essential things: the perfect awareness of one's total dependence upon God Most High, and perfect imitation of the

> Messenger of God. It is in this that the ego-self finds neither respite nor rest.[64]

Submission to correct conduct relates directly to the adherence to the Qur'ān and the *Sunna*. This comprehension goes beyond the prescriptive nature that is often associated with the idea of correct conduct (*ādāb*). *Ādāb* represented an attitude of total detachment from one's needs and desires, while at the same time being totally committed to a spiritual attitude of effacement. *Ādāb* was the means of intimately knowing God. In this quote by Sulamī from *Darajāt al-ṣādiqīn* the inner and outer facets of the view of *ādāb* are well expressed:

> The comportment (*ādāb*) which brought them to this station and this degree consists of their practicing upon themselves various spiritual exercises. [After having realized] before this sound repentance (*taṣḥīḥ al-tawba*), perfect detachment (*tamām al-zuhd*), turning from all other than God (*i'rāḍ 'an al-khalq*), from the world and its occupants, the abandonment of all they own, distancing themselves from their personal inclinations, departure upon long journeys, denial of outward passionate desires, constant watchfulness over their inner mysteries (*murāqabat al-asrār al-bāṭina*), deference towards the masters of the Path, service to brethren and friends, giving preference to others over themselves (*īthār*) in worldly goods, person and spirit, perseverance in [their] efforts, and regarding all their actions or states that may arise from them inwardly or outwardly with contempt and disdain.[65]

From this quote one sees that *ādāb* as an inner attitude constituted a normative basis of conduct for the aspirant.

For the Malāmatīya correct conduct was the means of counteracting and opposing the ego-self's natural inclination towards pride, love of recognition, and self-satisfaction. For them correct conduct was an affirmation of the "nature of mystical reality" and the means of attaining a direct and personal knowledge of God. Ḥamdūn al-Qaṣṣār, when asked the true meaning of Sufism, summed it up as correct attitudes, saying:

> Sufism is made up entirely of correct attitudes (*ādāb*); for each moment there is a correct attitude, for each spiritual station (*maqām*)

> there is a correct attitude. Whoever is steadfast in maintaining the correct attitude of each moment, will attain the degree of spiritual excellence, and whoever neglects correct attitudes, is far from that which he imagines near, and rejected from where he imagines he has found acceptance.[66]

The Malāmatīya have been seen by some scholars to be an ascetic or pietistic tendency within Islam.[67] If we define pietism as a religious attitude of devotional feeling[68] and asceticism as renunciation[69] (neither of which goes beyond the performance of "works"),[70] Sulamī, in the texts we have at hand would seem to refute this assertion. The Malāmatīya never visualized normative conduct as the performance of "works" or a *via purgativa* as an end in itself. Normative conduct was the means of sincere submission to God, the only path to intimate discourse with God. *The Humble Submission of Those Aspiring* (*Bayān tadhallul al-fuqarā'*) highlights the essential role played by conduct in spiritual aspiration (*sulūk*). *Stations of the Righteous* (*Darajāt al-ṣādiqīn*) treats the attendant attitudes for such conduct and how these attitudes are founded in the spiritual alertness of the aspirants themselves.

The most salient characteristic of the Malāmatīya was disdain for the ego-self (*nafs*). Rather than being an ethical statement however, their disdain for the ego-self was based primarily upon the metaphysical understanding of the deficient nature of all manifestation. The ego-self was also seen as the center of the ego, which in the traditional Qur'ānic view was the *al-nafs al-ammāra bi-al-sū'* (the soul which incites evil). The Malāmatīya did not believe that spiritual discipline and ascetic practices could purify this ego-self. They taught that the sole means of disciplining the ego-self was by subjecting it to constant blame and abasement. This blame had to be of a twofold nature, as mentioned earlier, both from external agents and from the *malāmī* himself. Sulamī reported this trait as being among the basic tenets of the Malāmatīya, saying:

> Among the tenets of the Malāmatīya is that they reproach their ego-self under all circumstances, whether it is amenable or retreats, shows signs of obedience or not, and [they show] a minimum of satisfaction with it [i.e. the ego-self] or inclination towards it.[71]

This awareness is self-substantiating as Sulamī's narration in the *Risālat al-malāmatīya* emphasizes:

> He who wishes to understand the waywardness of the ego-self (*nafs*) and the corruption of its instinctual nature, let him listen to one praising him. If he notices that his ego-self transgresses its bounds, even minutely, he should realize that it has no means for realizing the Truth. For the ego-self either finds repose in the praise of that which lacks all truth, or is unsettled by blame of that in which there is no truth [either]. Were he to face it at times with the disdain (*tadhlīl*) it deserves, it would neither be affected by praise nor pay attention to blame. Then it would enter the states of *malāma*.[72]

The ego-self, distracted by its innate self-interest, which it manifests through its love of praise and aversion to blame,[73] is unable to realize the truth of objectivity that stems from self-scrutiny. This explains why Abū Yazīd said—when asked what he most desired from the world—"That I might see myself through the eye by which people see me."[74] Disdain for the ego-self was not however, directed at one's interior state alone. Everything that the ego-self touched, be it devotional acts or spiritual states, became suspect for the Malāmatīya.

Disdain for the ego-self led the Malāmatīya to abandon all pretension to piety and spiritual states. Since they held their ego-self in disdain, they avoided displaying any signs of piety or spiritual states, seeing them as imperfections of sincerity. The following quote of Abū Yazīd al-Bistāmī illustrates how the deceptive tendencies of the ego-self veil us from a true appraisal of our states and acts:

> Whoever does not regard their attestation [of the truth] (*shāhidihi*) as pure compulsion (*iḍṭirār*), their [spiritual] moments as pure deception (*ightirār*), their interior states as a pitfall of which they are heedless (*istidrāj*), their speech as pure falsehood (*iftirā'*), and their devotions as pure self-satisfaction (*ijtizā'*) such a person has missed the mark.[75]

This awareness of the negative tendencies of the ego-self led the Malāmatīya to scrutinize their conduct and states, which they regarded as never being free of ostentation, self-satisfaction, and pretension. The renunciation of any claim to piety and or a spiritual state in order to attain *perfect servanthood* is the theme of *Tadhallul al-fuqarā'*, from which the following passage is taken:

> Know, may God gladden your joy with the light of His grace, that utter need (*faqr*) is one of the traits of *servanthood*. In servitude there is neither arrogance nor pride, but rather humble submission and compliance. God—May He be exalted—says, *God coined a similitude: (on the one hand) a (mere) chattel slave, who is capable of nothing* [16:75]. Therefore, one who imagines that he is capable of something, and claims for himself a spiritual state, station, or degree, is devoid of the traits of servitude, one of which is utter need.[76]

Any claim to a spiritual state or station is seen as a form of self-satisfaction and therefore a flaw in one's sincerity. Sulamī draws our attention to this in the following passage as he writes:

> Most of their teachers warn their companions against enjoying the taste of devotional acts and obedience. They consider this a major transgression (*min al-kabā'ir*). For when a human being finds anything to be sweet and enjoys it, it becomes exalted in his eyes; and whoever deems any of his actions as good or pleasing, or regards them with satisfaction, falls from the degree of the great ones.[77]

The humble manner in which they regarded themselves was crucial to the path of abandoning any pretense to individual inclinations in their everyday conduct.

The necessity for humility and the abandonment of all pretense led the Malāmatīya to the "secreting" their states in God. This means living a life in anonymity among one's fellows, while inwardly having intimate discourse with God. Anonymity was necessary because the deceptive nature of the ego-self had profound repercussions upon the attitudes it manifested and upon the acts it instigated. This awareness on the part of the Malāmatīya brought them to view their devotional acts and states as valueless. They disclaimed any outward show that might distinguish them in any way from other people. They intentionally avoided many of the outward aspects of the Sufis, from the very name of *sufi*, to distinctive forms of dress,[78] vocal *dhikr*,[79] sessions of *samā'*,[80] and even public religious rites; though they were known to be meticulous in their adherence to the *Sharī'a*. They neither proselytized nor wrote treatises setting forth their principles,[81] nor did they profess a speculative mysticism about the unity of being.[82] Their desire for anonymity led them to meet in the homes of their teachers. Their emphasis on disclaiming any spiritual state led them to earn their living among the people of the marketplace. As Ahmed Karamustafa points out, "the overwhelming concern for social conformity rendered the Path of Blame into an ideal mode of religiosity for artisanal and merchant classes."[83] Ḥamdūn al-Qaṣṣār, for example was a fuller and bleacher of cloth while Abū Ḥafṣ al-Ḥaddād was a blacksmith. In their anonymity, the Malāmatīya achieved a harmony of both their outward and inward aspects. The generality did not recognize them from their outward appearances due to their conformity with social norms, nor did they know them by their inner states. When Ḥamdūn al-Qaṣṣār was asked about the Malāmatīya he replied:

> They are a folk that outwardly have no signs that distinguish them from people, nor do they inwardly make claims with God - May He be exalted. That which lies between them and God in their inner most soul (*sirr*) is perceived by neither their inner hearts (*af'ida*) nor their outer hearts (*qulūb*).[84]

This rapport of the inner and outward aspects of their spirituality, coupled with their living among people as one of them reminds one of the model of the "normative Sufi", which was to mark later western scholarship.

Holding the spiritual ideal of *secreting one's state*, the Malāmatīya avoided any outward signs of poverty or need. A well-known saying among them was, "Allow your house, on the day of your death, to be a moral lesson for others, rather than show poverty during your lifetime."[85] The Malāmatīya sought effacement through their lives among people. They adopted a life style at one with the generality of pious believers. Sulamī points out that this effacement among the generality has profound mystical repercussions.

> The *malāmatīs* are those whose innermost states (*asrār*) God keeps watch over, drawing over their innermost states the curtain of formal appearances. Outwardly they participate in all the activities performed by their fellows, keeping company with them in the marketplaces and in earning a means of livelihood, while in Truth (*al-ḥaqīqa*) and Divine Sovereignty (*al-tawalli*) they are with God–Most High.[86]

This ideal is reminiscent of the doctrine of the hidden and unknown saint that later plays a major role in the writings of Ibn 'Arabī, but which is already prefigured in the work *Khatm al-awliyā'* (*The Seal of the Saints*)[87] by Ḥakīm al-Tirmidhī. This led to the doctrine in Sufism of a hierarchy of invisible saints, without which the world could not subsist.

In *Darajāt al-ṣādiqīn* Sulamī affords us a rare glimpse of these saints hidden in God. He narrates:

> Among them are those whom He hides from the eyes of creation, from their eyes, their hearts, and their inward secrets; they exist among people as one of them. They eat, drink, and mingle with others. God has allowed their exterior aspect to face creation while keeping their inner state exclusively to Himself. No one perceives their inner perfection, while He is completely aware of them. This is because of God's jealousy over them, for He is too jealous to allow other than Himself the knowledge of His elect saints.[88]

The attitudes and the incumbent conduct founded upon the above criteria formed an integral unity whose goal was the perfection of sincerity, seen by the Malāmatīya as the key to knowledge of God as Divine Unity. Their teachings would remain as relevant to Sufism throughout its long history as they were to the Malāmatīya of 10th century Nishapur in the form of "powerful subcurrents within the fabric of subsequent Sufi thought and practice... rather than as a termination during the course of the fourth/tenth century."[89] This centrality of the teachings of the Malāmatīya to the ultimate goal of all Sufis, the intimate knowledge of God, explains how a Sufi of Baghdad, Abū al-Ḥasan al-Ḥuṣrī (d. 371/982),[90] could have said, when informed of the Malāmatīya of Nishapur, "Were it ever possible that a prophet should appear in our times, he would be from among them (i.e. the Malāmatīya)."[91]

SULAMĪ AND THE MALĀMATĪYA

The close ties that link Sulamī to the Malāmatīya, his esteem for their mentors, his early training as well as his teachings and writings demonstrate that he himself was an heir to their tradition and a transmitter of their ideals and doctrines. His ties to the Malāmatīya were through his grandfather Ibn Nujayd, his father, and his many mentors, who were companions and disciples of all the major figures among the Malāmatīya. He also had direct relationships and narrated from other disciples of the Malāmatīya such as

Aḥmad al-Farrā',[92] 'Abdallāh ibn Muḥammad al-Mu'allim ibn Faḍlūya[93] and Abū 'Amr ibn Ḥamdān Muḥammad ibn Aḥmad.[94] A careful study of *Darajāt al-ṣādiqīn, Tadhallul al-fuqarā'* and several newly edited manuscripts, recently published in Iran[95] leave little doubt that Sulamī had inherited the tradition of the Malāmatīya. The body of his works indicate that he continued to exemplify and transmit their teachings and disciplines from the small lodge (*dwayra*) that he had built in his native city of Nishapur until his death and from which Muḥammad Ibn Bākūya al-Shirāzī (d.428/1037),[96] a disciple of Ibn Khafīf al-Shīrāzī (d. 371/982) continued to teach after him.

The earliest mention of the Malāmatīya we have, as well as the most definitive work on the their doctrine and practices, is Sulamī's *The Treatise of the People of Blame*.[97] In this treatise Sulamī places the Malāmatīya at the summit of the spiritual hierarchy.[98] In his introduction he divides the spiritual aspirants into three basic groups: the exoterists (*ahl al-ẓāhir*) or scholars of the Law (*'ulamā' al-sharī'a*), the Sufis or people of gnosis (*ahl al-ma'rifa*) and the Malāmatīya,[99] in ascending order. Sulamī then presents the methodology of the Malīmatīya and the Sufis. Subsequently he evaluates the lot of the Sufis and their *murīdīn* (aspirants of the path) from the standpoint of the Malāmatī. In a word the Sufis do not appear in a very positive light.[100] In elucidating how the Malāmatīya of Nishapur viewed the Sufis of Iraq there are few better textual examples.

Even more pertinent to the argument at hand is the light that the *Treatise of the People of Blame* sheds on how Sulamī portrays the "self-criticism" and "submission to correct conduct" of the Malāmatīya, and the manner in which he relates these teachings to the stations of mystical knowledge. This relationship is the central theme of the majority of his other works written for aspirants. It is through an understanding of how *blame* relates to "gnosis" within the context of the *Treatise of the People of Blame* that we can determine to what extent *Darajāt al-ṣādiqīn* and *Tadhallul al-fuqarā'* are examples of Sulamī's exposition of Malāmatī methods. In the *Treatise of the People of Blame* Sulamī stresses first and foremost the education of the aspirant. This education embodies: adherence to the Qur'ān and the Sunna, inner spiritual attitudes and correct conduct under all circumstances, disdain for miracles and any attachment to spiritual states as well as for the ego-self and all its claims and finally, when the aspirant has attained sincerity in his aspiration, he is taught to secret his state while assiduously following the precepts of the religion. In contrast to the aspirant of the Malāmatīya, Sulamī felt that the *murīd* disciplined by others became self-deluded into believing that they are achieving nearness to God when, in fact, their efforts only distance them from God and his path. He consistently criticizes the tendency among some Sufis to be preoccupied with miracles and spiritual states and those shaykhs who support this preoccupation in their aspirants. As this significant section of this treatise has never been translated into English and as it provides a picture of formative Sufism seldom glimpsed, I quote it here in its entirety:

> When aspirants frequent the "people of blame" they guide them to that which is evident, of compliance (to the injunctions of the law, *al-sharī'a*) and the application of the *Sunna* at all times, and constancy in correct comportment (*ādāb*) both inwardly and outwardly under all circumstances. They do not allow them claims [of spirituality], and stories of signs and miracles, nor dependence upon them; instead they stress correct comportment [towards others], and constancy in discipline. Thus the *murīd* learns their path (*ṭarīq*), and becomes accustomed to their manner of comportment. Should they see exaltation on his part of any of his acts or states, they would explain to him his defects and guide him to the elimination of his fault, until he ceases to deem worthy any of his acts or to rely upon them. When a *murīd* among them claims a state or a spiritual station for himself, they belittle it in his eyes until he attains sincerity in his aspiration; and spiritual states manifest themselves to him. Then they instruct him in their practice of secreting of [ones] states, while manifesting correct conduct in regard to the ordained and forbidden [aspects of the religion]. Thus he attains all the stations while still on the path of aspiration. For them [the Malāmatīya] it is through the perfection of spiritual endeavor that one achieves all the spiritual stations, except the station of mystical knowledge. The *murīd*, when disciplined by others [apart from the Malāmatīya] is permitted spiritual claims while still an aspirant. He takes the states of the founders [of the Path] as a veil for himself, and claims them as his own, the passage of days increases them only in retreat and distance from God (*al-Ḥaqq*), and His path. For this reason the mentor of this way, Abū Ḥafṣ al-Naysabūrī, may God sanctify his spirit, says as it was told me by Muḥammad ibn Aḥmad ibn Ḥamdān, he said, I heard my father say, I heard Abū Ḥafṣ say, "The disciples of the Malāmatīya lead a life of nobility, there is no danger for their

> ego-selves, nor is there any means for the faults which might appear from them to intrude upon their stations; because their outward is for all to see, while their true states are veiled. Whereas the disciples of the Sufis exhibit rash claims and miracles, that make anyone who has reached realization laugh, for their claims are many while the realities of their states are few."[101]

In this passage Sulamī transmits and holds up as ideal Malāmatīya doctrines about the aspirant's proper relationship to God, the world, his community of fellow aspirants, and the community of believers.

More evidence of Sulamī's Malāmatī perspective is his concise exposition of "constancy in correct comportment" and of the central role of blame and "secreting one's state." Here Sulamī portrays the synthetic whole of the path: form and meaning, self-effacing comportment and intimate knowledge of God. This reflects the essence of the Malāmatīya teachings. Even his tendency to avoid expressing his own views explicitly is in accord with Malāmatīya doctrine, which stresses that intimacy with God requires effacement before His creation, and a reluctance to speak of one's own spiritual state, which is the meaning of secreting one's state in God. An example of this is his citation of Yaḥyā ibn Mu'ādh, who said, "One who is sincere with God does not want to be seen nor have his words narrated."[102]

Darajāt al-ṣādiqīn and *Tadhallul al-fuqarā'*

Darajāt al-ṣādiqīn and *Tadhallul al-fuqarā'* are complementary works of differing natures. As stated above, both represent the heritage of the Malāmatīya of Nishapur as taught and transmitted by Sulamī. They differ, in that *Darajāt al-ṣādiqīn* is more psychologically and metaphysically subtle, while *Tadhallul al-fuqarā'* is more concretely an example of 'applied Sufism.' While *Darajāt al-ṣādiqīn* provides the metaphysical tenets upon which the teachings of the Malāmatīya are based, *Tadhallul al-fuqarā'* shows how these tenets are to be implemented. *Darajāt al-ṣādiqīn* is representative of Sulamī, the teacher in his own right, employing a minimum of narrative material. *Tadhallul al-fuqarā'* is an example of practical advice (*naṣīḥa*) given by Sulamī, richly interpolated with the narratives of both Malāmatī and Sufi sources. In *Darajāt al-ṣādiqīn* Sulamī affirms the intrinsic unity of *malāma* and Sufism, in *Tadhallul al-fuqarā'* he provides us with the thread that unites them, *faqr* (innate poverty). These two texts provide an exemplary exposition of both the inner and outer dimensions of the teachings of the Malāmatīya.

The precepts emphasized in both *Darajāt al-ṣādiqīn* and *Tadhallul al-fuqarā'* are the fundamental principles of the Malāmatīya. Both *Darajāt al-ṣādiqīn* and *Tadhallul al-fuqarā'* deal with a precept central to *malāma*, the flawed nature of the phenomenal world. *Darajāt al-ṣādiqīn* expresses the idea as a concept. *Tadhallul al-fuqarā'* applies it within the realm of conduct. The uniqueness of *Darajāt al-ṣādiqīn* lies in its highlighting the defective nature of created being that is consistent with the Malāmatīya understanding of the very nature of the universe. This theme runs through the text, giving life to their doctrine and providing a key to the comprehension of the precepts of this important school of Islamic spirituality. This statement of metaphysical doctrine elevates the Malāmatīya from a being a spiritual tendency based upon a pessimistic view of the human state or one having an overly negative view of the ego-self to being a mode of perceiving the creation on all its levels.

In *Darajāt al-ṣādiqīn*, Sulamī presents this concept through the eyes of the traveller who has attained to the divine presence. All else is demeaned to him by his vision of divine reality, such that he sees that, 'the locus of created being is never free of defects.' *(maḥal al-ḥawādith lā takhlū min al-'ilal).*[103] *Tadhallul al-fuqarā'* provides the means by which such a perception of reality can be incorporated into the conduct of the aspirant. Given the flawed nature of creation and the innate negative tendencies of the ego-self, the aspirant has no grounds for claiming for himself any state, station, or personal merit; any such claim is nothing but a deception of the ego-self. *Tadhallul al-fuqarā'* represents the *malāmī* response to their vision of the imperfect nature of creation, a response embodied in correct inner attitudes and conduct.

A comparative overview of both texts elucidates the relationship between the *malāmatī* view of creation on the one hand, and their attitudes towards conduct on the other.

1. The Qur'ān and *Sunna*, being divinely inspired, are the only sources of knowledge free of defects and are thus the only sound foundations for the path to mystical knowledge (*Darajāt*: sec. 18; *Tadhallul*: sec. 3, 6, 19, 21, 33, 34, 39).[104]

2. Submission to correct comportment is the only means of freeing oneself of the defects inherent in self-oriented aspirations (*tadbīr*), for through abandonment of self-oriented aspirations (*tark al-tadbīr*), one attains

sincere submission to God. As Abū 'Uthmān Ḥīrī said, "Right conduct is the mainstay of the spiritual aspirant and the beauty of the wealthy"[105] (*Darajāt* sec. 7; *Tadhallul* sec. 3, 6, 8, 12, 17, 18, 21-25, 30, 32-34, 36-39, 41-44).

3. When one understands the defective nature of phenomena and the self's tendency to become deluded, one can only feel disdain for the ego-self. Such is the meaning of Abū 'Uthmān's words, "Everything that pleases the ego-self, be it obedience or disobedience, is passion"[106] (*Darajāt* sec. 4; *Tadhallul* sec. 4, 8, 9, 10, 13, 26, 31, 32, 37)

4. Likewise, one will regard with disdain his deeds and states, firm in the knowledge that they too are susceptible to the defective nature of all that is other than God. Thus the second distinctive trait of the Malāmatīya was a general disclaiming of all pretensions to piety or spiritual states. This was expressed by Abū 'Uthmān, who said, "Fear of God will bring you to God, pride and self-satisfaction will sever you from God, and scorn for people will afflict you with a disease for which there is no cure"[107] (*Darajāt* sec. 3; *Tadhallul* sec. 2-11, 14, 15, 19, 20, 24, 27, 29, 35, 37, 40, 41, 45).

5. When defects are the inherent nature of created being, where does one seek refuge? Refuge can only be sought in "secreting one's states from creation" and seeking repose in God's perfect knowledge of our state of sincere submission to him (*Darajāt* sec. 17; *Tadhallul* sec. 2-4, 10, 16, 22, 28, 41). In a few concise lines Sulamī expressed the inner consequences of ostentation and the central role of anonymity to realizing sincerity.

> Were a *faqīr* to forsake an outward means of livelihood, he would surely be driven to importunity in seeking aid (*alḥafa*).[108] Were he to don the 'patched frock' or show outward signs of *faqr*, he would likewise be showing importunity. Were he to make a show of his *faqr* before the wealthy, he would only be showing [his] esteem for the world and its place in his heart. For were there no esteem in his heart for the world, he would not flaunt his renunciation of it before others. Of such a one it has been said, "Verily, for one who esteems the world, God has no esteem."[109]

From this brief comparison we see how the two texts mirror and complete one another. This complementary balance of inward and outward dimensions was among the most salient aspects of the teaching tradition of the Malāmatīya of Nishapur.

The clear exposition in *Darajāt al-ṣādiqīn* and *Tadhallul al-fuqarā'* of the relationship between the doctrine of the defective nature of created being and the attitudes central to the Path (as visualised by the founders of the Malāmatīya) makes these works salient examples of the teachings of Sulamī. In both works he maintains a balance between the inward and the outward aspects of the quest for intimate knowledge of God. He allows neither to dominate the other. In *Darajāt* he discusses the interior attitudes, calling upon the aspirant to bring his inward aspects into a conformity with the Real (*al-Ḥaqq*) and to abandon all spiritual claims and pretensions; knowing the defective nature of all but the Real (*al-Ḥaqq*). In the more outwardly oriented *Tadhallul* he stresses the necessity of abasing the ego-self and unconditionally accepting the humility that is innate to the human state. For in renouncing any claim to a spiritual state, the aspirant renounces his own will, and submits to the will of God. Then, in *Darajāt*, the aspirant, by divine grace, is granted knowledge and nearness and embarks upon the traversing of the mystic states of gnosis. Finally, from the intimacy that has made him a stranger to creation, he is returned to dwell with people, either as a saint, hidden among them, or as a source of light and wisdom for those in quest of God. In contrast, *Tadhallul* gives the aspirant the keys to this mode of conduct and the essential attitudes by which he may live among others as one of them. His inward state resides in proximity to God, while his outward state has been bestowed upon creation. These two texts are of a reciprocal nature which is reflective of the equilibrium inherent in Sulamī's method and style, a reciprocity of spiritual attitude and correct conduct. Through the windows of these precious texts the reader may discern the nature of the teachings of the Malāmatīya of Nishapur as well as the role of Sulamī as the spiritual heir and transmitter of these teachings.

THE MANUSCRIPTS

Mas'alat darajāt al-ṣādiqīn fī al-taṣawwuf

Both Brockleman (Supplement 1/955; GAL 1/219) and Ritter (Oriens, vol. 7, 1954; p. 399) have mentioned this treatise by the name *Mas'alat darajāt al-ṣādqīn fī al-taṣawwuf*; Sezgin makes mention of it (GAS p. 673), though he has given its title as *Mas'alat darajāt al-ṣālḥīn*; the manuscript citation of all three is the same, Fātiḥ 2650/3 59a-68b. Yūsuf Zīdān in his edition of *al-Muqaddima fī al-taṣawwuf* (1407/1987) lists *Mas'alat darajāt* among the unpublished works of al-Sulamī. Dr. Süleyman Ateş published it based upon the Fātiḥ manuscript in his collection of nine of Sulamī's texts (Ankara, 1401/1981). Unfortunately this edition, being based on only one manuscript, left something to be desired and has a lacuna of one page that went unnoticed in the original editing. I have based the present translation on my recent critical edition based upon two newly discovered manuscripts not cited in the above mentioned reference works and the Fātiḥ manuscript.

1. The manuscript on which I based my critical edition is from the library of Muhammad ibn Saad Islamic University in Riyadh. The catalog number of this Islamic Manuscript is 2118, under the name of Sulamīyāt, from folio 53a to 57b. The manuscript is written in an ancient *naskhī* script, and dated 474/1082. The manuscript bears signs of having been correlated with an original that may have dated to the time of Sulamī himself, for this reason I made it the base manuscript from which I worked. I have referred to this manuscript in the critical apparatus as **R**.

2. The second manuscript on which the present translation is based is from the Fātiḥ Library of Istanbul, Turkey in a compilation of works on Sufism number 2650/3 comprising 11 folios. The text entitled *Mas'alat darjāt al-ṣādiqīn fī al-taṣawwuf* is from fol. 59 to fol. 70. The manuscript was copied in a clear *naskhī* script, with the title in red by Muḥammad 'Abd al-Raḥmān al-Qārī and dated 876/1471. Each page is 17 cm x 13 cm of thirteen lines, with approximately ten words a line with a good margin. This manuscript has a lacuna of one folio that was evidently lost before the compilation was rebound and its pages numbered. The missing folio would have occurred between folio 68/b and 69/a. I have referred to this manuscript as **F**.

3. The third manuscript on which I based this translation is from the Ibn Yūsuf Manuscript Collection, Marrakech, Morocco; catalog number: 1208 located in Compilation 91 on works of Sufism, comprising 141 folios. The text (91/6), the last in the compilation; although untitled is listed in the catalog *as Kitāb al-farq bayn al-taṣawwuf wa al-malāma*, comprises 7 folios from fol. 136 to fol.141. Each page is 23 cm x 15 cm of nineteen lines, with approximately ten words a line with a good margin. It is undated, but paper and style, plus the fact that the compilation includes a copy of Ibn 'Abbād's *Rās'il al-ṣughrā* indicate that is was written some time after 14th century, perhaps in the 15th or16th centuries. I have referred to this manuscript as **B**.

4. Another manuscript, also from the Ibn Yūsuf Manuscript Collection, Marrakesh; catalog (Compilation 387), 123 folios, copied ca. 936/1530, was helpful in filling in some of the damaged portions of the three main manuscripts. The text, which is untitled, is from fol. 1-fol. 4. The manuscript is incomplete, lacking two folios; 18.5 cm x 14 cm, twenty lines a page, approximately nine words a line, the margin being badly worm eaten was reduced in rebinding. I have referred to this manuscript as **B/2**.

Kitāb bayān tadhallul al-fuqarā'

Both Brockleman (Supplement 1/955; GAL 1/219) and Ritter (Oriens, vol. 7, 1954; p. 399) have mentioned this treatise under the name *Bayān zalal al-fuqarā'*. Sezgin makes mention of it (GAS p. 673), though he has given its title as *Bayān zalal al-fuqarā' wa-mawājib ādābihim*; the manuscript citation of all three is the same, Fātiḥ 2650/4 (77a-99b, 9. Jh.H.). Yusuf Zīdān in his edition of *al-Muqaddima fī al-taṣawwuf* (1407/1987) lists *Bayān zalal al-fuqarā' wa-manāqib ādābihim*; among the unpublished works of Sulamī. Dr. Ateş published his critical edition of this treatise based upon the Fātiḥ manuscript in his collection of nine of al-Sulamī's texts (Ankara, 1401/1981). When my good friend Mustapha Naji of Rabat directed me to a second manuscript at the Ibn Yūsuf Library in Marrakech, Morocco I decided to undertake a second edition of the text. Subsequent to this critical edition Dr. Pourjavady generously provided me with a third manuscript dated 740/1340 and entitled *Kitāb bayān tadhallul al-fuqarā'*. This manuscript's early date, archaic calligraphic style and linguistic eloquence led me to make it the basis for a new critical edition published Tehran in 2009 in volume three of *The Collected Works of al-Sulamī*, edited by Nasrollah Pourjavady and Mohammed Soori. The present translation is based on this revised critical edition and bears the title of the Baku manuscript.

1. The manuscript on which I based this edition is from the National Manuscript Archives of Azerbaijan in Baku. The catalog number of this manuscript is 2785/Ṭ4410 under the title: *Kitāb bayān tadhallul al-fuqarā'*. The manuscript comprises 17 folios, from fol. 18 to fol. 33. The al-Mājid University's Center for Culture and Heritage, division for reproductions made the microfilm. The manuscript was written in an early *naskhī* script by Awḥad b. Maḥmūd b. Abī Bakr al-Madanī and dated in the month of Ramadan, 740/1340. The manuscript is the earliest of the three I employed and bears the closest resemblance, in the language and style, to other early Sulamī texts I have worked from. For this reason I made it the base manuscript for this edition. The title *Kitāb bayān tadhallul al-fuqarā'* resonates with the subject matter of the treatise itself and I have therefore given it preference over the title, *Bayān zalal al-fuqarā'*, by which this treatise has been previously cited among the works of al-Sulamī. I have referred to this manuscript as **B**.

2. The second manuscript on which the present translation is based is from the Fātiḥ Library of Istanbul, Turkey; it is located in the same compilation as *Darajāt al-ṣādiqīn*, number 2650/4 comprising 24 folios. The text entitled *Bayān zalal al-fuqarā wa mawājib adābihim* is from folio 77a to fol. 99b. The manuscript was copied in a clear *naskhī* script, with the title in red by Muḥammad 'Abd al-Raḥmān al-Qārī and dated 876/1471. Each page is 17 cm x 13 cm of thirteen lines, with approximately ten words a line with a good margin. I have referred to this manuscript as **F**.

3. The third manuscript on which I based this edition is from the Ibn Yūsuf Manuscript Collection, Marrakech, Morocco; catalog number: 1205 located in Compilation 91/3; 141 folios. The text, which is titled *Bayān zalal al-fuqarā' wa-ādābihim*; is located in the same Compilation as *Darajāt al-ṣādiqīn,* and comprises 14 folios from fol. 83 to 97. I have referred to this as manuscript **M**.

4. I have employed an additional manuscript in editing the final sections of *Bayān tadhallul al-fuqarā'* entitled *Sulūk al-'ārifin,* that Sulamī added it to complete this treatise. This manuscript is located at Dār

al-Kutūb al-'Arabīya, in the al-Taymūrīya collection under *Taṣawwuf* number 74 (18a-30a). I have employed pages 23a-25a.

I owe a debt of gratitude to Dr. Ateş, whose first editions of *Mas'alat darajāt al-ṣādqīn* and *Bayān zalal al-fuqarā'* in his *Nine Works on Sufism and Zuhd of al-Sulamī* (Ankara 1401/1981) first attracted my attention to these texts and led me to seek out and find the other manuscripts I have employed in the critical editions I have based the present translations upon.

First folio of *Mas'alat darajāt al-ṣādiqīn fī al-taṣawwuf*, Ms. 2118, folio 53b, (*Sulamīyyāt*) from The Islamic University of Muhammad Ibn Saud in Riyadh, The Kingdom of Saudi Arabia.

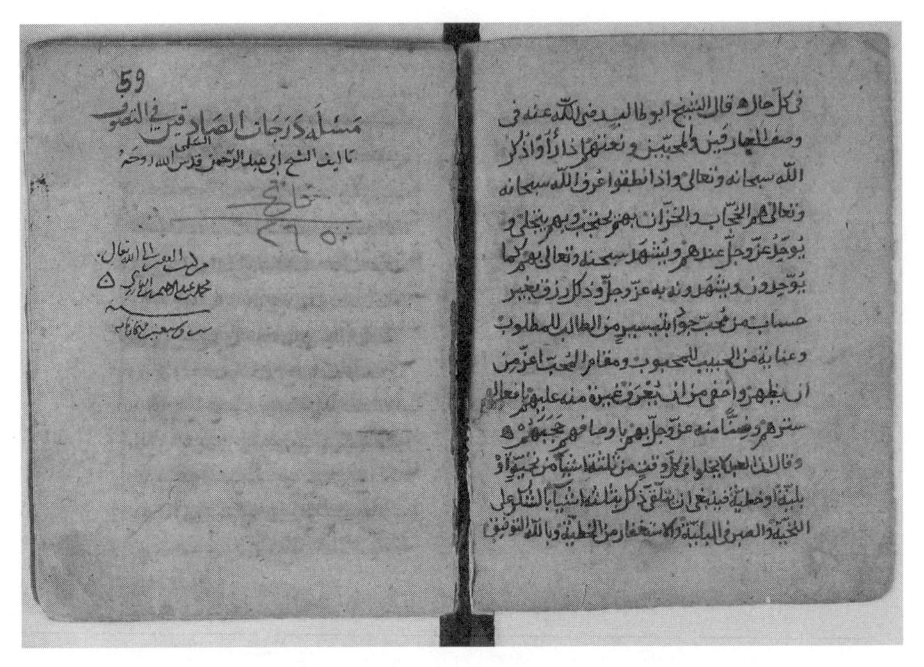

Title page of *Mas'alat darajāt al-ṣādiqīn fī al-taṣawwuf*, MS 2650/3, folio 59a, from the Fātiḥ Collection in Istanbul, Turkey

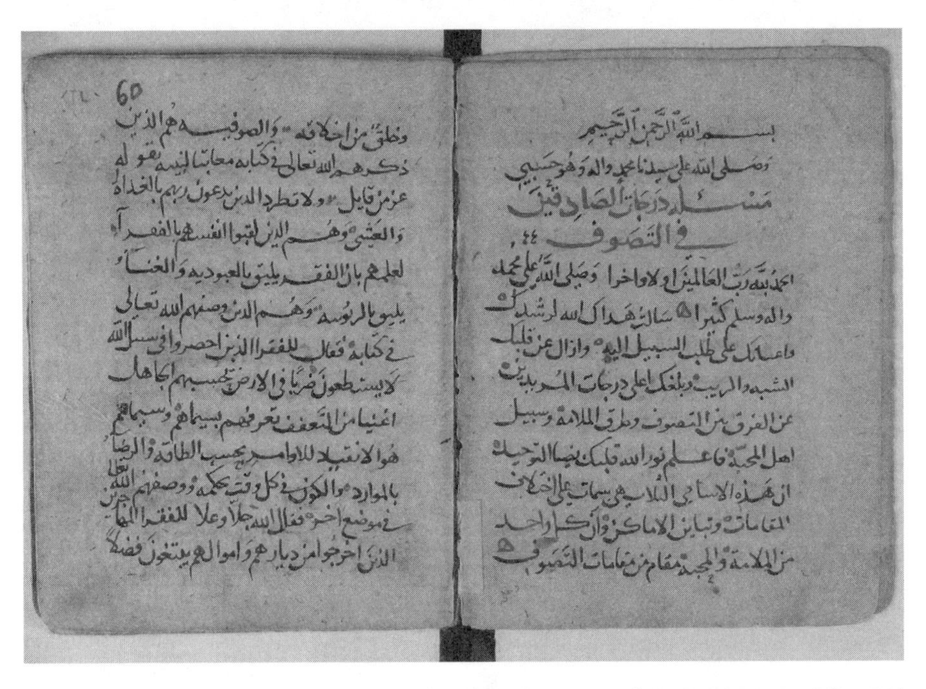

First folio of *Mas'alat darajāt al-ṣādiqīn fī al-taṣawwuf*, MS 2650/3, folio 59b, from the Fātiḥ Collection in Istanbul, Turkey.

قدوة للمكتفين وشمايله زينة للمريدين ...
النبي صلى الله عليه وسلم من تواضع رفعه الله وهذا
آخر الفصول ... والحمد لله

الحمد لله رب العالمين أولا وآخرا وصلى الله على سيدنا
محمد وآله وسلم كثيرا. سألت هداك الله لرشدك وأعانك
على طلب السبيل إليه وأزال عن قلبك الشبه والريب وبلغك
أعلى درجات المريد عن الفرق بين التصوف وطريق الملامتية
وسبيل أهل الصحبة فاعلم نور الله قلبك بضياء التوحيد
أن هذه الأسامي الثلاث هي سمات على اختلاف المقامات
وتباين الأماكن وأن كل واحد من الملامتية والصحبة من مقامات
التصوف وخلق من أخلاقه والصوفية هم الذين ذكرهم
الله تعالى في كتابه مخاطبا لنبيه صلى الله عليه وسلم بقوله
ولا تطرد الذين يدعون ربهم بالغداة والعشي يريدون وجهه
وهم الذين لقبوا أنفسهم بالفقراء لعلمهم بأن الفقر يليق
بالعبودية والغنى يليق بالربوبية وهم الذين وصفهم الله
تعالى فقال للفقراء الذين أحصروا في سبيل الله لا يستطيعون
ضربا في الأرض يحسبهم الجاهل أغنياء من التعفف تعرفهم
بسيماهم هو الانقياد للأوامر بحسب الطاقة والرضى

First folio of *Mas'alat darajāt al-ṣādiqīn fī al-taṣawwuf*, Ms. 91, folio 227a, from the Ibn Yusuf Collection, Marrakech, Morocco.

الفتح فيفنى في الولاية بعده حالا فحالا أو درجة فدرجة وأيضا
الانتهاء في المقامات الا بصحة الابتداء فمن لم يصح ابتداء
سلوكه على الكتاب والسنة لا يبلغه الانتهاء الى شيء من
المعارف واذا صح له ابتداؤه صح له انتهاؤه واذا صح له
الانتهاء رجع من مقام الاقبال على الله الى اقبال الله عليه ومن
مقام التقرب الى الله الى مقام قرب الله منه ومن مقام الاختيار
لنفسه الى مقام اختيار الله له فهنيئا لهذا العبد حاله
ومقامه وما اكرمه به من الفضل العظيم والشرف الرفيع فلا
يزيده الله رفعة بحال من الاحوال الا ازداد في نفسه تواضعا
واستكانة لعلمه ان من تواضع لله رفعه الله فهو يطلب
بتواضعه زيادة الرفعة من ربه وانا اسأل الله تعالى ان يمن
علينا بما من به على اوليائه واهل صفوته وان لا يحرمنا زوائد
فضله بمنه وسعة رحمته انه قريب مجيب والحمد
لله رب العالمين

انتهى بحمد الله وحسن عونه وصلى الله على
سيدنا ونبينا ومولانا ونبيه محمد
وعلى آله وصحبه وسلم تسليما

Final folio of *Mas'alat darajāt al-ṣādiqīn fī al-taṣawwuf*, Ms. 91, fol. 232b, from the Ibn Yusuf Collection, Marrakech, Morocco.

كتاب بيان تذلل الفقراء
للشيخ الامام السالك المحقق
ابو عبد الرحمن محمد بن الحسين
السلمي النيسابوري
روح الله روحه

Title page of *Kitāb bayān tadhallul al-fuqarā'*, MS 4410 / Ṭ 2785, folio 18a, from the National Archives of Azerbaijan in Baku.

بسم الله الرحمن الرحيم
الحمد لله اولا واخرا وصلى الله على محمد
النبي واله وسلم كثيرا اما بعد فانه
لما ظهر في فقراء الوقت من التعزز بالفقر
والتكبر به والصول على الخلق فزاد على
[illegible] الاغنياء وتكبرهم وتجبرهم غار بعض
مشايخنا تولى الله رعايته على ما احدثوه
من الرسوم الطبيعية التي هي خلاف
اخلاق مشايخهم وسالني ان اجمع فصولا
ابين فيه سبل الفقر وطريقته واخلاقه
وادابه ومن اين ضلوا مع سواء السبيل
وتوهموا الباطل حقا والخطا صوابا
فاستخرت الله في جميع حروف وفصول
منه على حد الاختصار يستدل به
الناظر على طريقة الحق في الفقر والتر[illegible]
به من غير حقيقة واستعنت بالله
فيه وهو خير معين فاعلم اسعدك
الله بنور التوفيق ان الفقر احد
اوصاف العبودية وليس في العبودية
تعزز وانكبار انما هو الانقياد والخضوع
قال الله تعالى ضرب الله مثلا عبدا
مملوكا لا يقدر على شيء فمن ظن انه يقدر
على شيء او حال او مقام او درجة فهو خارج
من اوصاف

من اوصاف العبودية التي احد اوصافها
الفقر والفقر لباس يورث الرضا اذا
تحقق العبد فيه والفقر ثوب سداه القناعة
ولحمته التواضع والفقير اذا ترك ظاهر
الكسب فقد الحف في السوال واذا لبس
المرقعة فقد الحف واذا اظهر الفقر فقد
الحف واذا تكبر بفقره على الاغنياء فقد
اظهر محل الدنيا وانبايها في قلبه لانه لو لم
يكن للدنيا في قلبه قدر لما كان يتكبر على
الخلق بتركها وقد قيل ان من تكون للدنيا
في قلبه قدر لا يكون له عند الله قدر والفقير
من يجهله من ليس في درجته ومقامه قال الله
تعالى في صفة الفقراء يحسبهم الجاهل اغنياء
من التعفف وذلك لصيانتهم فقرهم ولسكونهم
الى عدم المالوفات وتركهم اظهار فقرهم و
استكانتهم بحال ثم قال الله تعالى تعرفهم
بسيماهم وانما يعرفهم من في الجملة درجتهم
من الفقراء دون غيرهم وذلك لسيماء خشوع
بواطنهم وخضوع ظواهرهم واستكانتهم في
احوالهم وتذللهم في انفسهم ونصيحتهم للاخوان
واحترامهم للمشايخ ورحمتهم على من بلاه الله
بما توهمهم عنه ثم قال لا يسألون الناس الحافا
كلت السنتهم عن السوال من تملك الكل رضاهم

First and second pages of *Kitāb bayān tadhallul al-fuqarā*, MS 4410 / Ṭ 2785, folio 18b and 19a, from the National Archives of Azerbaijan in Baku.

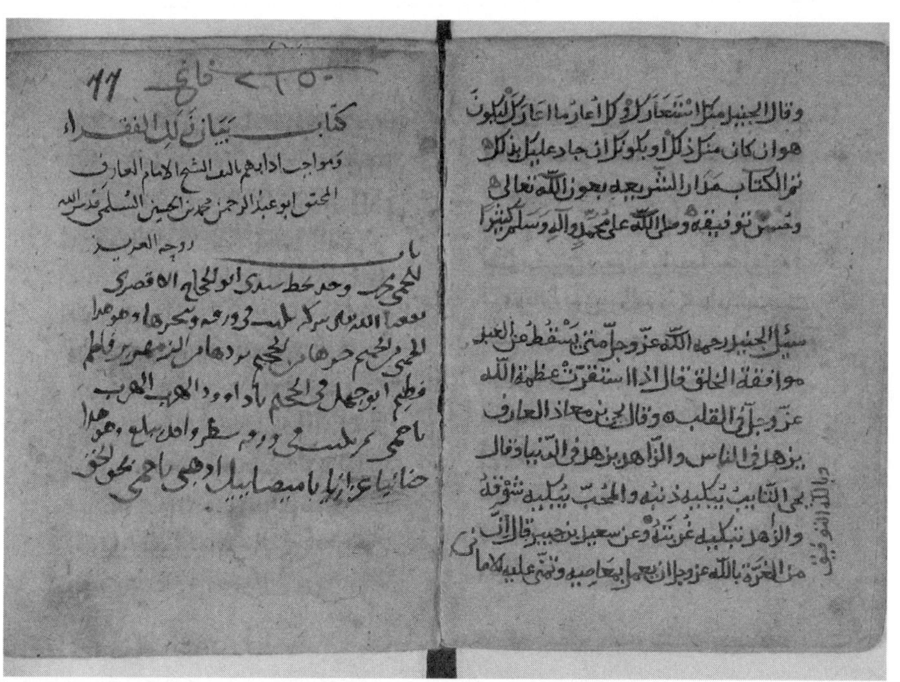

Title page of *Kitāb bayān zalal al-fuqarā wa mawājib ādābihim,* MS 2650/4, folio 77a, from the Fātiḥ Collection in Istanbul, Turkey.

First two pages of *Kitāb bayān zalal al-fuqarā wa mawājib ādābihim,* MS 2650/4, folio 77b &78a, from the Fātiḥ Collection in Istanbul, Turkey.

بسم الله الرحمن الرحيم صلى الله على سيدنا محمد وعلى آله وسلم

بيان زلل الفقراء وآدابهم

الحمد لله أولا وآخرا وصلى الله على سيدنا محمد
أما بعد فإنه لما ظهر في فقراء الوقت من التعزز بالفقر
والتكثر به والصول على الخلق ما زاد على تيه الأغنياء وكبرهم
ونبههم [illegible] بعض مشايخنا قول الله [illegible] على ما أحدثوه
من الرسوم الطبيعية التي خالف أخلاق مشايخهم وسألني
أن أجمع فصولا أبين فيها سبيل الفقر وطريقته وأخلاقه
وآدابه ومن أين ضلوا عن سواء السبيل [illegible]
حقا والخطأ صوابا فاستخرت الله تعالى في جمع حروف وفصول
منه على حد الاختصار يستدل به الناظر على طريقة [illegible]
الفقر والتشبه به من غير حقيقة واستعنت بالله فيه وهو
خير معين فاعلم أسعدك الله بنور التوفيق أن الفقر
أحد أوصاف العبودية وليس في العبودية تعزز ولا تكبر
إنما هو الانقياد والخضوع قال الله تعالى ضرب الله مثلا عبدا
مملوكا لا يقدر على شيء فمن ظن أنه يقدر على شيء وله
حال أو مقام أو درجة فهو خال من أوصاف العبودية التي أحد

First folio of *Kitāb bayān zalal al-fuqarā wa ādābihim*, Ms. 91, fol. 174b, from the Ibn Yusuf Collection, Marrakech, Morocco.

الفقر صعب لأنه حال النبي صلى الله عليه وسلم والصفوة من
الأيمة والسلف الطاهرين رضي الله عنهم فمن توسم به وطالب
نفسه بالصدق فيما ادعاه كثر ذلك او رثه بركات التحقق فيه قال
الله تعالى يقول والذين جاهدوا فينا لنهدينهم سبلنا وروي
عن النبي صلى الله عليه وسلم انه قال من عمل بما يعلم اورثه
الله ما لم يكن يعلم وقد بينا في هذه الفصول التي ذكرتها
مختصرا ما يستدل به الموقف على طريقة القوم وادابهم
وشمايلهم واخلاقهم وانا اسأل الله الكريم هنا بركات ما
نوينا فيه وسعينا له بفضله وسعة رحمته انه قريب مجيب

انتهى بحمد الله وحسن عونه
وصلى الله على سيدنا محمد نبيه وعبده
وعلى آله وصحبه وسلم تسليما
احب مجالسة المشايخ
وحفظ حرماتهم

بسم الله الرحمن الرحيم صلى الله على سيدنا محمد

اعلم وفقك الله لمتابعة العلوان الله تعالى ذكره
امر الطاعة باتباع الاكابر والتأدب باداتهم بقوله تعالى
واتبع سبيل من اناب الي اي من رجع الي من جميع مراداته

Final folio of *Kitāb bayān zalal al-fuqarā wa ādābihim*, Ms. 91, fol. 187b, from the Ibn Yusuf Collection, Marrakech, Morocco.

Abū al-Ḥasan al-Būshanjī said, "One who humbles himself, God raises in stature, but one who exalts himself God humbles in the eyes of men." The [true] *faqīr* is the one who has neither deed that pleases him, nor any state in which he finds repose, nor any moment (*waqt*) to which he returns. His innermost soul is a witness to the Truth (*al-Ḥaqq*). He lacks the means to go backward or forward. [The circumstances of each of] his moments (*waqt*) render him incapable of describing his state or his station; he neither takes shelter in anything known [to him] nor does he find rest in any beloved thing. *Faqr* is true servanthood; its sign is constant awareness of one's inadequacy and inability to reach the goal [by one's own effort]. Such is the truth of *faqr*.

His preoccupation with the reality of each of his moments keeps him from paying attention to those of his brothers, and he sees other people's merits by being aware of his own short-comings. He acts with noble character towards strangers, to say nothing of how he acts with his brothers and companions. He respects spiritual mentors (*mashā'ikh*), is generous to his companions, and compassionate towards aspirants (*murīd*). He does not seek to fulfil his needs through relationships with any secondary causes [such as people or worldly interests] except in the instance of necessity, and then only from a place where his soul finds repose.

[53a]

In the Name of God, the Merciful, the Compassionate
My Lord is my sufficiency and in Him lies my trust

STATIONS OF THE RIGHTEOUS

(*Mas'alat darajāt al-ṣādiqīn fī al-taṣawwuf*)
[Abū 'Abd al-Raḥmān al-Sulamī]

1 From the beginning and ultimately, all praise is due to God, Lord of all worlds, alone; and may His blessings be upon our Master Muḥammad and his family.

You have asked—may God bring you to right guidance, aid you on your way to Him, and rid [53b] your heart of all ambiguity and doubt, bringing you to the highest degrees of the aspirants—of the difference between Sufism (*taṣawwuf*),[1] the paths of blame (*ṭuruq al-malāma*),[2] and the way of the people of love (*sabīl ahl al-maḥabba*).[3]

2 Know well—may God illumine your heart with the light of oneness—that these three names refer to outward characteristics of differing spiritual stations (*maqāmāt*)[4] and varied points of view, when in fact, [the path of] blame and [the path of] love are each a station and innate characteristic [experienced] in Sufism. The Sufis are those mentioned by God in His book, in the verse reproving His Prophet—may peace be upon him—*Repel not those who call upon their Lord at morn and evening, seeking His countenance* [6:52]. They are those who have called themselves the poor (*fuqarā'*), for they know that utter need (*faqr*) corresponds to the state of servitude, while [the quality of] self-sufficiency and independence (*ghinā'*) corresponds to the state of Lordship (*rubūbīya*).[5] They are those people that God described in His book saying, *for the poor, who being wholly occupied with the cause of God cannot travel in the land [for trade]. The unthinking man thinks them wealthy because of their restraint [from asking for alms]. You know them by their distinguishing marks* [2:273]. Their marks are utmost obedience in their accomplishment of religious duties, acceptance (*riḍā*) of divine decree, and constancy in the wisdom (*ḥikma*) of each moment. God has referred to them in another verse saying, *for the poor [among] immigrants, who have been driven from their homes and their belongings, seeking bounty from God and His grace* [59:8]. We

are informed [in this verse] of their [distinguishing] quality, being that their hopes are not fixed upon some safe haven or on anything known to them; on the contrary their support and their reliance is upon the bounty of God. They have been divested of their actions, their individual qualities, their words, their invocations [of God], and their acts of obedience. They find no repose in any of those things nor do they regard them with esteem. This is because they have passed away (*li-fanā'ihim*) from the totality of their own individual attributes.

3 Among the comportment (*ādāb*) that brought them to this station and this degree is the spiritual discipline (*riyāḍāt*) they impose upon themselves, preceded by sound repentance (*taṣḥīḥ al-tawba*), then perfect detachment, turning from all other than God—from the world and its inhabitants—the abandonment of all they own, distancing themselves from all familiar things (*ma'lufāt*), departure upon long journeys, denial of outward passionate desires, constant watchfulness over their innermost secrets (*al-asrār al-bāṭina*), deference towards the masters of the Path, service to brethren and friends, preference to others over themselves in worldly goods (*arfāq*), person, and spirit, perseverance in [their] efforts at all times, and regarding all that may arise from them inwardly or outwardly—of their actions or their states—[54a] with contempt and disdain.

4 Then the ascent from this degree (*daraja*) is made by insisting that the ego-self (*nafs*) place total trust (*tawakkul*) in God in all states. The lowest degree of trust in God is trusting (*thiqa*) [that one will receive] one's daily bread (*rizq*), while its true foundation is turning to God in all things, until one sees neither benefactor nor malefactor other than He. Then [with time] this trust becomes certainty (*yaqīn*); subsequently, reliance upon God; then entrusting all one's affairs to Him (*tafwīḍ*); whereupon [it becomes] total submission (*taslīm*) in the face of all that arises from the unseen [realm] (*ghayb*), bring it joy or sorrow. Then one attains patience in the face of trial and tribulation. After this one meets tribulation with gratitude. Thereupon one [attains a state of] inner repose in tribulation—with neither complaint nor pretence—as if one were reposing in a state of ease, until finally, one finds pleasure in tribulation above that which one found in ease. Next comes inward and outward contentment (*riḍā*) with all that befalls one [from one's destiny], then respect for all Muslims. Subsequently one regards all creatures with the eye of Truth (*bi-'ayn al-Ḥaqq*). All of these states are the degrees of the stations of the aspirants. Then, after all this, there arises the

fear that all this is but being led on by degrees (*istidrāj*) and deception (*makr*), then fear of one's shortcomings in fear, then fear of lack [of awareness] of one's shortcomings, then fear of lack of sincerity [in fear]. After this, one attains hope which is [both] the heart's repose—away from the assaults of fear—in God's promise of beneficence towards His servants and trust in His goodwill knowing that He will, through his benevolence, cleanse them of the deficiencies of these stations and shield them from areas of corruption (*mawāḍiʿ al-fasād*).

5 After this follows the return from the end [of the way] to its beginning when the aspirant has traversed them [i.e. the stations] a second time. [This occurs] when he has become sound in his journeying (*sulūk*) and has clearly understood God's elucidation of it (*bayān al-Ḥaqq*). Thus Abū Yazīd al-Bisṭāmī[6] said, "Whenever I imagined I had reached the end, I heard a voice saying," "This is the beginning." I also heard Shaykh Abū 'Uthmān al-Maghribī[7] say, "I traversed the stations three times, whenever I reached the end [i.e. of the path], it was said, 'Return him to the beginning, that he not remain ignorant.'" Abū 'Uthmān said, "I then asked one of real knowledge (*mutaḥaqqiqūn*) of journeying about this and he told me, 'That is the way with one who has been blessed, he is returned from the end to the beginning to efface him of any attitude of ignorance or pretension.'"

6 Then from this station, one is raised to a subtle mystical state wherein he is able to discern inspiration (*ilhām*), temptation (*waswasa*), passing thoughts (*khāṭir*), inclination (*ṭabʿ*) [54b], miracles (*karāma*), self-deception (*ightirār*), certainty (*yaqīn*), and being led on by degrees (*istidrāj*); and these [states] too, are among the principle states of the Folk [i.e. travelers of the path].

7 At last one reaches the state of stability and rectitude (*istiqāma*), wherein he resides in God's presence having attained stability of the ego-self, stability of innermost soul (*sirr*), stability of will (*irāda*), stability of natural inclination (*tabʿ*), stability of thought, stability of reflection; stability at the beginning and the end. Only the Prophet himself has ever been directly addressed as having perfectly attained this state; as God states, *So dwell in stability as you have been commanded* [11:112]. The Prophet said to his community—knowing the deficiency of their states compared to his, "Keep to the straight path, but do not keep accounts."[8] All these [states] are among the stations of servitude (*'ubūdīya*). A servant possesses no right to choose for himself until he has attained a position of trust, even then, he may act only with the permission of his Lord within His domain. The servant has no purposes he calls his own

(*tadbīr*) nor goal (*murād*), because his decisions are made for him and his goal is that which has been decided for him. His states are never perfected, because he is subject to whatever changes in state His Master decrees [not as he himself might choose].

8 Then, after this, the first of the stations of knowledge (*ma'rifa*) appears. This knowledge is also a branch of the branches of Sufism. It is the aspirant's passing away from all of these states, stations, degrees and all else besides. He manifests qualities that he has not fully realized. He is not void of states, yet he does not manifest a specific state. He has become purified [divested] of his ego-self, his actions, his words, his states, and all that relates to him and has become—as I heard 'Abd al-Wāhid ibn Muḥammad say, "Bundār ibn al-Husayn[9] said—when asked about the meaning of [the word] *sufi* [10]—that, 'it refers to [one] who has been purified of all that he had by the expanses (*bawādī*) of divine lights that entered [his being] from God (*al-Ḥaqq*), so that his innermost soul is unveiled and he is able to move freely within the realm of the unseen and relate its secrets in accord with the decrees of destiny.'" This is one kind of intuitive knowledge (*firāsa*) about which the Prophet spoke when he said, "Beware of the intuitive glance of the believer, for he sees by the light of God."[11] After this, the traveler's state is purified until he is able to confirm authoritatively the [mysteries] of the unseen; just as he [formerly] would relate that which he had been informed of. This was the case when the 'most veracious' [Abū Bakr][12] [55a] told [his daughter] 'Ā'isha,[13] just before his death, "They are your two brothers and two sisters."[14] [In doing so] he foretold that his wife would bear a daughter.[15] This is the subtlest of judgements.

All of these stations are among the first stations of knowledge. True knowledge (*ḥaqīqat al-ma'rifa*) is the denial of all but the known (*al-ma'rūf*), the Only Real (*wa-huwa al-Ḥaqq*). As al-Junayd[16] said, "Knowledge is denial." (*al-ma'rifa inkār*). Therefore knowledge is never realized until one has denied all other than the known. In a like manner, each individual thing is realized in [reference to] its opposite; thus, knowledge of God is ignorance of all other than He. As long as you claim knowledge for yourself of a refuge, joy or sanctuary other than God, you are not a person of knowledge (*'ārif*). [You can achieve this state] only if you know Him through denial of all other than He. The servant knows not His Lord until all his objects of knowledge have fallen away from him, all but the knowledge of He who is the Known to the people of knowledge.

9 As to that which has been related concerning the saying of one of the early mentors that, "He who knows himself, knows His Lord;" it means that one cannot know one's Lord with knowledge of oneself. Thus when he forgets himself, he knows His Lord. Sahl [ibn 'Abdallāh][17] said, "The life of the heart is in the knowledge of God alone [not of another]." Abu 'Uthmān [al-Ḥīrī][18] and Abū Turāb al-Nakhshabī[19] said, "One who is ignorant of God's decrees (*aḥkām*) cannot be one knowledgeable of God." No one attains true knowledge of God while being ignorant of God's decrees and commands. How might one who has attained knowledge of God be ignorant of His decrees and commands?! When one knows His Lord, knows His decrees and commands, and lives by them to the best of his ability, he will manifest the signs of sincerity and be counted among the sincere (*ṣādiqīn*). Then, [in time] he will become firmly established in sincerity and will subsequently be counted among the veracious (*ṣiddiqīn*).[20] This is one of the enviable stations [of the path], about which the Prophet said, "Among God's servants there are those that are neither prophets nor martyrs; they are envied by the prophets and martyrs."[21] One of the people of spiritual knowledge (*ma'rifa*) was asked about this hadith of the Prophet's, "they are envied by the prophets and martyrs." "How might the prophets envy them when they [referring to the prophets] are above them in rank?" To which he answered, "Because the prophets were occupied with the obligation of the proclamation [of their message] and being witnesses to all created beings, while those [who are envied] bore not that burden, hence nothing distracted them from God. For this reason the prophets envy them, even though the state of prophecy is higher and more perfect."

10 Once he is established in the station of sincerity—in the intimate knowledge and awareness of God and subsistence in Him (*al-baqā bihi*) through extinction from all other than He and collectedness in Him through separation from all that is not He—[the aspirant] enters the fields of union (*wasla*) [55b] and communion (*ittiṣāl*) and becomes known as one who has arrived at the Truth (*wāṣil bi-al-Ḥaqq*) through his separation from all that is other than God. Therein he embarks upon the transversing of the ninety-nine stations, which accord in number with the Divine Names.[22] To each of these stations corresponds a state in which the traveler is in direct relationship with one of these names, the grace (*baraka*) of which becomes apparent upon his person. That name is the place from which he drinks (*mashrab*), his spring (*mawrid*), and his place of origin (*maṣdar*). Each of these stations bathes him in its own light and luminosity, no one resembling the preced-

ing one, until the traveler reaches the outermost limits [of his path] (*aqsā al-nihāyāt*). Here he has traversed all the stations and subsists with God (*al-Ḥaqq*), having neither station, locale, name, form, quality, pretence, desire, sight, vision (*mushāhada*), endeavour nor goal (*ṭalab*). He is as it has been said, "The servant is as though he had never been, and God is as He has never ceased to be." It has also been said, "The Sufis are like children in the lap of God (*al-Ḥaqq*)." When one of them was asked about the qualities of the Sufis he said, "God (*al-Ḥaqq*) has brought to naught their qualities and assumed their protection with His qualities."

11 From here the traveller gains awareness of the knowledge of hidden things (*al-'ilm al-bāṭin*) among the secrets of Divine Reality (*asrār al-Ḥaqq*), secrets that He only makes known to the most trusted of the saints (*awliyā'*). This is the mystic knowledge (*al-'ilm al-ladunī*) spoken of by God in the Qur'ān, *Then they found one of our servants to whom we had shown our mercy and had taught him knowledge from our presence* [18:66]. This form of knowledge overcomes the listener; the one who gives it needs neither proof nor argument [to convince the listener of what he has been told]. Have not you seen [in the Qur'ān] how Moses deferred the decrees of his law before the mystic knowledge of al-Khiḍr. Even though Moses was superior and more perfect in state and station, he was overwhelmed by mystic knowledge, not by his perception of al-Khiḍr or of his actions or decrees.

12 Then the knowledge of innermost secrets of the hidden realm (*'ilm bāṭin al-bāṭin*) are opened to the traveler. This is knowledge of unseen matters regarding divine degrees and destiny, as yet unmanifest, but which God (*al-Ḥaqq*) will manifest. They behold [these secrets] by the purity of their inward mysteries, the strength of their states, and their extinction from their own qualities. This is exemplified by the saying of 'Abdallāh ibn 'Abbās,[23] "God bless Omar[24] it is as though he views destiny through a thin veil." Similarly, it has been recounted that one day al-Jarīrī[25] asked his disciples, "Is there one among you who knows what will arise from the unseen before it appears?" [56a] When they answered "No," he said, "Weep over hearts brought far from God." Al-Junayd likewise said, "When God (*al-Ḥaqq*) intends to manifest something hidden (*ghayb*) or a decree of His unseen realms, He rouses an intuition (*ẓanīn*) within the inner mysteries of the elect of his saints and through this [intuition] they become aware of the unfolding of unseen matters."[26] Those are hearts that are never absent from the divine presence; they are never unaware of God (*al-Ḥaqq*), nor do they mingle in companionship with others.

13 From these states the aspirant ascends to a state in which he deems miracles insignificant. This is the moment of witnessing of God's glory, omnipotence, and magnificence. All else appears deprecated in his eyes, and through his perception of the defective nature of all appearances he realizes that the locus of created being (*maḥal al-ḥawādith*) will never be devoid of defects.[27] Thus, upon witnessing divine design (*al-ṣun'*) he is intimately drawn to its freedom of all imperfection. When he witnesses the locus in which the divine design appears, he feels estranged, conscious of the defects [inherent in creation]. This is among the stations of the illustrious and the masters [of the path]. This is a time in which impurities are found in purity and purity in impurities. Like the quest of Moses for fire,[28] whereupon he was directly spoken to [by God] and addressed; while Adam's quest of the tree, aspiring for eternal life, brought him only expulsion from his rank and station.[29] This is the moment wherein permission is granted [the traveler] to hear (*samā'*) [divine discourse] and to have its meanings unveiled (*kashf*) to him. He is honored by the understanding of what he hears, by being addressed, and by witnessing the inner meaning of hearing and cognition thereof, increasing his proximity and intimacy. God said, *Lo! Therein verily is a reminder for him who has a heart or has listened attentively while witnessing (shāhīd)*. [50:37] [This is also] the moment of finding (*wujūd*) repose (*rawḥ*) in the innermost secret (*al-sirr*), heavenly fragrance (*rayḥān*) in the heart, light in the innermost secret, and illumination (*ḍiyā'*) in the breast. God said, *Thus if he is of those brought nigh, then [he shall find] divine bliss (rawḥ), heavenly fragrance (rayḥān), and a garden of bounty* [56:88-89]. Thus divine bliss brings deliverance to their innermost secrets from [the distractions of] creation through union with its Creator; while the heavenly fragrance, here refers to the repose of their hearts in God (*al-Ḥaqq*) at the commencement and at the end [of their journey]. The garden of bounties is their joy in the proximity of their Lord, in witnessing Him, and in their freedom from that which occupies the people of paradise; as God said, *Lo! those who merit Paradise this day are happily occupied.* [36:54]

14 When one has truly attained these stations and grown steadfast in them, refuge (*amn*) is afforded him, either through inspiration (*wahyī*), the word of a prophet (*akhbār al-nabīy*), the intuition of a saint (*firāsat walī*) [56b], witnessing of the unseen (*mushāhdat al-ghayb*), or personal intuition (*musāmarat khāṭir*). God said, *Verily the friends of God know no fear nor do they grieve* [10:63]. That is like the Prophet's informing the Ten [of his Companions] of the Quraysh [that they would attain] Paradise, and like his saying about Ḥāritha

[ibn al-Nuʿmān], "I heard his recitation [of the Qur'ān] in paradise."[30] This, after he had been martyred in the Prophet's presence. Likewise when he said to Jābir ibn 'Abdallāh, "God has addressed your father face to face."[31] His foretelling of the sanctity of 'Uways al-Qaranī[32] was similar to this, and there are many other instances like these.

15 When God has brought one of His servants to the station of realized sainthood (*taḥqīq al-wilāya*) through truthful knowledge, he is freed of leanings towards fear; whereas solemn awe (*ḥayba*) never leaves him. Those in these states vary in degree. Some of them are brought from a state of fear to a state of apprehension (*khashiya*), while others, of subtler state, are brought to the state of fearful awe (*ruhba*), while still others, of [even] subtler state are brought to solemn awe. This is because the locus of phenomena cannot possibly be freed of defects [even] through [the attainment of] a mystical state. However, it may be possible that certain elements of the virtue of fear may gain ascendancy over one, and thereby his qualities will fade away. This is as God mentioned in His venerable book, *We purified him with a pure thought, remembrance of the hereafter. Verily in our sight they are of the elect, the excellent.* [38:47-48]. The state of one whose attributes are thus is that his attributes become embodied in an attribute of these [Divine] attributes, until the servant is freed of all his attributes and inclinations. He speaks from pure truth (*ṣirf ḥaqq*), and communicates the purity of a Divine reality (*ṣafā ḥaqīqa*). This [state] however is but a flash of lightning and will not endure. If it were of any duration it would completely enrapture and annihilate him. How many there are, mad with love (*hā'im*) annihilated (*fānin*) in this [state].

16 Then, once God has brought a servant among his servants to these degrees, given him refuge in a place of proximity to Him, bestowed upon him the intimacy of His remembrance, and made him a stranger to all other beings, He may reveal him to people as a model and a refuge to which aspirants might turn in their quest for Him. In this He permits the outward aspect [of the servant] to turn towards mankind as a mercy from Him to them. For were they to lose [access to] his knowledge, inner attitudes, and disciplines they would stray in their journey and their quest and fall into self-delusion. By the lights of those masters, they seek illumination, and by their counsel they are rightly guided in their efforts to reach their goal. [Those returned to awareness of creation] are the masters of the people of divine Reality (*ahl al-ḥaqā'iq*). They are the lords of hearts and lofty degrees. [57a] They

are the points of reference for the travelers of the path, in them they find a model and refuge, in the same manner the generality of believers find a refuge concerning questions of law in the jurists. When God shows one of his saints to humankind, He causes temptation to fall away from him. Thus he neither deludes others nor is he deluded.

17 Among them are those whom He hides from the eyes of creation, from their eyes, their hearts, and their inward secrets; they exist among people as one of them. They eat, drink, and mingle with others. God has allowed their exterior aspect to face creation while keeping their inner state exclusively to Himself. No one perceives their inner perfection, while He is completely aware of them. This is because of God's jealousy over them, for He is too jealous to allow other than Himself the knowledge of His elect. Should one of the saints made apparent to men err, by a glance or a word—and he could not err beyond this—the hidden saint would return him to the straight way. He would either reveal himself to him and restore him to rectitude or befriend him, while remaining veiled, and restore him to equilibrium by [the authority of] his inner attitudes (*akhalaq*). And there shall always be a Pole (*quṭb*)[33] among the saints watching over them. The Pole restores he who swerves from the Truth (*al-Ḥaqq*), to his path by either his inner attitude or the overwhelming nature of his authority. Have not you seen how [Abū Bakr] al-Siddīq—the most esteemed individual among the Islamic community after the Prophet himself—brought everyone [to the straight way] by his overwhelming authority when they differed with him on waging war against the apostates,[34] until 'Umar [Ibn al-Khaṭṭāb] stated, "When God opened Abu Bakr's heart to war, I knew it was the true way." Thus is the authority of the realized saints after him [Abu Bakr] from state to state and degree to degree.

18 There can be no successful completion of the journey through the spiritual stations without a sound beginning. He who has not founded his journey upon the Qur'ān and the practice of the Prophet (*al-sunna*) will in the end attain nothing of intimate knowledge of God. If his commencement is sound, his culmination will be sound. If the culmination of his journey is sound, he will be brought from the station of turning towards God (*iqbāl*), to the station of God's turning towards him, and from the station of drawing near God (*taqarrub*), to the station of God's proximity (*qurb*) to him, and from the station of choice for himself, to the state of God's choosing for him. Glad tidings to this servant, for his state and station, and the mag-

nificent rank [57b] and lofty respect that God has granted him. His degree could not be elevated by any state, unless he be increased in humility and abasement, knowing, that [as the Prophet said,] "He who humbles himself before God, God elevates [in degree]."[35] Thus asking his Lord, in humility, he seeks to be upraised.

I ask God most high to favor us with that which He has favored His saints and the people of Purity. May He not deprive us of His increased blessings by His generosity and His boundless mercy. He is indeed the Near, He who answers. All praise is due to God alone, and may the blessings of God and peace be upon our Master Muḥammad and his family.

[18/a]

THE BOOK ON THE HUMBLE SUBMISSION OF THOSE ASPIRING

(*Kitāb bayān tadhallul al-fuqarā'*)

by

The Imām, the Realized Wayfarer, Shaykh Abū 'Abd al-Raḥmān Muḥammad b. Ḥusayn al-Sulamī al-Nīsābūrī
May God grant his eternal soul (*rūḥahu*) repose

In the Name of God, the Merciful, the Compassionate

[18/b] At the beginning and ultimately, all praise is due to God, may His blessings be upon our Master Muḥammad.

1 Now to our topic: When self-exaltation and pride in poverty (*faqr*)[1] appeared among the aspirants (*fuqarā'*) of our time and they began to act aggressively towards people, [a situation] which only increased the haughtiness of the wealthy[2] as well as their arrogant and despotic behavior; one of our mentors (*mashā'ikh*)—may God keep him under His protection—took exception to the purely human modes of conduct (*al-rusūm al-ṭabi'īya*) these aspirants had innovated, [modes of conduct] that were contrary to the noble character of their mentors, asked me to assemble some chapters elucidating the *path of poverty* (*sabīl al-faqr*), its way, its essential character traits (*akhlāq*), and requisite conduct (*ādāb*), and clarifying therein where those [who had innovated] had erred from the straight path and had imagined falsehood, truth and error, correct guidance. Thereupon, I sought guidance from God—be He exalted—in assembling some concise statements and chapters concerning the path of poverty, so that the reader might, through this treatise, discern between the real path of poverty and an empty parody of it [which is] devoid of substance. In so doing I sought help from God; indeed He is the best of helpers!

2 Know, may God gladden you with the light of His grace, that utter need (*faqr*) is one of the traits of servanthood. In servanthood there is neither arrogance nor pride, but rather humble submission and compliance. God—be He exalted—says, *God coined a similitude: [two men, on the one hand] a [mere] chattel slave, who is capable of nothing and a [free] man upon whom we*

have bestowed goodly sustenance [as a gift] from Ourselves, so that he can spend thereof [at will, both] secretly and openly. Can these two be deemed equal? [16:75]. Therefore, one who imagines that he is capable of something, and claims for himself a spiritual state, station, or degree, is devoid [19/a] of the traits of servanthood, one of which is utter need. *Faqr,* when truly realised, is a garment which bestows acceptance [of divine decree] (*riḍā*).[3] *Faqr* is a fabric, the warp of which is contentment (*qanāʿa*) [with God], and the weft of which is humble submission (*al-tawāḍuʿ*). Were a *faqīr* to forsake an outward means of livelihood, he would surely be driven to importunity in seeking aid (*alḥafa*).[4] Were he to don the 'patched frock' or show outward signs of *faqr,* he would likewise be showing importunity. Were he to make a show of his *faqr* before the wealthy, he would only be showing [his] esteem for the world and its place in his heart, for were there no esteem in his heart for the world, he would not flaunt his renunciation of it before others; of such a one it has been said, "Verily, for one who esteems the world, God has no esteem."

3 The *faqīr* is only recognized by someone of his own degree and station, even as God—be He exalted—said in describing the *fuqarā',* *He who is unaware [of their condition] might think them wealthy because of their restraint [from asking for alms]* [2:273]. That is because they guard their *faqr,* find repose in the absence of any familiar means [of relief] (*ma'lūfāt*), and give up displaying both their *faqr* as well as any complaint concerning it. God—be He exalted—then said, *You will recognise them by their distinctive marks* [2:273]. Verily, the only one able to recognize them by their distinctive marks is one of the *fuqarā'* who is of their degree. Those distinctive marks are their inward humility, their outward obedience [to the law], their submission in their [various] states, their self-effacement, their counsel to their brothers, their respect for spiritual mentors, and their compassion for those whom God has afflicted with that which He has enabled them to transcend. God—be He exalted—then said, *They do not beg of men with importunity* [2:273]. Their tongues are ever silent, not petitioning the One Who Possesses all, because of their contentment (*riḍā*) [19/b] with the state they are in and their repose in Him. How could they then petition someone who possesses nothing? That [state] is due to their knowledge that *faqr* is one of God's secrets, which He only entrusts to the trustworthy among his servants, those who hide their *faqr* and intimately repose in it. They do not arrogantly divulge it to people. For the [true] *faqīr* only makes his *faqr* known to the One Who has the ability to make him independent [of others] and bring him by the

path of *faqr* to his goal. Thus, one who makes his *faqr* known to people and assails them with it has indeed left the ranks of the *fuqarāʾ* and entered the ranks of the destitute.

4 Humility in the *faqīr* is that he perceives the excellence (*faḍl*) of those around him while witnessing his own flawed nature. This is because he is certain of his own deficiencies whereas the faults of others are but supposition. Therefore anyone who is satisfied with the state of his ego-self after gaining knowledge of it is [in fact] only displaying his own ignorance. [This is because] a person will act arrogantly only to the degree of their satisfaction with their ego-self, for when a person is satisfied with his state, he esteems it highly; and anyone who highly esteems [even] a fraction of his states, God belittles and brings low therein. One of the signs of someone who markets his *faqr* is that he seeks recognition and stature through it. While the signs of one who has realized true *faqr* is that he seeks to be anonymous, to be among people, outwardly as one of them and also that he seeks an increase in that [relationship] which is between him and his Lord, through his requisite conduct (*ādāb*) in *faqr*. He is outwardly like one of the generality, inwardly like one of the favored saints.

5 Praiseworthy *faqr* consists of emptying the innermost recesses of the soul (*sirr*) of the world (*al-kawn*) and all that is in it, while being ever in a state of utter need for God, both outwardly and inwardly. Blameworthy *faqr* consists of forsaking the world and turning away from it [20/a] while attacking those who are of the world and regarding his fellow man with scorn; and this derives from highly esteeming one's own state. Indeed, one who highly esteems even a fraction of his states will be deprived of their blessing and will be brought to disastrous ostentation. A *faqīr* is one who adorns his *faqr* with his [unassuming] ego-self (*nafs*), not one who adorns his ego-self with his *faqr*. The world in its totality is two things: seeking recognition and love of rank (*riyāsa*). One who loves these has seized the world, imagining he has renounced it. Worldly people seek to attain these two stations (recognition and rank) by expending their possessions. But *fuqarāʾ* who seek these qualities have surpassed the worldly in worldliness. The worldly are better off than such *fuqarāʾ*, for while the worldly seek rank and recognition through conventional means (*asbāb*), the *fuqarāʾ* seek them by means of religion (*dīn*).

6 One attains to the reality of *faqr* only after he enters therein by its principles (*waja*) and resides therein by its requisite conduct. The principle of entering

it is to let go of all attachments from one's innermost soul while putting into practice formal religious knowledge outwardly (*fī ẓāhir*).[5] The requisite conduct necessary for residing [in contrast to merely entering] therein are tranquillity (*sakīna*), sobriety (*wiqār*), humility, selfless generosity (*īthār*), relinquishment of the ego-self's pleasures, abandonment of natural inclinations, belittlement of the self while honoring others, putting into practice proper inner attitudes (*akhlāq*), detachment from sustenance (*arfāq*),[6] and trust in the One Who Suffices (*al-Kāfī*); which in fact is sincere reliance on the guarantee of the One Who Suffices.

7 *Faqr* consists of emptying [oneself] of all natural tendencies [20/b] (*akhlāq al-ṭabi'īya*) and abandoning all base actions, speech and states, the basest of these being pride. The Prophet said, "The man who flaunts his indigence is cursed."[7] A slave would only take pride in his states if he took pleasure in them or deemed them sweet, and such a state is considered abject. Similarly I heard through Abū 'Umar ibn Maṭar that Abū 'Uthmān al-Ḥīrī[8] said, "Everything that pleases the ego-self, be it obedience or disobedience, is passion (*shahwa*)."[9]

8 The dignity of the *fuqarā'* is in humility and abasement, just as the arrogance of the wealthy is in the display of severity and haughtiness. A *faqīr* arrogant in his *faqr* is lower [in status] than the wealthy person who is proud of his wealth. I heard Abū Zayd Muḥammad ibn Aḥmad *al-faqīr* [...][10] say that Ibrāhīm ibn Shaybān[11] said:

> God bestows no greater honor upon any of His servants than the honour of showing him the abject nature of his ego-self (*nafs*), and God abases no servant with a greater abasement than when He veils him from the abject nature of his ego-self.

It is certain that the arrogance of a *faqīr* is born of his forsaking ascetic discipline while still a novice and of his failing to be initiated into the Path by the Masters of the Path, thus his ego-self (*nafs*) dominates him and does not submit to guidance. If he were to impose ascetic discipline upon it and hold it in disdain, it would not make a show of arrogance. I heard 'Abdallāh ibn Muḥammad al-Rāzī say that Muḥammad ibn al-Faḍl[12] said, "The foundation upon which *faqr* is based is renunciation of [both] the world and the ego-self, while holding them both in disdain."

9 A *faqīr* has truly realized the station of *faqr* when he comes to recognize his inadequacies in fulfilling the obligations of [the path of] *faqr* and his inability to practice its tenets and until he sees the wealthy more worthy [of praise] than himself. Indeed the best of people are those who see the best in others. I heard through my grandfather [Ibn Nujayd]—may God bless him—that Abū 'Abdallāh al-Sajazī[13] said, "You have merit as long as you do not see your merit. If you see your merit, you have no merit." A *faqīr* does not become aware of his inadequacies regarding the true obligations of *faqr* until he reflects upon the venerable forefathers (*salaf*) [22/b] from among the Companions. God—be He exalted—spoke in His book of their *faqr* saying: *For the poor immigrants (al-muhājirīn) who have been driven out from their homes and their belongings, who seek bounty from God and help His messenger.... They are the righteous* [59:8]. *And also: For the indigent, who are totally occupied in the way of God* [2:273]. And let him ask himself whether any one [of the Companions] grew arrogant in that state, or haughtily raised his head, or whether God's praise of their traits increased them in anything but humility (*khuḍū'*) and submission (*istikāna*). They are the first who tread the path of *faqr*, those who have realized it, and its exemplars. No one of them ever flaunted his *faqr*, nor acted arrogantly [on account of it]. Consequently one whose state is less than theirs—and it would be impossible for anyone to reach the state they realized, as is testified to by the true word of God—[14] and behaves with arrogance and pretension, is nothing but one with whom Satan has toyed, who has acquiesced to the lower nature (*ṭab'*) and the follies of the ego-self.

10 A *faqīr* has truly reached the state of *faqr* when he has been cleansed of all excessiveness (*taklīf*)[15] and adheres to that which knowledge dictates for him at each moment. I heard through 'Abdallāh ibn 'Alī that Muḥammad ibn Qāshbūn heard Ibrāhīm al-Qaṣṣār[16] say, "For thirty years I have not placed a patch (*khirqa*) upon a patch,[17] nor have I asked [anything] of anyone, [but] neither have I opposed [any offer of assistance]."[18] Concerning the requisite conduct necessitated by *faqr*, I heard 'Abdallāh ibn Muḥammad al-Rāzī say that Abū 'Alī al-Jūzjānī[19] said:

> The fruits of lofty states are among the consequences of embracing *faqr*, which itself is the quest for knowledge of the imperfections of ego-self and the right remedies for their maladies, vigilant observance of the heart, and intuitions (*mawārid*)[20] which descend upon it. Blessed is the one who has the good fortune to accept the true

intuitions (*mawārid*). Cursed [23/a] is the one who discerns not between them, finding delight in each incoming thought, and deluded by each token of grace (*karāma*) until he forgets the awareness of gratitude (*minna*), becomes proud and overbearing, and assails his own kind. Of such [deluded souls] God—be He exalted—has said: *Satan has gained mastery over them, and has caused them to forget the remembrance of God* [58:19].

11 To the degree that a *faqīr* retains any self-interest in his ego-self, or is dependent upon a conventional means of livelihood, or entertains expectations of anyone, he is devoid of the requisite conduct of *faqr*. Similarly I have it ʿAbdallāh ibn Muḥammad al-Dimashqī say that he heard Ibrāhīm ibn al-Mawlid[21] say:

> I asked Abū ʿAbdallāh ibn al-Jalāʾ,[22] "When is the *faqīr* worthy of the name *faqīr*?" Whereupon he answered, "When there is naught of *faqr* left to him." So I said to him, "O my master, how can that be?" To which he answered, "When it is *his*, it is not his, and when it is not *his*, it is his."

12 The *faqīr* is one who holds steadfastly to the requisite conduct of *faqr* and does not avail himself of dispensations therein by [employing] terms invented by those ignorant of its true demeanor or its spiritual realities. Yielding to such dispensations only debases the *faqīr* from the spiritual degree of *faqr,* it brings him back to dependence upon habit (*ʿāda*) and instinct.[23] I heard in Merv, through Muḥammad ibn ʿAbd al-ʿAzīz al-Marwazī that Abū Bakr al-Wāsiṭī[24] said:

> They call offensive comportment *sincerity* (*ikhlās*), the greed of their ego-selves *expansion* (*iminbiṣāṭ*) and their base ambitions *sweetness* (*ḥalāwa*). They are thus blind to the Path, treading only on its narrow defiles. Neither life nor [useful] discourse springs from what their assertions (*shawāhidhim*).[25] If they speak, it is in anger; if they preach it is with pride.[26]

I found in my father's handwriting—may God bless him—that he heard Abū al-ʿAbbās al-Dīnawrī[27] say:

> With names they have invented they have pulled down the corner stones of Sufism and *faqr* destroying both of these paths. They call greed *increase* (*ziyāda*), offensive conduct *sincerity* and deviation from the truth *ecstatic utterance* (*shaṭḥ*). [They call] taking pleasure in blameworthy things *natural inclination* (*ṭabī'a*), the pursuit of passions *a trial from God* (*ibtilā'*) and turning back to the world *arrival* (*wuṣūl*). [They call] baseness of character *fervor* (*ṣawla*), avarice *steadfastness* (*jallāda*), begging *striving* (*'amal*), and bawdy language [a means of following] the *path of blame* (*malāma*). This was not the path of the folk (*al-qawm*)![28]

13 Vanity and pride arise from a lack of knowledge of the ego-self. People who know who they are, from whence they came, and what is demanded of them in each [21/a] moment and state, and people who know how incapable they are of fulfilling what is demanded of them are free of pride. I heard Abū Bakr al-Rāzī[29] say, "Vanity prohibits one from knowing the true merit of the ego-self."[30] Abū 'Uthmān al-Ḥīrī said, "When a *faqīr* shows arrogance, he has divulged his own base state; for he has donned the raiment of humility and lowliness, and anyone who is arrogant in such raiment becomes a demon."

14 When the *faqīr* arises in the morning, he must see his need of God and of other creatures (*khalq*), while not imagining himself to be in a position wherein anyone has need of him.[31] For if he does not manifest dependence in his totality, both inwardly and outwardly, his station of *faqr* would be unsound. Whereupon [a state of] freedom from conventional needs may envelope him; when— through his Lord— he becomes independent of all created beings. It is then that he enters the ranks of the contented (*rāḍīn*), at which time his perception of creatures and his preoccupation with them falls away. Or as Abū 'Abdallāh ibn al-Jalā' said:

> When a servant has realized the state of true *faqr*, he dons the raiment of contentment, and in so doing increases his compassion for others, such that he conceals their faults, prays for them, and shows them mercy.

This is one of the stations of the sincere *fuqarā'*. Therefore if you see the *faqīr* looking with disdain—because of his *faqr*—on one of the wealthy or someone of worldly rank, he has demonstrated how important the world and its contents are to his heart. He believes that by abandoning the world he has attained a [worthy] degree, station, or rank.

The Truly Sincere *Faqīr*

15 The *faqīr* who is truly sincere in his *faqr* prefers the honor of others to his [own] honor, [21/b] and his [own] abasement to the abasement of others. I heard from Muḥammad ibn ʿAbdallāh al-Rāzī that al-Ḥusayn ibn ʿAlī al-Qirmīsīnī said:

> ʿĀṣim al-Balkhī sent a [gift] to Ḥātim al-Aṣamm[32] (d. 230/851), who accepted it. When he was asked why he had accepted it, he replied, "In accepting it I found my abasement and his honor; while in refusing it, his abasement and my honor. I preferred his honor to mine and my abasement to his."

When the *faqīr* boasts of his *faqr* and is arrogant on account of it, he falls from the rank of *faqr*; since he desires recognition and praise while manifesting contempt for other people on account of his [pride in his] *faqr*. That [feeling of pride] is the price [for which he has sold] his *faqr*. Were he sincere, he would hide his *faqr* so that no one would be aware of it. A certain *faqīr* visited a master who asked him, "What are you?" Whereupon he answered, "I am a *faqīr*." He said, "You have lied. *Faqr* is God's secret, He entrusts it only to those who do not reveal it."

16 When a servant attains true sincerity in any of his states, his state is raised aloft and his regard falls not upon it, nor does he rely upon it, because that which is accepted is elevated [and hidden from general view].[33] I heard this from my grandfather Ismāʿīl ibn Nujayd—may God bless him—who heard from ʿAbdallāh ibn Muḥammad ibn Muslim al-Isfarāʾinī[34] that Abū Saʿīd al-Miṣrī heard ʿAlī ibn al-Ḥusayn—may God be pleased with him—say, "Every one of your actions that connects with your perception, that is proof that it has not been accepted [by God], for accepted actions are upraised and unseen by you. That which has been detached from your perception, [22/a] that is proof of its acceptance."

17 The basest of the *fuqarāʾ* is one who has neither realized the station of *faqr*, nor learned the conduct required therein, and yet he acts haughtily and makes pretentious claims about his *faqr*. I heard Muḥammad ibn Aḥmad

al-Farrā'[35] say that Abū Bakr al-Shāshī al-Ḥakīm[36] said, "The sign of hypocrisy is that the ego-self (*nafs*) is sinful and the heart has turned away [from God], while entertaining pretensions of spirituality." One is not a *faqīr* [23/b] if he cannot find contentment—in the beginning [of his path]—with the constraints of a profession, then after that [he is not a *faqīr* if he is not content with] the abasement of begging and standing in the face of refusal without antipathy. I heard through 'Abdallāh ibn Muḥammad al-Mu'allim that 'Abdallāh ibn Munāzil[37] said, "There is no excellence in one who has not tasted the abasement of earning a livelihood, begging, and the humility of rejection."

18 It is obligatory for the *faqīr* that his *faqr* be [based] upon knowledge. If his *faqr* is based upon knowledge, he will attain repose therein and experience a minimum of distress. He will also be granted contentment with the adversities that he encounters, and [in addition will be endowed with] humility of ego-self, and a minimum of pretension regarding his *faqr*. That is why when a certain *shaykh* was asked for counsel he replied:

> I advise you to seek the company of a *faqīr* [who has] knowledge of the requisite conduct of *faqr*, who teaches right conduct through his own excellence of character (*akhlāq*), who gives good counsel through [the example of] his dealings with others, who advises you with sympathetic speech, and who blames not the negligent, nor resents anyone who disagrees with him.

19 The [true] *faqīr* is one who humbles himself in such a manner that no one could compare to him in his humility. Abū Ja'far Muḥammad ibn Aḥmad ibn Sa'īd al-Rāzī informed me that al-'Abbās ibn Ḥamza said that he heard Aḥmad ibn Abū al-Ḥawārī say that he heard Abū Bakr al-Rāzī say that Abū Sulayman al-Dārānī[38] said, "I have not been satisfied with myself for even the blink of an eye. Were all the people of the earth to come together to humble me as I have humbled myself, they would not be able to."

20 Among the signs of a true *faqīr* is that he is humbled after [knowing] honor, is hidden after [knowing] prominence, is rejected after [knowing] approval, and forsaken after being shown compassion. This is because of the exaltedness of the demands of *faqr*, for it deprives him (*yufqiduhu*) in every state of what it has demanded of him.[39] I heard [24/a] Abū al-Qāsim Ja'far ibn Aḥmad al-Rāzī[40] say:

> The first blessing of entering *faqr* and Sufism is humility and the abandonment of arrogance, delight with *faqr*, service to one's companions while recognizing their virtues, and beneficence towards others whether they are believers or unbelievers, as long as one does not violate the law (*sharī'a*) nor commit any reprehensible action (*makrūḥ*).

Baseness on the part of a *faqīr* occurs when his *faqr* induces [in him] pride and arrogance. I heard from Shaykh Abū al-Walīd al-Faqīh, may God bless him, that Muḥammad ibn al-Mundhir al-Harawī reported that 'Uthmān ibn Kharazzad said that he heard from 'Abd al-Raḥmān ibn 'Abd al-A'lā that al-Aṣmā'ī said, "When the noble man becomes devout he acts with humility, while the ignoble man, when he becomes devout, grows haughty."

The Obligations and Comportment Expected of a *Faqīr*

21 As for the requirements of *faqr* and its conduct, I heard Manṣūr ibn 'Abdallāh say that al-Ḥasan ibn 'Allawayah heard Yaḥya ibn Mu'ādh,[41] when asked at what point a *faqīr* may [truly] claim [to be upon the path of] Sufism, say:

> Not until he has prevailed over his ego-self in the following traits. He totally abandons the world even while holding those who seek it in respect. At all times he is occupied with mandatory acts of devotion (*farḍ*), *sunna* or supererogatory acts (*nāfila*). He is too occupied with his devotions (*awrād*) to be concerned with [his] acceptance or rejection by others and he accumulates nothing. He stores away nothing (*iddakhar*), there is neither deceit in his heart nor malice towards anyone, [the sincerity] of his actions is not sullied [24/b] by people's awareness of him, self-pride does not arise in him when praised, nor does he slacken [in his devotions] when they turn from him.

22 After this you should know that anyone who claims to be a *faqīr*, who has mastered a trade and then forsakes his trade is acting with importunity (*ilḥāf*). He is not to be confused with one who has withdrawn [from the world] and lives on alms (*'alā al-futūḥ*), but experiences no avidity, desire, or ambitions. Such a one, on the contrary, has withdrawn with God to

the degree of [his] satisfaction [with God]. Neither is he disturbed by the absence [of things], nor does he repose when they are present. For him, the two states are one. [In this regard] I heard ʿAbdallāh ibn Muḥammad [ibn Faḍlawayya al-Muʿallim] say that ʿAbdallāh ibn Munāzil heard Ḥamdūn al-Qaṣṣār[42] say, "To give up one's work [for spiritual reasons] is importunity in begging alms." Then, after [realizing] this [state of satisfaction with God's decrees], he looks upon what is given him without asking, and with neither avidity nor desire, as a trial and tribulation, except in a time of dire necessity. I also heard from Muḥammad ibn ʿAbdallāh al-Ṭabarī that Khayr al-Nassāj[43] said:

> I entered a certain mosque wherein there was a *faqīr* that I had known. As soon as he saw me he took hold of me and said, "O master have pity on me for my tribulation is great!" I said to him, "What is your tribulation?" He said, "I have ceased to be afflicted and have been fortified with health. And you know that this is a terrible affliction." Then I looked into his affair and found that he had come into some worldly goods.

23 The wise must surely know that whoever mentions the failings (*ʿuyūb*) of his brethren God will make his failings apparent. To that effect I heard from Muḥammad ibn ʿAbd al-ʿAzīz that ibn Yazdān al-Madāʾinī said:

> In times past I frequented people and I saw among them those who had no failings, [25/a] but they then criticized others and ended up acquiring faults [themselves]. And I saw people who had failings but kept quiet about the failings of other people. Then God concealed their failings and rid them of those failings.

24 The *faqīr*, when he truly realizes *faqr*, is too taken up by the delight at finding the sustenance of *faqr* to be concerned about others' approval or rejection of him, let alone their praise or blame. In this regard I heard Ibrāhīm al-Naṣrābādhī say that Abū ʿAlī al-Rūdhbārī[44] said:

> Abū Bakr al-Zaqqāq asked me, "Why is it that the *fuqarāʾ* do not take [from the alms given to the poor] in order to meet their needs?" I replied, "As I see it, they favor the Giver over the given." He said, "No, rather they are a people who are not harmed by want since

> God is their sustenance; they do not strive to acquire [possessions], since they have found God.[45]

So the joy of their gain and the grief at their need [God's presence] preoccupies them, distracting them from secondary causes deriving from other than God.

25 It is obligatory for a sincere *faqīr* to use the outer dimension of each of his moments to assist others while not seeking assistance from them; for every action performed for others is excusable. I heard from Abū Bakr Muḥammad ibn 'Abdallāh that Abū al-'Abbās ibn 'Aṭā'[46] said:

> It is more beneficial towards a person's attaining redemption to act hypocritically for twenty years towards gaining a position of rank so that one of his brothers might live a single day [because of his rank], than to practice sincere devotion for twenty years, desiring therein one's own redemption.

He [Abū Bakr Muḥammad ibn 'Abdallāh] also said, "I heard Abū al-'Abbās ibn 'Aṭā' say, 'Place [25/b] your every moment at the disposal of whomever you may of God's creatures, other than placing them at the disposition of your ego-self (*nafs*).'" He [Abū Bakr Muḥammad ibn 'Abdallāh] also said that Abū al-'Abbās ibn 'Aṭā' said:

> The origin of every temptation (*fitna*) is in forgetting God (*al-Ḥaqq*); for one who forgets Him, He causes to forget his own ego-self. As God—be He exalted—has said: *Be not as those who have forgotten God, and whom He therefore causes to forget themselves.* [59:19].

26 If God has afflicted one with forgetfulness [of the true nature of] his ego-self, of witnessing its baseness and insignificance; it is evidence of the beginning of God's chastising him for having turned away from Him. Then, on account of his deficient perception of his own frailty and forgetfulness of God's omnipotence, he becomes ever more insolent. For such a one there is no hope of well being, for there is no sign [in him] of well being and support. The signs of support are those that God—be He exalted—has taught us in His book, in his words dealing with the traits of those who have gained His pleasure saying: *Surely God gave you support and aid at Badr and you were [among the] lowly* [3:123]. Here God clearly made apparent the

signs of His support (*nuṣra*) and turn of good fortune (*dawla*). Therefore one who does not seek wellbeing and support through lowliness and utter need will never attain them. To pursue God's favor through [attaining] power is to contend with God's Lordship; and anyone who contends with the Lord is brought low. Abū Yazīd al-Bisṭāmī—foremost of the gnostics of his time, of exalted station and lofty rank, well known for his ascetic practices, detachment, and journeys—relating of himself, as I heard 'Alī ibn Aḥmad ibn Ja'far say that al-Ḥasan ibn 'Allawayah said, "When Abū Yazīd was asked what he most desired from the world, he replied, "That I might see [26/a] myself through the eye by which people see me."

27 It is obligatory for a *faqīr* to seek betterment of his ego-self, betterment of his comportment, station, or state and that he never be satisfied with his ego-self and that which it encompasses. For if one is not seeking to better his state, his state is in decline. But as for one who is aware of his short-comings and seeks betterment at all times, that [awareness] will preoccupy him [freeing him] from concern with anything else. Anyone who exalts his ego-self and acts arrogantly is satisfied with it. Yet anyone who witnesses the ego-self as it is [i.e. its true nature] banishes pride from his self. I heard Manṣūr ibn 'Abdallāh al-Harawī say that al-Nahrajūrī[47] said:

> Among the signs of one whose states God has taken in hand is that he attests to the inadequacy of his sincerity, the heedlessness of his invocation, the imperfection of his truthfulness, the laxness of his striving, and his lack of observance of what is required in *faqr*. Thus all of his states are unsatisfactory to him. In both his aspiration and his journeying, he feels evermore his need of God until he passes away from all else but He. For such a one, the mundane portions that people seek, praise and blame have fallen away.

28 It is also obligatory for a *faqīr* to know the precepts of his sustenance, so that he takes sustenance only from where he knows he is not using his religion as a means of earning his daily bread. I heard from 'Abd al-Wāḥid ibn Bakr that Aḥmad ibn 'Aṭā' reported hearing from Muḥammad ibn al-Zabarqān that Abū Yazīd, when asked how many ways of gaining sustenance were blameless and whether attaining one's daily-bread by means of religion was justifiable, replied:

> Sustenance is blameless from only three sources; from [26/b] [the fruits of] a lawful profession, from what is provided by a brother in God who is firm in his religion, or from that which is permitted according to knowledge [of the Law]. All else is attaining one's daily bread by means of religion [and that is not permitted for a *faqīr*].

29 Among the traits of a true *faqīr* is that which I heard [Abū] Naṣr ibn Muḥammad al-Ṭūsī [al-Sarrāj] report from 'Umar ibn Muḥammad al-Baghdādī, who said that he heard Manṣūr al-Ḥīrī say that Bishr al-Ḥārith[48] said, "True *faqr* is holding fast to privation (*qilla*), seeking affinity with abasement, and habitual solitude." One who seeks prominence through *faqr* shows, thereby, that his striving is out of need (*faqr*), not out of a sense of obligation to [the path of] *faqr* or love for it. That is because he [whose striving is out of obligation] will find in *faqr* that which he will not find through wealth and worldly pursuits. The truly sincere *faqīr* is one that lives by *faqr* as an obligation not as a means [of worldly gain]. Thus, whoever inclines in his *faqr* towards a worldly motive abides in his motive not with *faqr*.

30 Among the conduct required of a *faqīr* is the acceptance of abasement with neither complaint nor contention; for outward *faqr* is abasement before people, while its inner reality is abasement before God. I heard Aḥmad ibn 'Alī ibn Ja'far say that Fāris heard Yūsuf ibn al-Ḥusayn[49] say:

> I had a friend who died, and whom I later saw in a dream. I asked him what God had done with him and he replied "God—be He exalted— said, 'I have forgiven you on account of [the humiliation you experienced in] your going back and forth to those mundane ones for a loaf of bread, before they gave you one.'"

31 The poorest of the *fuqarā'* is one that has been veiled from regarding his own deeds and character. For one who truly knows the true nature of his ego-self disdains [27/a] in taking pride in it or in any of its states. He will be preoccupied with the [constant] rectification of each of his moments. I heard Muḥammad ibn al-Ḥasan al-Baghdādī say that Abū 'Amr al-Ṣammāk heard al-Ḥasan ibn 'Umar al-Sabī'ī quote Bishr al-Ḥārith as having said:

> I suffer from a disease, and as long as I have not treated myself I am not free to treat another; when I have treated myself, I will be free to treat others. Even were assistance to reach me, I could not

> discern the affliction from the cure. Then he [Bishr] said, "You are the affliction! I see the faces of a people who fear not, those who take lightly the affairs of the afterlife."

32 [Also] among the conduct required of a *faqīr* is that he begins by disciplining himself. Only then, when he has completed this task, might he concern himself with the disciplining of others. And how can the servant [of God] complete the task of disciplining himself, since his ego-self is the locus (*maḥal*) of calamity and affliction, and it is that which incites one to do evil (*al-amāra bi-al-sū'*). Aḥmad ibn 'Abdallāh ibn Yūsuf al-Qirmīsīnī informed me in writing by his authorization (*munāwalatan*)[50] that his father reported from 'Alī ibn 'Abd al-Ḥamīd al-Ghaḍāyarī that al-Sarī [al-Saqaṭī][51] said, "Anyone not capable of disciplining his own ego-self is still less capable of disciplining others."

33 The true *faqīr* is one who feels compassion towards the wealthy because he is aware [of the burden] of their preoccupation with worldly affairs and the account they face in the Hereafter. He thus prays for them and does not scorn them. When Shaqīq al-Balkhī[52] was asked how a person could recognize a true *faqīr* he responded:

> By his steadfastness in *faqr*, his compassion, sympathy, and supplication for the worldly, his recognition of God's grace upon himself for not [27/b] afflicting him with what He has afflicted them, and his [constant] thanks for that grace.

The best [comportment] of a *faqīr* is [his] practicing noble character in his relationships with others, following the example of the Messenger of God—may God's peace and blessings be upon him—in the Divine Law (*al-sharī'a*), and actualizing the intimate knowledge of God with regard to the Absolute Truth (*ḥaqīqah*).

34 The required conduct of *faqr* includes what was narrated from Abū Ḥafṣ[53] when he was asked about the precepts and requisite conduct of *faqr*:

> Upholding the veneration of the masters [of the path], interacting nobly with one's brethren, counseling the young, accepting counsel from elders, abandoning contention over sustenance, being constant in giving precedence [to others], avoiding accruing [worldly goods]

> and associating with those not in one's [social or spiritual] rank, and assisting others in both religious and worldly affairs.

The contention [that occurs] between *fuqarā'* and the wealthy is due to the importance the world holds in their eyes. For this reason Ḥamdūn al-Qaṣṣār said, "Attach little importance to the world, until neither its inhabitants nor those who possess it have any importance in your eyes."

35 A *faqīr* will have never totally complied with the obligations of *faqr* until he has renounced what is due him.[54] I heard Abū Naṣr [al-Sarrāj] al-Ṭūsī say that he heard Aḥmad ibn 'Aṭā' relate from his uncle that al-Junayd said, "You will never achieve what is required of you until you have renounced that which is due you. No one is capable of that but a Prophet or one of the *utterly sincere* (*ṣiddīq*)." The source of contention between the *fuqarā'* and the wealthy is covetousness [on the part of the *fuqarā'*] and the fact that the wealthy prevent them from attaining what they are seeking [of wealth and worldly rank]. I saw in the book of Abū Ja'far ibn Ḥamdān that he heard Abū 'Uthmān say, "The root of enmity lies in three things: coveting possessions, coveting deference, and desire [28/a] for the approval of others." He also said, "A man's faith does not attain perfection until four things are equal in his heart; withholding and giving, honor and abasement." He also said, "Probity of heart is attained through four qualities; humility towards God, utter need (*faqr*) of God, fear of God, and hope in God." There is nothing more disruptive to the conduct of the *fuqarā'* than self-satisfaction, pride and scorn for others. I saw in the book of Abū Ja'far ibn Ḥamdān that he heard Abū 'Uthmān say, "Fear of God will bring you to God, pride and self-satisfaction will sever you from God, and disdain for people will afflict you with a disease for which there is no cure."

36 Right conduct is the adornment of the *fuqarā'*. Abū 'Uthmān [al-Ḥīrī] said, "Right conduct is the mainstay (*sanad*) of the *fuqarā'* and the ornament of the wealthy." Among the incumbent comportment of the *faqīr* is chivalrous conduct (*futūwah*). In this regard, when asked about the noble character of the *fuqarā'*, Ruwaym[55] said, "It is that you find excuses for your brothers' mistakes, while behaving with them in a manner that requires no excuses [from them]." And Ruwaym also said:

> One of the precepts of *faqr* is allowing a broad interpretation of the rules where one's brethren are concerned, while enjoining strict-

> ness upon oneself. This is because granting latitude to them is in accordance with religious teachings (*'ilm*), while being demanding of oneself is among the precepts of moral responsibility (*wara'*).

Ruwaym said as well:

> Associating with any people is preferable for you than associating with the Sufis. For while everyone else associates [with others] according to outward forms, the Sufis relate to one another according to absolute truths; and while everyone else seeks to put themselves in conformity with the outward aspects of the Law, they [the Sufis] seek to realize within themselves true moral comportment [28/b] and constant sincerity. Therefore, one who associates with them and then does not conform to them in that which they have realized, God takes the light of faith from his heart.

37 [Also] among the necessary conduct of both the wealthy and the indigent is [this saying of] Muḥammad ibn al-Faḍl al-Samarqandī:[56]

> The basest of the *fuqarā'* is a *faqīr* who flatters a wealthy man and humbles himself before him, while the noblest of the wealthy is a wealthy person who humbles himself before a *faqīr,* who [in return] humbles himself before him.

And Muḥammad ibn Abī al-Ward[57] said:

> Part of the requisite conduct of a *faqīr* is abstaining from blaming and condemning those who are afflicted by seeking [gain in] the world, having compassion and sympathy for them, as well as praying that God give them repose from their fatigue. [...[58]]

A true servant of God is not afflicted by people's evil deeds unless he begins to regard his own actions as commendable, wherein will be his destruction. Maḥfūẓ ibn Maḥmūd[59] said:

> Whoever gives regard to the virtues of his own ego-self will be afflicted by the vices of people, but whoever looks to his own faults will be free of mentioning the vices of people.

Muḥammad ibn Ḥāmid[60] said, "I have never belittled anyone without finding a deficiency in my own faith and my knowledge of God." I heard Abū al-Qāṣim al-Dimashqī say that he heard Abū 'Alī al-Rūdbārī say:

> Assailing one who is below you [in station] is weakness, while assailing one who is above you is arrogance. No one is raised [in station] except through humility; while no one is brought low except through pride.

Abū al-Ḥasan al-Būshanjī[61] said, "One who humbles himself, God raises in stature, but one who exalts himself God humbles in the eyes of men." The [true] *faqīr* is the one who has neither deed that pleases him, nor any state in which he finds repose, nor any moment (*waqt*) to which he returns. His innermost soul is a witness to the Truth (*al-Ḥaqq*). He lacks the means to go backward or forward. [The circumstances of each of] his moments (*waqt*) render him incapable of describing his state or his station; he neither takes shelter in anything known [to him] nor does he find rest in any beloved thing. *Faqr* is true servanthood; its sign [30/b] is constant awareness of one's inadequacy and inability to reach the goal [by one's own effort]. Such is the truth of *faqr*.

Among the forms of chivalrous conduct (*futūwah*) of the wealthy is that they serve the *fuqarā'* [and provide for them] while being aware that [the *fuqarā'*] are superior to them and that they [themselves] cannot reach their degrees [of piety]. Whereas the *futūwah* of the *fuqarā'* is that they realize their own incapacity to fulfil the obligations of *faqr,* that they recognize the virtues of the wealthy, have compassion for them, and pray that God may alleviate them of the tribulations of wealth.

38 Among the traits of the true *faqīr* is that he only harbors enmity towards another for the sake of the religion and that he envies no Muslim; for such envy is the behavior of someone seeking the world. So when love of the world falls away from one's heart, it becomes free of worldly enmities, rivalry with worldly people, and the mention of their vices. Among the traits of the *faqīr* is that his garment is contentment (*riḍā*), his nourishment is righteousness (*taqwā*), his conduct selfless regard for others (*īthār*) and generosity. He is an example of submission (*khushū'*), humility (*khuḍū'*) and a humble manner. His [chief] attribute and disposition is his acceptance of all that befalls him with a smiling face and an open welcoming heart. It has reached me that when Abū Ḥafṣ asked a new arrival who he was, the man answered, "I

am a *faqīr*." Abū Ḥafṣ responded, saying, "All people are *fuqarā'*, show me someone in the world that is independent of need (*ghanī*), that you should be praised for your *faqr*. Know well, that the people are all *fuqarā'* without pretensions and you are a *faqīr* with pretensions." Another of them said, "When a servant has been true in his *faqr*, God bestows him with worthy attributes. Among them are satisfaction [with the basic necessities] (*qanā'a*), virtuous comportment, awareness of people's merits through his awareness of his own deficiencies, and respect for God's saints." [31/a]

39 When Abū 'Alī al-Juzjānī was asked about the distinguishing traits of the *fuqarā'* he said:

> Obedience to God is their sweetness; love of God is their companion; God is their need and He is their protector. God-wariness is their nature; with God is their commerce; upon Him they depend; with Him is their intimacy; and in Him is their confidence. Hunger is their sustenance, nakedness their dress, renunciation their gain, virtuous comportment their discerning trait, humility their disposition, and an open smiling face their adornment. Generosity is their profession, intimate fellowship their companionship, the intellect their leader, patience their driving force, and abstinence their provision. The Qur'ān is their speech, gratitude their ornament, the invocation of God their booty, contentment [with God] their repose, and sufficiency [with little] their possessions. Worship is their profession, Satan their enemy, the mundane world their refuse heap, modesty their garment, and fear their natural temperament. The night is their meditation, the day their admonition (*'ibra*), wisdom their sword, and The Truth their guardian. Life is their place of alighting [on their journey], death is their way station; the grave is their citadel; and the Day of Judgment their feast day. [To stand] before God is their most ardent desire, in the shade of The Throne is their gathering place, in [the paradise of] Firdaws is their dwelling and the vision of God the object of their destiny.

When a *faqīr* holds steadfast to these norms of conduct and imposes these character traits upon his ego-self, he is among the sincere *fuqarā'* whom God has raised to such lofty stations. His companionship with people is founded upon mutual well being; people are safe from him, [...][62] while he [too] is secure from the whisperings of his ego-self and its passionate nature.

Abū 'Abdallāh ibn al-Jalā' said:

> Companionship with *faqr* is [attained] by practical experience, not by making claims to it. Therefore, whoever travels the path of aspiration through practical experience will acquire submission, humility, self-abasement, and compassion; but whoever travels it by empty claims will acquire pride and arrogance.

Abū Turāb al-Nakhshabī[63] said:

> God adorns the inhabitants of each time (*zamān*) with that which corresponds to them. There has been no time nobler than the epoch of Muḥammad—may the peace and blessings of God be upon him—nor has there been a people nobler than those who were his companions and who believed in him. God adorned them with *faqr* and their garment of *faqr* imparted to them humble comportment outwardly and contentment with divine decrees inwardly. They were the noblest of people and theirs was the noblest of character.

40 Know well, that God—be He exalted—attributed [29/a] to Himself [the attributes of] pride and might, saying: *He is the All-compelling (al-Jabbār) the Proud (al-Mutakkabir)* [59:23]. Those are among His praiseworthy attributes, for pride and might coincide with absolute self-sufficiency that can be overcome from no quarter and He alone is capable of rendering self-sufficient whomever He wishes among His servants. The Prophet—may the peace and blessings of God be upon him—related from his Lord, "Majesty is My upper garment and might My lower; anyone who would strip from Me either, I will destroy."[64] God imposed upon His servants the appellation of *faqr* saying: *You are the poor (al-fuqarā'), towards God.* [35:15]. Their *faqr* is an [absolute] indigence (*faqr*) that self-sufficiency can in no way impinge on. Pride and arrogance in indigence are blameworthy attributes, for the cloak of *faqr* requires abasement and anonymity. The attribute of true self-sufficiency negates pride and arrogance, therefore whoever manifests pride and arrogance in his *faqr* has repudiated the attributes of servanthood and *faqr*. A man once asked al-Junayd, "Who is the most excellent *faqīr*?" He responded, "He who gains sustenance by means which accord with correct conduct, not out of craving." Sahl ibn 'Abdallāh[65] said:

> God created people and decreed *faqr* for them and self-sufficiency for Himself; He made the garment of *faqr* submission and abasement and the garment of self-sufficiency magnificence and pride. Therefore whoever acts arrogantly in his *faqr* has indeed left the comportment of servanthood and entered into contention with lordship.

41 I have already mentioned in *The Wayfaring of the Gnostics (Sulūk al-'ārifīn)*[66] the requisite comportment of *faqr* and its obligations. [29/b] I thus felt obligated here to restate what I had written in order to better complete my objectives in the present work dealing with *faqr*.

42 Among its obligations and requisite comportment is that the *faqīr* fears [the loss] of his *faqr* more than a wealthy person fears [the loss] of his wealth. Thus he jealously safeguards it, not showing it [to anyone], and should something of it become evident, he strives to conceal it. He does not frequent *fuqarā'* in such a manner that his *faqr* becomes known, nor does his conduct diverge from that of the wealthy in such a manner that the signs of *faqr* are apparent. He associates with people, behaving with integrity, manifesting neither wealth nor poverty. He is among people as one of them, indiscernible from them except by the steadfast discipline of his journeying; he has states in which he withdraws [from people] enjoining upon himself sincerity in [those of his acts] which he reveals and makes known to other people. His ego-self dwells in a state of hardship [from his constant vigilance], while people are in repose from him. He discloses his outer manner to people, while he safeguards from them his inner state. He finds no repose in any familiar means [of comfort], nor does he grieve at the absence thereof. Should, through God's omnipotence (*al-qudrah*), sustenance (*rifq*) be provided him he accepts it knowing that God (*al-Ḥaqq*) has provided it for him, albeit in a manner free of all blame (*sabab munazzah*) and by means of which he does not transgress the boundaries of [religious] teachings (*sharṭ al-'ilm*).[67] He does not solicit that which is not present, nor does he pursue an aim out of self-interest. He does not seek excessively; nor does he frequent a particular place by which he may be known, nor does he wear garments that discern him from his own kind. Outwardly he follows a livelihood, while inwardly he trusts [in God alone]. If he speaks, it is within the bounds of knowledge, if he is silent it is with sobriety and forbearance; and if he partakes of nourishment, it is with deference for the other. If he speaks, it is with counsel; if he is quiet, it is in reflection; if he listens, it is with intense involvement (*wajd*). If he enjoins [30/a] [anything],

it will be the good (*ma'rūf*); if he forbids [anything], it will be evil (*munkar*). His preoccupation with the reality of each of his moments keeps him from paying attention to those of his brothers, and he sees other people's merits by being aware of his own short-comings. He acts with noble character towards strangers, to say nothing of how he acts with his brothers and companions.[68] He respects spiritual mentors (*mashā'ikh*), is generous to his companions, and compassionate towards aspirants (*murīd*). [31/b] He does not seek to fulfil his needs through relationships with any secondary causes [such as people or worldly interests] except in the instance of necessity, and then only from a place where his soul finds repose.[69] His friendship is for his fellow journeyers first and foremost. He bears vexation from his companions but vexes them not; he upholds their precepts, but does not judge them. Should the discourse be of teachings, he gives counsel [not didactic discourse], and when he speaks with them, it is with affection (*uns*). He seeks excuses for the unintentional errors of his companions. If an excuse presents itself, and his heart does not accept it, he knows that he is at fault, not them. He conceals their iniquities from them. In fact, he sees no iniquity in them unless they commit a breach in the Law or something that may lead to it. He frequents them out of his natural inclination, otherwise he knows he does not merit their companionship. He enjoins his ego-self to act in accord with the Law and requisite comportment. He does not neglect acts of supererogatory worship, nor does he take the *Sunna* lightly. He vigilantly observes his heart when he offers the canonical prayers; he does not see himself fit to demand anything of his Lord; among his needs are petitions for atonement, pardon, and forgiveness.

43 He shares of his sustenance at all times. He does not demean the *fuqarā'*. Neither does he treat lightly the wealthy, nor defer to them for reasons of sustenance. His conviction is that God alone is the One Who withholds and the One Who provides, his indigence is turned away from created beings (*al-akwān*); his sufficiency is the Creator. He is compassionate towards those tried with tribulation, while asking his Lord for forgiveness. He is jealous of no one and harbors no malice towards any Muslim. Neither does he envy his brothers, nor does he rejoice at their misfortunes. He does not break a promise nor does he violate any agreement. He relies on nothing, while everything relies [32/a] on him; he is familiar with no one, whereas everyone is familiar with him, he does not seek intimacy with anyone, whereas all seek intimacy with him. Outwardly he is an exemplar of the requisite comportment of those aspiring on the path, inwardly a mirror of the lights

of those who know God intimately (*'ārifīn*). None but his peers [on the path] know his *faqr* or his degree. He does not travel for his own purposes, instead [he travels] to perform the pilgrimage, to strive in sacred combat, to visit a *shaykh*, to discipline his ego-self, to keep a friend company, to seek learning, or to visit a brother. He learns what is indispensable to fulfilling the obligations of religion, maintains a study of the Qur'ān in private, and fills the greater part of his time with the invocation of God. Neither does he feign weakness in his *faqr* [to display it], nor does he complain—for the complaints of an aspirant on the path of *faqr* could be endless—but [rather] he keeps up his spiritual discipline (*mujāhadah*) both inwardly and outwardly.

44 His most precious possession is his present moment (*waqt*) [so] he uses it only for the most precious things: constant meditation (*murāqaba*), following the [divine] commands, and seeking his Lord's contentment. The moments in which he has the most hope [of acceptance by his Lord] are those in which he is serving his brethren. He prefers the welfare of his companions to his own in sustenance and he relieves them of hardship. He does not see himself as superior to anyone of the creation. He assiduously maintains himself in correct conduct so that others in his presence might learn it. He turns in repentance to his companions when they err, excuses them when they sin, picks them up when they stumble, and pardons them when they slip. He is arrogant with those who are arrogant to the *fuqarā'*, but is kind towards those who respect them or treat them with kindness. He is lenient in respect to the precepts [of *faqr*] when they apply to his brethren, [but] strict when they apply to himself. He abandons what does not concern him, occupies himself with [32/b] what does, learns right conduct from *mashā'ikh*, and imparts it to his companions. He does not associate with adolescents. He avoids the offerings (*arfāq*) from women and shuns intimately associating with or befriending them, or [even] talking to or about them, [for] he knows that they are lacking in both reason and religious practice, and he knows that the Prophet—may the peace and blessing of God be upon him—said, "Whenever a [single] man and woman are alone together, the Devil is the third."

45 His innermost soul (*sirr*) is at ease with the absence [of any familiar means of relief]. He does not rely on sufficiency when he has adequate provisions; he relies, rather, on the One Who Suffices (*al-Kāfī*). He embraces patient endurance (*ṣabr*), is an enemy to passion, stays apart from lusts, and dons the robe of contentment. His speech is counsel, his silence contemplation (*fikr*).

He frequents only his brethren and keeps company only with his peers. He frequents no one for the purpose of self-gratification, nor does he place himself at ease with worldly people so as to acquire their sustenance. He keeps his *faqr* free of any mingling or associating with them and does not incline toward the generality, seeking through his *faqr* to join their company. He learns right conduct from an *imām*, keeps the *Sunna*, and keeps company with those who follow it. He avoids innovation and those who practice it. He does not wear a patched robe except out of absolute necessity and does not marry except out of fear that he might violate the sacredness [of the Law]. He does not sit at the head of an assembly, nor does he address people [while in one]. He does not frequent assemblies where ecstatic poetry is chanted (*majlis al-samāʿ*).[70] He does not accumulate wealth nor return to familiar habits and customs; and he never uses his *faqr* as a means to gain recognition by the worldly.

46 And he knows, above all, that everything [we have mentioned] are but the outward forms of *faqr*, not its realization. Reaching the reality of *faqr* [33/a] is [exceedingly] difficult; because such was the state of the Prophet—may the peace and blessing of God be upon him, the elect among leaders [of this path] and the pious elders (*al-salaf al-Ṣāliḥīn*)—may God be pleased with them. And yet for anyone who conforms to the path of *faqr* and searches his ego-self for sincerity in the manner we have discussed, [his embrace of *faqr*] will bestow upon him the blessings of its realization. Indeed God—be He exalted—has said: *As for those who strive in Us, We surely guide them to Our Paths* [29:69], and the Prophet-may the peace and blessings of God be upon him—said, "He who acts upon what he knows, God will endow with what he did not know."

47 Thus, in these chapters, in a brief and summary manner, I have set forth whatever guidance an aspirant on the path of the folk might seek, and [I have elucidated as well] their conduct, their attributes, and character traits. We ask God that He not deprive us—in virtue of His generosity and vast mercy—of the blessings that we have aspired to in this work and that we have striven for. Verily, He is the One Who is Ever Near and He is the One Who Answers Prayers. All praise is God's alone, Lord of all the worlds. May God bless His Prophet, the best of His creation and his family in its entirety.

The Book on The Humble Submission of Those Aspiring (*Kitāb bayān tadhallul al-fuqarā'*) has been completed at the hand of the needy servant, full of hope for the benediction of his Lord, the Totally Independent (*al-Ghanī*), Awḥad ibn Maḥmūd ibn Abu Bakr al-Madanī, on the ninth of the revered month of Ramadan, 740 (March 9, 1340).

We praise Him and ask for blessings on the Prophet.[71]

Sufism is made up entirely of correct attitudes (*ādāb*); for each moment there is a correct attitude, for each spiritual station (*maqām*) there is a correct attitude. Whoever is steadfast in maintaining the correct attitude of each moment, will attain the degree of spiritual excellence, and whoever neglects correct attitudes, is far from that which he imagines near, and rejected from where he imagines he has found acceptance.

NOTES

INTRODUCTION

1. R.A. Nicholson, *Studies in Islamic Mysticism* (1921; reprint Cambridge: Cambridge University Press, 1967) 14.

2. Al-Sulamī, *Futuwah: Traité de Chevalerie Soufie,* ed. and trans. Faouzi Skali (Paris: Editions Albin Michel, 1989) 7.

3. Karamustafa, Ahmet, *Sufism: The Formative Period* (Edinburgh University Press, 2007) 63.

4. His full name was Muḥammad ibn al-Ḥusayn ibn Mūsā ibn Khālid ibn Sālim ibn Zāwīya ibn Sa'īd ibn Qabīsa ibn Sarrāq al-Azdī al-Sulamī al-Naysābūrī. He was of Arab origin and known by the name Abū 'Abd al-Raḥmān al-Sulamī. The appellation Sulamī was his mother's tribal affiliation to the al-Sulamīyīn, a well known tribe that has migrated to Nishapur at an early date.

5. In the present biographical survey I will only touch on the aspects of Sulamī's life that lend relevance to the texts under consideration. For a detailed accounts of Sulamī's life and works see, Böwering "The Qur'ān Commentary of Al-Sulamī", in W.B. Hallaq and D.P. Little (eds.), *Islamic Studies Presnted to Charles J. Adams* (Leiden 1991) 41-56; Sulamī *Ṭabaqāt aṣ-ṣūfīya*, ed. J. Pedersen (Leiden 1960); idem. ed. Nūr ad-Dīn Sharība (Cairo 1969); Cornell, Rkia, *Early Sufi Women* (Fons Vitae, 1999) 15-37.

6. For a profile of the intellectual and political life of Nishapur see Richard Bulliet, *The Patricians of Nishapur* (Cambridge, Mass.: Harvard University Press, 1979).

7. Of the four references to his father, Al-Ḥusayn ibn Muḥammad ibn Mūsā al-Azdī (d. 348/959), in Sulamī's *Ṭabaqāt al-ṣūfīya,* two are narrations of Ibn Munāzil, a disciple of Ḥamdūn al-Qaṣṣār *Shaykh al-Malāmatīya* (see *al-Risālat al-qushayrīya*, ed. Ma'rūf Zarīq and 'Alī 'Abd al-Ḥamīd Balṭajī (Beirut: Dār al-Khayr,1993) p.435, and one of Abū 'Alī al-Thaqafī, a disciple of both Ḥamdūn al-Qaṣṣār and Abū Ḥafṣ. Ibn al-Mulaqqin (d. 804/1401) cites Sulamī's father as being among those who frequented Ibn Munāzil and others, saying also that he encountered al-Shiblī. In this citation his father is said to have based his *sulūk* upon "correct comportment *(ḥusn al-khuluq)*, continual striving (*dawām ijtiḥād*), and discerning speech in the science of human relationships (*lisān al-ḥaqq fī 'ulūm al-mu'āmala*)," *Ṭabaqāt al-'awlīyā'*, Ibn Mulaqqin, ed. Nūr ad-Dīn Sharība (Cairo: Maktabat al-Khānjī, 1973) 189. All these are fundamental traits of the Malāmatīya.

8. Sulamī writes, "Abū 'Amr ibn Nujayd Ismā'īl ibn Nujayd ibn Aḥmad ibn Yūsuf ibn Sālīm ibn Khālid al-Sulamī was my grandfather on my mother's side-may God bless him. He associated with Abū 'Uthmān al-Ḥīrī. He was one of his most eminent companions and the last of the companions of Abū 'Uthmān to die. He met Junayd. He was among the most illustrious *mashā'ikh* (spiritual teachers) of his times. He was unique in his practice of the path, on account of his concealment of his interior state and the manner in which he guarded his intimate moments [with God]. He heard, narrated, and dictated *hadith.* He was a reliable narrator (*thiqqa*). He died in 360/971, al-Sulamī, *Ṭabaqāt al-sūfīya*, 454-457, all subsequent mention of *Ṭabaqāt al-sūfīya* will be to the edition of Nūr ad-Dīn Sharība (Cairo 1969).

9. Sulāmi narrates that Abū 'Uthmān al-Ḥīrī al-Naysābūrī (d. 298/910-11), was originally from al-Ray. He frequented in the beginning [of his path] Yaḥyā ibn Mu'ādh al-Rāzī and Shāh ibn Shujā' al-Kirmānī. He then came to Abū Ḥafṣ in Nayshāpur, remained with him, and took up his *malāmatīya* path In his time he was unique among the masters in his comportment, through him Sufism spread in Nishāpur. *Ṭabaqāt al-ṣūfīya*, 170.

10. *Ṭabaqāt al-sūfīya*, 115.

11. Tāj al-Dīn al-Subkī, *Ṭabaqāt al-shāfi'īya al-kubrā*, 6 vols. (Cairo, 1324/1906) 3:61. For a list of the scholars that Sulamī studied under see *Ṭabaqāt al-ṣūfīya,* 19-27.

12. Tāj al-Dīn al-Subkī, *Ṭabaqāt al-shāfi'īya al-kubrā*, 6 vols. (Cairo, 1324/1906) 3:61. For more biographical information on Abū Ṣahl al-Ṣu'lūkī see *al-Risālat al-qushayrīya* 65, 134, 251, 252, 283, 334, 342, and 370.

13. See *Ṭabaqāt al-sūfīya*, 361.

14. See *Ṭabaqāt al-sūfīya*, 123.

15. 'Abd al-Raḥmān al-Jāmī, *Nafaḥāt al-uns,* ed. M. Tawḥīdīpur (Tehran, 1337/1918-19) 311.

16. Sibṭ ibn al-Jawzī,, *Mir'āt al-zamān*, vol. 11, fol. 3, the events of 412 H. (quoted Sharība, intro. to *Ṭabaqāt al-sūfīya* 31).

17. Abū Nu'aym al-Iṣbahanī, *Ḥilyat al-awlīyā'* (Beirut: Dār al-Kutub, 1988) vol. 2, 25.

18. Al-Dhahabī, *Sayr a'lām al-nubalā',* ed. Shu'ayb al-Arna'ūt and Muḥammad Nu'aym al-'Irqasūsī (Beirut: Mu'assasat al-Risāla, 1994) vol. 17, 247.

19. *Abdāl* (pl. of *badal*), one of the highest ranks in the Islamic hierarchy of the saints. *Abdāl* are those figures whose role is to maintain equilibrium in the nature of affairs in this world, they represent on the human level, the hierarchy of divine manifestation. For an in-depth insight into the *abdāl* and the other members of the hierarchy of saints in Islamic traditional literature and particularly that of Ibn 'Arabī. Michel Chodkiewicz, *Seal of the Saints: Prophethood and Sainthood in the Doctrine of Ibn 'Arabī* (Cambridge: The Islamic Text Society, 1993) 91.

20. *Mir'āt al-Zamān*, vol. 11, fol. 3, events of 412 H. (quoted from Sharība, 46).

21. Ibn 'Abbād al-Runda, *Sharḥ kitāb al-ḥikam* (Cairo: Matba' Wādī al-Nīl al-Miṣrīya, 1277) 44.

22. For a detailed account of the fluctuations of the fortunes of Nishapur during this period see Richard Bulliet, *Islam The View from the Edge* (Columbia University Press, New York, 1994)129-144.

23. Danner, "The Early Development of Sufism," in *Islamic Spirituality: Foundations*, ed. Seyyed Hosein Nasr (New York: Crossroads, 1987) 250-256.

24. For more on the *madrasa* in early times see George Maksisi, *The Rise of the Colleges* (Edinburgh University Press, 1981) 9-32.

25. Ibid. 1-9.

26. On the ascetic and mystical currents existing in fourth/tenth century Nishapur see Sara Sviri, "Ḥākīm Tirmidhī and the Malāmatī Movement," *Classical Persian Sufism: from its Origins to Rumi*, ed. Leonard Lewisohn (London, New York: Khaniqahi Nimatullahi Publications, 1993) 584-586; see also Claude Cahen, "Mouvements populaires et autonomisme urbain dans l'Aise musulmane du Moyer Age," in *Arabica* 6, (1959) 27 ff. C. E. Bosworth, *The Ghaznavids*, (Edinburgh, 1963) 163-71.

27. The Tāhirids were known to be loyal to the Abbasids who in turn sanctioned their authority in Khurasan. The Tāhirids were also a bastion of Sunni Islam at a time when

the Shi'ites had begun to seek influence in the area. See Bosworth, *The Islamic Dynasties*, (Edinburgh: University of Edinburgh Press, 1967) 99-100;103-06; idem. "The Tāhirids and Ṣaffārids," *The Cambridge History of Iran: 4*, ed. R. N. Frye (Cambridge: Cambridge University Press, 1975) 90-135.

28. For more information on the final destruction of Nishapur see Bulliet, *Patricians of Nishapur*, 85-89.

29. Margaret, Malamud, "Sufi Organisation and Structures of Authority in Medieval Nishapur," *International Journal of Middle East Studies* 26 (1994): 429.

30. On the Karramites and their place in Khurasan, see C.E. Bosworth, "The Rise of the Karrāmīya in Khurasān," *Muslim World* (1960) 6-14; also see Karamustafa's comments in, *Sufism: The Formative Period*, 61 on the tensions that existed between the Malāmatīya and the Karrāmīya in Nishapur.

31. "The importance of the *malāmatī* trend in Khurāsānian Sufism, constituting an evolutionary development of the pure asceticism of the earlier generation, goes back to the precedence of Ḥamdūn al-Qaṣṣār (d. 271/885), a master of Nishpur, who put his stamp on the Sufi practice of the region, and stressed the importance of sincerity, declaring, 'God's knowledge of you is better than people's.'" Terry Graham, "Abū Sa'īd ibn Abī'l-Khayr and the School of Khurasān" in *The Heritiage of Sufism*, vol.1, ed. Leonard Lewisohn, (Oneworld:Oxford, 1999) 128.

32. For the Malāmatīya see: EI2, art. "MALĀMATIYYA," Fr. de Jong, Hamid Algar, and Colin Imber; Abdülbākī Gölpinarli, *Melāmīlik ve Melāmīler* (Istanbul: Devlet Matbaasi, 1931); al-Sulamī, *Risālat al-malāmatīya*, ed. Abū al-'Alā al-'Afīfī (Cairo: Dār Ihyā' al-Kutub al-'Arabīya, 1945); Sara Sviri, "Hakīm Tirmidhī and the Malāmatī Movement," in *Classical Persian Sufism: from its Origins to Rumi*, ed. Leonard Lewisohn (London: Khaniqahi Nimatullahi Publications, 1993), 583-613; Fritz Meier, "Khurasīn and the End of Classical Sufism," in *Essays in Islamic Mysticism and Piety*, trans. John O'Kane and Berndt Radke (Leiden: E. J. Brill, 2000), 215-217; Alexander, Knysh, *Islamic Mysticism, A Short History* (Leiden: E. J. Brill, 2000), 94-99; Hakīm Tirmidhī, *Kitāb ithbāt al-'ilal*, ed., Khālid Zahrī (Rabat: Muhammad V University, 1998), 24-25; also see the collected presentations from the International Conference on the *Malâmatiyya and Bayrâmī* Orders held in Istanbul in June, 1987 in *Melâmis-Bayrâmis*, ed. N. Clayer, A. Popovic, and T. Zarcone, (Istanbul: Les Editions Isis, 1998). For a recent analysis of the Malāmatīya and their role within the context of formative Sufism see Ahmet T. Karamustafa's *Sufism: The formative period*, (Edinburgh Press, 2007), multiple citations throughout the work.

33. *al-Risāla al-qushayrīya*, 226. Fritz Meier has drawn our attention to this distinction as being the key to understanding the reticence among the Malāmatīya to discuss doctrinal matters, as was common among the Sufis of Iraq, "Khurasān and the End of Classical Sufism," 214.

34. Sulamī, *Risālat al-malāmatīya,* ed. Abū al-'Alā' al'Afīfī (Cairo: Dār Iḥyā' al-Kutub al-'Arabīya, 1364/1945) 86-87.

35. See Melchert, Christopher, 'Sufis and competing movements in Nishapur,' in Iran 39 (2001), 239-40, the term 'fusion' is Melchert's. Also see J. Chabbi, "Remarques sur le développement historique des mouvements ascétiques et mystiques au Khurasan", *Studia Islamica*, Paris (1977), 41, note 1; and Knysh, Alexander, *Islamic Mysticism: A Short History*, 96, and Sviri, 'Hakim Tirmidhī, 599; and Karamustafa, *Sufism: The Formative Period*, 61.

36. Cognates of LWM are used in the Qur'ān fifteen times all centering on the context of blame.

37. For a concise survey of the degrees of the soul within the Qur'anic context see, *The Degrees of the Soul*, Shaykh Abd al-Khaliq al-Shabrawi, trans. Mostafa al-Badawi (London: The Quilliam Press, 1997).

38. Hujwīrī (d. 456/1063-4), the author of one of the first Sufi compendiums, in his commentary on this verse (Qur'ān 5:54), points out that this verse referring to the prophets and the eminent of the community (those who have intimate discourse with God) and he explains why they are blamed by "the whole world." "Such is the ordinance of God, that He causes those who discourse of Him to be blamed by the whole world, but preserves their hearts from being occupied by the world's blame. This He does in His jealousy: He guards His lovers from glancing aside to 'other' (*ghayr*), lest the eye of any stranger should behold the beauty of their state; and He guards them also from seeing themselves, lest they should regard their own beauty and fall into self-conceit and arrogance. Therefore He hath set the vulgar over them to loose the tongues of blame against them, and hath made the 'blaming soul' (*nafs-i lauwāma*) part of their composition, in order that they may be blamed by others for whatever they do, and by themselves for doing evil or for doing good imperfectly." *Kashf al-maḥjūb*, 62).

39. Hamid, Algar, *The Path of God's Bondsmen from Origin to Return*, (Delmar, New York: Caravan Books 1982)108-109. I would like to express my thanks to Dr. Algar for sending me an advanced copy of his article, "Elements de Provenance Malāmatī dans la Tradition Primitive Naqshbandī," in which he brought this reference to the *malāmatīya* to my attention.

40. Muslim ibn Ḥajjāj al-Qushayrī al-Naysābūrī, *Isnād Muslim*, ed. Muḥammad Fuæād 'Abd al-Bāqī (Beirut: Dar Iḥyā' al-Turāth al'Arabī, 1972) vol. 4, 1995 *Bāb taḥrīm al-ẓulm*. In *Concordance de la Tradition Musulmane* by A. J. Wensinck and J. P. Mensing, p. 153-54 seventeen, traditions employing cognates of LWM are cited.

41. 'Alī ibn 'Uthmān al-Hujwīrī, *The Kashf al-maḥjūb*, Translated by Reynold A. Nicholson. Gibb Memorial Series, no. 17, new edition (London: Luzac and Company, 1976) 62.

42. Ibn 'Arabī, *al-Futūḥāt al-Makkīya*, (Cairo: Dār Ṣādir 1329) III 35.28.

43. This bifurcation has tended to mark the writings of later Sufism as well as the modern scholarship derived from the study of Sufi texts.

44. *Risālat al-malāmatīya,* 91.

45. See comments by 'Afifi, in introduction to *Risālat al-malāmatīya*, 48. Also see Julian Baldick, *Mystical Islam* (New York, London: New York University Press, 1989) 57.

46. Abū Ḥafṣ was a native of Nishapur. His full name was 'Amr ibn Salam or some said 'Amr ibn Salma. Sulamī recorded the latter as being more correct. He frequented 'Ubaydallāh ibn Mahdī al-Abī Wardī, and 'Alī al-Naṣrābādhī. He was also a friend of Aḥmad ibn Khaḍrawayh of Balkh. His best known disciples were Shāh al-Kirmānī, Abū 'Uthmān [Ḥīrī], and Sa'īd ibn Ismā'īl. He was known for his *futūwah* and as one of the *mashā'ikh* of the Malāmatīya of Nishapur. *Ṭabaqāt al-ṣūfīya*, 115-122, see additional biographical information there.

47. Cf. Sulamī, *Ṭabaqāt al-ṣūfīya,*115; Abū al-Qāsim, al-Qushayrī, *al-Risāla fi-'ilm al-taṣawwuf*, 406; *Kitāb al-luma'*, 108,188; *Risālat al-malāmatīya,* 88.

48. *Risālat al-malāmatīya,* 89.

49. M. Molé, "Autour du daré Mansour", *Revue des Études Islamique* 27: 1959, 53. Also see Trimingham, *The Sufi Orders in Islam* (Oxford: Clarendon Press 1971), "At the foundation of the *malāmatī* tendency is the absolute nothingness of man before God," 265.

50. One of the two texts translated in this edition.

51. Sulamī, *Darajāt al-ṣādiqīn,* sec. 13, page 131.

52. *Risālat al-malāmatīya,* 90.

53. The relationship between *blame* and gnosis is the subject of section 13 of *Darajāt al-ṣādiqīn.*

54. *Risālat al-malāmatīja,* pages 58/59,100. Also see Richard Hartmann, "As-Sulamī's Risālat al-Malāmatīja", *Der Islam,* 8 (1918): 164-165.

55. Sulamī considered Ḥamdūn al-Qaṣṣār (d. 271/884), a native of Nishapur, the founder of the Malāmatīya. He narrates: He was the *Shaykh* of the Malāmatīya of Nishapur; from him the Path of Blame spread. He associated with Salim ibn al-Ḥasan al-Bārūsī, Abū Turāb al-Nakhshabī, and 'Alī al-Naṣrābādhī. He was a scholar of jurisprudence, following the school of al-Thawrī (in jurisprudence). His spiritual path (*Ṭarīqa*) was a path particular to him. No one of his companions took his path from him like his companion 'Abdallāh ibn Muḥammad ibn Munāzil did. *Ṭabaqāt al-ṣūfīya,* 123-29.

56. *Risālat al-malāmatīya,* see tenets 8 and 9, 119.

57. See *Darajāt al-ṣādiqīn* sec. 9, page 129, for Sulamī's commentary on this well known Sufi saying.

58. *Risālat al-malāmatīya,* tenets 18 and 37.

59. Ibid. tenets 3, 6, 13, 14, 16, 22, 25, 28, 29, 30, 31, 34, 40, and 45.

60. Ibid. tenets 2, 3, 7, 8, 10, 12, 15, 19, 20, 26, 32, 35, 36, and 44.

61. Ibid. tenets 1, 11, and 27.

62. Ibid. tenets 5, 9, 17, 21, 23, 24, 38, and 42.

63. *Darajāt al-ṣādiqīn,* sec. 18, page 133.

64. *Risālat al-malāmatīya* 111.

65. *Darajāt al-ṣādiqīn,* sec. 3, page 126.

66. *Ṭabaqāt al-ṣūfīya,* 119.

67. Margaret Malamud, 429.

68. "Pietism," *Encyclopedia of Religion and Ethics,* ed. James Hastings (New York: Charles Scribners and Sons, 1928) vol. 10, 6.

69. "Ibrāhīm ibn Adham is credited with making the first classification of the stages of asceticism (*zuhd)* . . . (a) renunciation of the world, (b) renunciation of the happy feelings of having achieved renunciation, and (c) the stage in which the ascetic regards the world as so unimportant that he no longer looks at it" Annemarie Schimmel, *Mystical Dimensions of Islam* [Chapel Hill: The University of North Carolina Press, 1975] 36.

70. Ibn 'Arabī situates the ascetics as the first and lowest rank of the Men of Allah differentiating them from the Sufis and the *malāmatīya* in this very respect, i. e. that "they do not see anything beyond the works they perform" *al-Futūḥāt al-Makkīya* III, 34.28. Cited by W. Chittick, *The Sufi Path of Knowledge* (New York: State University of New York Press, 1989) 373).

71. *Risālat al-malāmatīya,* 100.

72. *Risālat al-malāmatīya,* 96.

73. The above citation by Sulamī seems to leave open the possibility of praise or blame that contained truth. Yet, as I have tried to portray in my translation, it is neither

the praise nor the blame that lacks truth. The object of the praise or blame lacks truth (*al-ḥaqīqa*). Therefore the ego-self's attachments to illusory objects of praise and its aversion to blame is the reason behind its inability to realize the objective reality of God the Truth (*al-Ḥaqq*). Were the ego-self to be subjected to abasement and disdain, it would realize the relative nature of manifestation and turn to God the Truth, and thus enter the states of *malāma*. This illustrates why the innate nature of the ego-self to seek appeasement in "Other" is always blameworthy, whether it is in obedience or disobedience. This is the more profound reason behind Abū 'Uthmān al-Ḥīrī's words, "Everything that pleases the ego-self, be it obedience or disobedience, is passion (*shahwa*)." See *Tadhallul al-fuqarā',* sec. 5, 6 and 7, pages 137-138.

74. *Tadhallul al-fuqarā',* sec. 26, page 147. Abū Yazīd Ṭayfūr ibn 'Isā ibn Shurūsān (d. 261/874-5) was among the most famous of the early mystically oriented ascetics and was well known for his ecstatic utterances. His tomb in Bisṭām (near Nishapur) is still venerated today. The Malāmatīya attribute many of their basic attitudes to Abū Yazīd, who is seen as one of the most central figures of the Khurasanian Tradition. See biographical notes in *Ṭabaqāt al-ṣūfīya,* 67-74.

75. *Risālat al-malāmatīya,* 105-106.

76. *Tadhallul al-fuqarā',* sec. 2, pages 135-136.

77. *Risālat al-malāmatīya,* 97.

78. *Risālat al-malāmatīya,* tenet 24. There is general agreement on this Malāmatīya habit, though one finds Molé ascribing to the Malāmatīya the patched frock (*muraqqa'a*) as being worn over the non-distinctive clothing of the market place. This does not seem in accord with the basic tenets expressed in the *Risālat al-malāmatīya.* Molé attributes this to a habit of Ḥallāj and sees it as another indication of his connection with the Malāmatīya although it appears to be a sign of his divergence from the Malāmatīya (Molé, *Les Mystiques Musulmans,* 76.) Also see Fritz Meier, p. 215.

79. *Risālat al-malāmatīya,* tenet 9.

80. *Risālat al-malāmatīya,* 103.

81. *Risālat al-malāmatīya,* tenets 21 and 37. One might suppose that the very fact that Sulamī was an extensive writer of Sufi treatises would have excluded him from *malāmī* circles. In an interesting aside though J. Baldick has unintentionally answered this question. "Sulamī wrote a treatise about them, [i.e. the Malāmatīya] *his method of abstaining from expression of his own beliefs,* while repeating respectable, isolated quotations from earlier Sufis, prevents us from obtaining a real picture of the *people of blame* (*Mystical Islam* 57-58, emphasis my own). Sulamī does not appear as a personality in his works. His teachings are dispersed between the quotations and in his choice of quote itself. This method is a living example of the anonymity taught by the Malāmatīya. Thus, the fact that Sulamī wrote treatises does not mean that he violated *malāmatī* principles, since he virtually effaced himself - as an author - from his works

82. Trimingham, *The Sufi Orders in Islam,* 266.

83. Karamustafa, *Sufism: The Formative Period,* 49, also see his comments on the relationship between the Malāmatīya, as craftsmen and traders and the ethical code of 'chivalry' (*futuwwa*).

84. *Risālat al-malāmatīya,* 90.

85. *Risālat al-malāmatīya,* tenets 23 and 41.

86. *Risālat al-malāmatīya,* 91.

87. Cf. Ḥakīm al-Tirmidhī, *Kitāb khatm al-awliyā'* ed. O. Yahia (Beirut: Imprimerie Catholique, 1965). For a linguistic study of the term *walāya* and its derivatives as well as an in-depth discussion on the hierarchy of saints in Islamic traditional literature see Michel Chodkiewicz, *Le Sceau des saints: Prophétie et sainteté dans la doctrine d'Ibn Arabī* (Paris: Gallimard, 1986), 29-78. Also see *The Concept of Sainthood in Early Islamic Mysticism: Two works by Al-Ḥakīm al-Tirmidhī*, Bernd Radtke and John O' Kane (London: 1996). This study is based on Radtke's revised edition of *Kitāb khatm al-awliyā'* under the new title *Kitāb sīyar al-awliyā'* (Beirut:1992).

88. *Darajāt al-ṣādiqīn*, sec. 17, page 133. Also see M. Molé, *Les Mystique Musulmans*, (Paris: Presses Universitaires de France, 1965) 77-78.

89. Karamustafa, *Sufism: The Formative Period*, 62.

90. Sulamī held Abū al-Ḥasan al-Ḥuṣrī in high esteem. He said of him in *Ṭabaqāt al-ṣūfīya*, "Shaykh of Iraq, and its spokesman, I have seen none among the masters more perfect of state than he, nor more eloquent or loftier in speech." *Ṭabaqāt al-ṣūfīya* , 489.

91. *Risālat al-malāmatīya* 119. Note that Jamī (following Anṣārī) cites Sahl Tustarī and Junayd as saying, "If it were possible for there to have been a prophet after Aḥmad [namely after Muḥammad] the divine messenger, he would have been from among those like (*az īshān-i*) Hamdūn al-Qaṣṣār," *Nafaḥāt al-uns*, vol. 1, p. 60 (I thank Dr. A. Godlas of the University of Georgia for this insightful note).

92. Abū Bakr Muḥammad ibn Aḥmad al-Farrā' (d. 370/980) was one of the great teachers of Nishapur. He associated with Abū 'Alī al-Thaqafī (d. 328/940) and Ibn al-Munāzil (d. 331/943) [both disciples of Ḥamdūn al-Qaṣṣār (d. 271/884) founder of the Malāmatīya of Nishapur]. *Ṭabaqāt* 507-8. Aḥmad al-Farrā' was one of Sulamī's direct sources for his narrations of the Malāmatīya; in *Risālat al-malāmatīya* he cites forty-seven citations from him. See Roger Deladrière, "Les premiers Malāmatiyya: les Gardiens du Secret" *Des acts du colloque sur les Mélamlis et les Bayramis* organized in Istambul (4-6 June 1987) by l'Institut Français Anatoliennes 2. My deepest appreciation to Prof. Deladrière for sending me an advance copy of this in-depth article on the Malāmatīya and Sulamī's relationship to them. Roger Deladrière subsequently translated Sulamī's *Risālat al-malāmatīya* under the title *La Lucidité Implacable: Épître des Hommes du Blâme*, trad. Roger Deladrière (Paris:1991).

93. 'Abd Allāh ibn Muḥammad al-Mu'allim ibn Faḍlūya was a disciple of Ibn Munāzil. He narrates 46 citations in *Risālat al-malāmatīya*. Deladrière, "Les premiers Malāmatīya, 2.

94. Abū 'Amr ibn Ḥamdān Muḥammad ibn Aḥmad was the son of Abū Ja'far ibn Sinān, a *malāmatī* in the line of Abū Ḥafṣ and Abū 'Uthmān. He narrates thirty-eight citations in *Risālat al-malāmatīya*. Deladrière, "Les premiers Malāmatīya, 2.

95. Sulamī, *Majmū'a-i-āthār-i-Abū 'Abd al-Raḥmān Sulamī*, ed. Naṣr Allāh Pūjavādī and Mohammed Soori, (Tehran: 2009) vol. 3.

96. Louis Massingnon states that Ibn Bākūyā, "to whom Sulamī bequeathed at the time of his death (in 412/1021) the directorship of his convent-library in Nishapur, was, like him [Sulamī], a traditionalist historian, whose perspectives, however, were narrower and method less solid, but whose inquisitiveness with regard to the behavioral eccentricities of mystics was sharp." 7, vol. 1; Louis Massignon, *The Passion of al-Hallāj, Mystic and Martyr of Islam*, trans. Herbert Mason, (Princeton: 1982). See the references cited there. Ibn Bākūyā was a major figure in the transmission of the works of Ḥallāj for this reason he is cited multiple times in *The Passion of Hallāj*. For Ibn Bākūyā, also see Bābā Kūhī, EIr: 293-4 (M. Kesheff).

97. There is interestingly enough no mention of the term Malāmatīya in the earlier existent compendiums on Sufism such as *Kitāb al-luma'* by Abū Naṣr Sarrāj (d. 370/980) nor in *al-Ta'arruf* by al-Kalābādī (d. 380/1000). Though both authors were from Khurasan, they rarely cited narratives from sources that were considered by Sulamī to be among the Malāmatīya.

98. This view was also held by Ibn 'Arabī who calls them the "masters and leaders of the folk" (*al-Futūḥāt al-Makkīya* (III:34.28) See William Chittick's superb translation of the passage in *The Sufi Path of Knowledge*, 372-375.

99. *Risālat al-malāmatīya* 86-87.

100. Sulamī writes that "Sufi aspirants manifest frivolous claims and miracles (*karāmāt*) that any realized person (*mutaḥaqqiq*) would laugh at." *Risālat al-malāmatīya* 89.

101. *Risālat al-malāmatīya* 88-89. This quote seems in contradiction to Fritz Meier's conclusion that Abū Hafṣ was not among the Malāmatīya, p. 216.

102. *Risālat al-malāmatīya* 91.

103. *Darajāt al-ṣādiqīn* sec. 13 and 15, pages 131-132. Jean-Jacques Thibon has called attention to this passage as the "basis for an explanation of the Malāmatīya distrust of miracles," Rachida Chih, Denis Gril, "Le Saint et Son Milieu, ou Comment Lire les Sources hagiographiques," Institut Français d'Archéologie Orientale, Cahier des Annales Islamogiques 19, 2000, 21.

104. The references to the texts are cited in bold according to the sections of the Arabic edition. I have chosen one reference from *Darajāt al-ṣādiqīn* that is representative of a statement of doctrine and multiple references from *Tadhallul al-fuqarā'*, which being more prescriptive lends itself more to explicit examples.

105. *Tadhallul al-fuqarā'*, sec. 36, page 150.

106. *Tadhallul al-fuqarā'*, sec. 7, page 138.

107. *Tadhallull al-fuqarā'*, sec. 35, page 150.

108. The root LḤF means to request or demand urgently, to solicit in such a manner that one makes a display of one's state of need. For the Malāmatīya to manifest a state of need to other than God was seen as unseemly comportment.

109. *Tadhallul al-fuqarā'*, sec. 2, page 136.

STATIONS OF THE RIGHTEOUS

1. Towards enriching the translation I include narrations from Sulamī's other works which relate to the text. "'Sufism,' as I heard my grandfather, Ismā'īl ibn Nujayd say, 'is patient perseverance under the permitted and the forbidden [in Islam].'" "I heard al-Ḥusayn ibn Aḥmad al-Rāzī say, 'I heard al-Kattānī say, "Sufism is inner attitude (*adāb*) he who surpasses you in *adāb*, surpasses you in Sufism."'" "Ibn Abī Sa'dān said, 'He who gains not in good character through Sufism is ignorant [of its true meaning]. Sufism is purity of state, thus he who is purified in his states and benefits from the entirety of his purity, he is a Sufi.'" Sulamī, *Darajāt al-mu'āmalāt,* in *Tis'at kutub fi uṣūt al-taṣawwfu wa al-zuhd*, ed. Sūleyman Ateş, (n.p. 1993) 173-74.

2. Abū Ḥafṣ replied, when asked the meaning of *malāmatīya* said, "The people of blame are those who stand constant with God (*al-Ḥaqq*) in protection of their every moment, and vigilance over their inward mysteries, they thus find worthy of blame all that

they may manifest of the various forms of intimacy and worship. They make apparent to others (*al-khalq*) the baseness wherein they [the *malāmatīs*] dwell, and hide from them their virtues; they come to be found blameworthy by others, and they blame themselves over that which they know of their own souls." *Risālat al-malāmatīya*, 89.

3. Sulamī narrates elsewhere that "Love is the dissolution of discernment. It has been called love because it erases all traces, and allows no footholds under any circumstances. The lover is wholly taken up in the Essence (*al-dhāt*), effaced of his qualities. When love wends its way into the inward mysteries [of the heart] it denudes and effaces it of all insight in its occupation with the Beloved. Love renders the lover silent, he voices not his state, his qualities, or his complaints." *Darajāt al-mu'āmlāt,* 178.

4. Stations are the degrees that the servant has realized of the disciplines [of the path] to which he has attained access through perseverant practice and realized through meeting requisites and constant applied effort; thus each person's station is the place they are situated within these [guidelines] and the discipline in which they are occupied. al-*Risālat al-qushayrīya,* 56.

5. Abū al-'Abbās al-Qāsim al-Sayyārī (d. 342/953-4) said, "*Rubūbīya* is the emulation of commands, the imposition of the will, and omnipotence and divine decree; *'ubūdīya* is knowledge of the worshipped and adherence to one's pacts" *Ṭabaqāt al-ṣūfīya,* 445.

6. See intro. note 74.

7. Sa'īd ibn Sallām from Qayrawān (d. 373/983-4), lived in Mecca a long time and became the most respected religious figure there. He frequented Abū Alt ibn al-Kātib and Ḥabīb al-Maghribī. He was unique in his devotion and asceticism. He was a vestige of the early masters and their epoch. None excelled him in nobility of state, or constancy in each moment. he was known for his intuition and spiritual awe. He immigrated to Nishapur and there he died. *Ṭabāqāt al-ṣūfīya,* 479.

8. Hadīth related by Aḥmad, Ibn Māja, al-Ḥākim, and al- Bayhaqī from Thawbān; and Ibn Māja and al-Ṭabarānī from Ibn 'Amr. see *Fayḍ al-qādīr,* vol. 1, p. 497. (ref. Sūleyman Ateş, *Tis'at kutub,* 372).

9. Bundār ibn al-Ḥusayn al-Shīrāzī (d. 353/964-5), He was an authority on the four foundations of Islamic jurisprudence, and famous for elucidating on divine reality. He was greatly respected by Abū Bakr al-Shiblī, who was the mentor of Sulamī's teacher in Sufism, Abū al-Qāsim al-Naṣrābādhī. This quote is to be found in its entirety in *Ṭabaqāt al-ṣūfīya*, 467.

10. Lit. "[The word *ṣūfī* is constructed according to the same verbal paradigm as is [the word] *ṣufiya*. Namely [it is like the passive perfect tense of the verb 'to purify' (*ṣafā*), and so] it refers to one who has been purified."

11. Cited by al-Qushayrī in his *Risāla,* 231. The hadith was narrated on the authority of Abū Sa'īd al-Khudarī, reported by al-Tirmidhī (hadīth 3125) in *al-tafsīr, 'bāb sūrat al-ḥijr.'* It was narrated by Jalāl al-Dīn al-Suyūṭī in *al-Durr al-manthūr* vol. 4, p. 103; al-Suyūṭī attributed this hadith to Ibn Jarīr, Ibn Abū Ḥātim, al-Bukhārī in *al-Tārīkh*, Abū Nu'aym under the heading '*al-Ṭibb.*'

12. Abū Bakr al-Siddīq ibn Abū Quḥāfa al-Taymī (d. 13/634). One of the earliest converts to Islam, known as the 'veracious' for his total confidence in all that the Prophet said. He accompanied the Prophet on his immigration to Medina, and was his closest friend and advisor. He became the first caliph; his short reign was marked by the suppression of the apostasies that occurred upon the death of the Prophet and by the beginnings of the conquest of Iraq and Syria. W. M. Watt, 'Abū Bakr al-Ṣaddīq,' *EI.*

13. 'Ā'isha bint Abī Bakr (d.58/678) The second wife of the Prophet. During his final illness he asked his other wives for permission to stay in her house, where he died. She played a major role in the community after the death of the Prophet, as a transmitter of hadith; she also played a political role and was involved in the revolt of Ṭalḥa and al-Zubayr against the caliph 'Alī. She ended her days quietly at Medina. W. M. Watt, "Ā'isha,' *EI.*

14. In *Jām'i karāmāt al-awliyā'* this *ḥadīth* is reported as being strong and was transmitted by 'Urwa ibn al-Zubayr, from 'Ā'isha. vol. 1, p. 128.

15. Lit. "[In doing so] he had confirmed authoritatively the fact that a female [fetus] was in the womb of his wife."

16. Abū al-Qāsim al-Junayd ibn Muḥammad al-Khazzāz (d. 298/910-11), born in Iraq, He was a scholar of hadīth and jurisprudence, he studied under Abū Thawr. He frequented his uncle al-Sarī al-Saqaṭī and al-Ḥārith al-Muḥāsibī and Muḥammad ibn 'Alī al-Qaṣṣāb al-Baghdādī. He is among the foremost Sufis of Baghdad and masters of the Path, respected by all. *Ṭabaqāt al-ṣūfīya,* 155.

17. Sahl ibn 'Abdallāh al-Tustarī (d. 283/896-7), one of the founders of Sufism, and one of the most knowledgeable, he spoke particularly on disciplines of the path, sincerity, and the defects that enter ones deeds. He frequented his uncle Muḥammad ibn Sawwār, he also saw Dhū al-Nūn al-Miṣī the year he made the Ḥajj. *Ṭabaqāt al-ṣūfīya,* 206.

18. See intro. note 9.

19. Abū Turāb al-Nakhshabī (d. 245/859-60), his name is 'Askar ibn Ḥusayn. He frequented Abū Ḥātim al-'Aṭṭār al-Baṣrī and Ḥātim al-Aṣamm al-Balkhī; he is among the most illustrious of the masters of Khurāsān, renown for knowledge and nobility of character (*futūwah*), reliance upon God, asceticism, and piety. *Ṭabaqāt al-ṣūfīya,* 146.

20. Al-Ghazālī places the station of veracity (*ṣidīqīya*) as the highest degree attainable before that of prophethood, which is for him definitively closed. *Ihyā 'ulūm al-din,* ed. Muḥammad al-Dālī Balta (Beirut: al-Maṭba'a al-'Aṣrīya, 1996) 3:99, 4:59. Ibn 'Arabī places an intermediary station between this station and the ultimate station of prophethood, the Station of Proximity (*maqām al-qurbā*). *al-Futūḥāt al-makkīya* vol. 2, p. 249. (ref. M. Chodkiewicz, *Le Sceau des Saints* (Paris: Gallimard, 1982) 77, 142.

21. Related in *Sunan al-Tirmidhī,* 239; also in *Sunan Imām Aḥmad* and *Abū Ya'lā* with good chains of transmission, and in *al-Ḥākim* who considered it 'strong.' *al-Targhīb* 2, 'Chapter on Love for the sake of God'. (ref. Süleyman Ateş, *Tis'at kutub,* 374).

22. Pertaining to the ninety-nine names of God see: *Muslim, Dhikr,* 6, al-Ghazālī, *The Ninety-Nine Beautiful Names of God,* trans. David B. Burrell and Nazih Daher (Cambridge: The Islamic Text Society, 1992), and for the Arabic text see al-Ghazālī, *Maqṣad al-asnā,* (Beirut: Dar el-Machreq, 1965).

23. 'Abdallāh Ibn 'Abbas, (d. 68/687-8) a cousin and close companion of the Prophet known for his righteousness and generally considered to be the first of the Islamic scholars; he was a narrator of hadith as well as the first to comment on the Qur'ān.

24. 'Umar ibn al-Khaṭṭāb (d. 23/634-5) He was the second caliph of Islam after Abū Bakr. He is respected for his unswerving devotion, while holding almost absolute authority. He continues to inspire Muslims today as an example of noble comportment and humble service to others.

25. Abū Muḥammad al-Jarīrī (d. 311/923-4) he was one of al-Junayd's greatest disciples, He also frequented Sahl ibn 'Abdallāh al-Tustarī. He succeeded al-Junayd because of his perfection of state and knowledge. *Ṭabaqāt al-ṣūfīya,* 259.

26. Lit. the unfolding of destined events before they occur.

27. Another understanding of the text which is harmonious with the Fatih ms. is as follows: "which he perceives through its appearance to him, since (*idh*) the locus of created being (*maḥal al-ḥawādith*) will never be devoid of defects."

28. This reference is to al-Qur'ān 27:7-10.

29. The Qur'ānic view of Adam's sin was in his disobedience to God's command not to approach the tree. Adam, however, desired to eat of the fruit after he had been told by Satan that the fruit of the tree would bestow immortality. See Qur'ān 20:120-123.

30. Dhahabī, *Siyar a'lām al-nubalāā,* vol. 2, p. 380.

31. Part of a long hadith related by al-Tirmidhī, who said it was reliable (*ḥasan*); and Ibn Māja in Jihād, citing a reliable chain as well; and al-Ḥākim, who considered its chain of transmission to be strong. (ref. Sūleyman Ateş, *Tis'at kutub,* 388).

32. 'Uways al-Qaranī, early ascetic, from Kūfa (d. 640/1243). The earliest mention of him is in Ibn Sa'd (d. 845). Uways has become an almost mythical figure in Islamic Sufic lore.

33. According to Ibn 'Arabī the Qutb was always chosen from the *malāmatīya. al-Futūḥāt al-makkīya,* vol. 3, p. 573.

34. The apostates (*ahl al-riḍḍa*) were the Arab tribes who refused the *zakat* they had given during the lifetime of Muhammad.

35. A hadith transmitted by 'Umar. ('Alī ibn Abū Bakr al-Haythamī (d. 807), *Majma' al-zawā'id,* vol. 8, p. 82 [Beirut: Dār al-Kitāb al-'Arabī, nd.]). A similar version is related in Aḥmad ibn Ḥanbal, *Masnad*, vol. 3, p. 76.

THE HUMBLE SUBMISSION OF THOSE ASPIRING

1. In a sense all the virtues are contained in spiritual poverty (*al-faqr*) and the term, *al-faqr*, is commonly used to designate the path of aspiration in Islam as a whole. Sufis in general do not refer to themselves as Sufis, rather they call themselves *fuqarā'*. The term *faqīr,* of which *fuqarā'* is the plural, refers to the aspirant on the path. "This *faqr* or spiritual poverty is nothing other than a *vacare Deo*, emptiness for God; it begins with the rejection of passions and its crown is the effacement of the *I* before the Divinity. The nature of this virtue clearly shows the inverse analogy that links the human symbol with its divine archetype: what is emptiness on the side of the creature is plenitude on the side of the Creator." Titus Burckhardt, *An Introduction to Sufi Doctrine* (Lahore: Sh. Moḥammad Ashraf Publishers, reprinted 1991) 110. Given the frequency with which the terms *faqr*, *faqīr*, and *fuqarā'* are used in the text, the term will be used in its transliterated form.

2. The word *ghinā'* refers to independence and freedom from want, wealth is therefore not only a state of material well being but could also refer to any state of self-sufficiency founded upon secondary causes. Independence founded upon God is not seen to be blameworthy for as in the hadith, "True wealth is wealth in God."

3. This saying was ascribed to Ibrāhīm al-Qaṣṣār. *al-Risālat al-qushayrīya,* 272.

4. The root LḤF means to request or demand urgently, to solicit in such a manner that one makes a display of one's state of need. For the Malāmatīya to manifest a state of need to other than God was seen as unseemly comportment.

5. Formal religious knowledge (*'ilm*) in this context refers to Islamic Law (*Sharī'ah*). Among the salient traits of the *Malāmatīya* was the stress they laid upon strict adherence to the *Sharī'ah* as a means of attaining total surrender to God.

6. The root RFQ appears multiple times in this text. The singular *rifq*, plural *arfāq*, is employed in this and many of Sulamī's other treatises to mean *rizq* or sustenance. See *Tadhallul* sections 28, 34, 40, 43, and 45. An example of the use of this term in both the plural and singular can be found in Section 28. Sulamī writes, "It is also obligatory for a *faqīr* to know the precepts of his sustenance (*arfāq*), so that he takes sustenance (*rifq*) only from where he knows he is not using his religion as a means of earning his daily bread."

7. Ibn al-Athīr, *Kitāb al-nihāya fī gharīb al-ḥadīth wa-al-athar* (Cairo: n.d.) vol. 2, 322.

8. Abū 'Uthmān al-Hīrī of Nishapur (d. 298/ 910) was the heir to the founder of the Malāmatīya, Abū Ḥafṣ (*Ṭabaqāt al-ṣūfīya* 170-75.) see Introduction, note 9. The birthplace and origins of the teachings of a narrator are of interest in reference to the sources that Sulamī drew upon. I will therefore briefly mention the principle narrators of each of the citations quoted in *Tadhallul al-fuqarā',* noting their birthplace and with whom they received their training. For the sake of clarity I will translate *ṣaḥaba* as *associated with* and only refer to discipleship if Sulamī has made a direct reference using the word *ustādh.* Instead of translating the term *shaykh* (pl. *mashā'ikh*), which basically refers to a person of spiritual eminence but not necessarily a mentor or a spiritual master or teacher, I will use the transliteration. By using transliterations of the terms mentioned I hope to avoid the ambiguity sometimes inherent in their translation. All references will be from Sulamī's *Ṭabaqāt al-sūfīya.* For more biographical material I advise the reader to look at the references cited there by Ben Sharība.

9. *Shahwa* (passion) from the point of view of Islamic teachings is any desire that contradicts the Law, or has an object that is not sanctioned by it. Thus the Qur'ān says, *Then there succeeded after them a later generation who has neglected prayer and followed passion* [19:59]. This quotation of Abū 'Uthmān reflects the degree of distrust with which the Malāmatīya regarded the ego-self.

10. Due to an error on the part of the scribe sections of the Baku manuscript are out of the order followed in the Fātiḥ and Ibn Yūsuf manuscripts. I have employed them both in re-establishing the Baku text. As this occurs twice in the Baku text, I will indicate the location of the misplaced sections by indicating the folio and the line and Arabic word where the misplaced text may be located. For this section see folio 22/a line 5 from [*yaqūlu samiᶜtu Ibrahim Mannān*] (correct: Shaybān), to folio 23/a line 22, [*tanmū shwā*]-*hidim.*

11. Ibrāhīm ibn Shaybān al-Qirmīsīnī (d. 330/941) was the *shaykh* of his time of the mountains of Iraq. He attained degrees of moral scrupulousness and righteousness beyond the possibilities of most people. He associated with Abū 'Abdallāh al-Maghribī and Ibrāhīm al-Khawwāṣ. He was unrelenting in his criticism of those who made pretentious claims. Ibrāhīm ibn Shaybān was held in high esteem by Ibn Munāzil (who according to al-Qushayrī was the *shaykh* of the Malāmatīya of his day, 435) who said of him, "Ibrāhīm is God's clear proof for the aspirants of the path (*fuqarā'*), the people of correct conduct, and piety. *Ṭabaqāt al-sūfīya,* 402-5.

12. Muḥammad ibn al-Faḍl al-Balkhī of Khurasan (d.319/932) was related to *futūwah* and well respected by Abū 'Uthmān al-Ḥīrī. He associated with Aḥmad ibn Ḥaḍrawayh (who was known for his *futūwah*). Aḥmad ibn Ḥaḍrawayh was also greatly respected by Abū Ḥafṣ, who said about him, "I have never seen anyone with more fervor for the path nor of a more sincere state than Aḥmad ibn Ḥaḍrawayh." *al-Risāla al-qushayrīya* 410. Sulamī reports that "Abū 'Uthmān al-Ḥīrī esteemed none of the *mashā'ikh* of Khurasan in the manner he esteemed Muḥammad ibn al-Faḍl al-Balkhī. He also reports, "I have it

from Muḥammad ibn 'Alī al-Ḥīrī that Abū 'Uthmān said, "If I had the strength, I would travel to my brother Muḥammad ibn al-Faḍl, for my innermost soul finds repose in seeing him." *Ṭabaqāt al-sūfīya,* 212-16.

13. Abū 'Abdallāh al-Sajazī associated with Abū Ḥafṣ and was one of the important *mashā'ikh* of Khurasan and those of the path of *futūwah.* He often sojourned in the desert trusting in God [i.e. taking no food or water with him]. *Ṭabaqāt al-sūfīya,* 254-55.

14. This is most likely a reference to The Qur'ān, Chapter al-Tawba, verse 100 which states: *And the first to lead the way (al-sābiqūn) of the Muhājirīn and the Anṣār, and those who followed them in goodness—Allah is well pleased with them and they are well pleased with Him.* [9:100] The companions of the Prophet were held in high esteem by the Sufis, as exemplars of spiritual conduct that went back to the beginnings of Islamic society. See Sarrāj, *Kitāb al-luma' fi al-taṣawwuf,* ed. R. A. Nicholson (London: Luzac, 1963) 119-121 for commentary on the above verse. Of the hadith that support Sulamī's statement that no one after the Companions could equal them in excellence, we have the following saying of the Prophet—May the Peace and Blessings of God be upon him, "Do not curse my Companions, for even if one of you donated [in God's name] an amount of gold the equivalent of Uḥud, he would never reach the measure of one of them, or even a half." (*al-Bukhārī ḥadīth number* 3673, from the chapter, 'The Virtues of the Companions of the Prophet.'

15. *Taklīf* (overburdening oneself) refers to actions that reflect a mistaken evaluation of one's capabilities. This creates a divergence of the interior and exterior states, between our innate inability to accomplish anything and our desire to manifest capability. In *taklīf* there is always some aspect of ostentation and "hoping to please," attitudes which the Malāmatīya saw as attempts to evoke a deceptive impression of one's interior state. The Malāmatīya regarded any manifestation of one's inner state worthless ostentation under any circumstances. On another level *taklīf* represents self-instigated action (*tadbīr*) the outcome of which is eagerly awaited, producing therefore a lack of effaced disinterest in the result of one's actions. Both the concept of renunciation of overburdening (*tark al-taklīf*) and renunciation of self-instigated action (*tark al-tadbīr*) are central tenets of the Malāmatīya.

16. Abū Isḥaq Ibrāhīm al-Qaṣṣār, (d. 326/937) was among the illustrious *mashā'ikh* of Shām (Syria). He was a contemporary of al-Junayd and Ibn al-Jalā'. *Ṭabaqāt al-sūfīya,* 319-21.

17. I take this to mean that he has not gone to the excess of repairing already worn and patched garments, a practice that would be indicative of extreme poverty.

18. This quote is indicative of the Malāmatīya attitude of total acceptance of the state of the moment and having no dependence upon habits; be they habits of dress, such as wearing a *patched frock,* (which was the sign of the wearer's following the mystical path), habits of comportment and attitude such as begging for alms as a means of affirming one's own *state of need,* or refusing assistance as a means of affirming one's *independence* in God.

19. Abū 'Alī al-Jūzjānī was one of the great *mashā'ikh* of Khurasan he wrote many well-known works. He spoke of the faults of the ego-self, discipline, and striving. He associated with Muḥammad ibn 'Alī al-Tirmidhī and Muḥammad ibn al-Faḍl and was close to them in age. *Ṭabaqāt al-sūfīya,* 246-48.

20. Ibn al-'Arabī defines the term *wārid* as "every praiseworthy incoming thought (*khāṭir*) which arrives at the heart without self-exertion; or, every affair which enters in upon the heart from any divine name." William Chittick, *The Sufi Path of Knowledge,* 266, citing Ibn 'Arabī, *al-Futūḥāt al-Makkīya,* vol. 2, 132.26.

21. Abū Isḥaq Ibrāhīm ibn al-Mawlid, was among the well known *mashā'ikh* of al-Raqqa, Iraq. He associated with Ibn al-Jalā' of Damascus, Ibrāhīm ibn Dāwūd al-Qaṣṣār al-Raqqī. He was among the most illustrious *mashā'ikh* in *futūwah* and the best of them in his comportment. *Ṭabaqāt al-sūfīya,* 410-11.

22. Abū 'Abdallāh ibn al-Jalā' (d. 306/918) was born in Baghdad and later lived in Damascus. Among the illustrious *mashā'ikh* of Shām (Syria), he associated with his father Yaḥyā al-Jalā', Abū Turāb al-Nakhshabī, and Dhū al-Nūn al-Miṣrī. Ismā'īl ibn Nujayd said, 'In this world there are three eminent leaders (*a'imma*) of the Sufis, there is not a fourth: al-Junayd of Baghdad, Abū 'Uthmān of Nishapur, and Abū 'Abd Allah ibn al-Jalā' of Shām.' *Ṭabaqāt al-sūfīya,* 176-79.

23. Having recourse to one's habit is indicative of the loss of the intuitive relationship with God, for instead of acting upon the living intuitive tenets of the path of *faqr* the aspirant is debased to dependence upon his own habits and customs which represent for the Malāmatīya the basest aspect of the ego-self.

24. Abū Bakr al-Wāsiṭī was among the earliest people to associate with al-Junayd and Abū al-Ḥusayn al-Nūrī. He moved to Khurasan at an early age where he began to teach the doctrines of Sufism. *Ṭabaqāt al-sūfīya,* 302-06.

25. The misarranged section from B ends here from folio 20/b line 12 [*mashā*]/*hidhim.*

26. Al-Qushayrī relates the same saying from Abū Bakr al-Wāsiṭī, but his additions clarify the rather unclear wording of both manuscripts used in the critical edition. For clarity's sake I have completed the saying in brackets from *al-Risālat al-qushayrīya.* Both manuscripts have the verb 'to lecture' or 'speak' in the passive, while *al-Risālat al-qushayrīya* employs the active voice, which is how I have translated it. *al-Risāla al-qushayrīya* 439-40.

27. Abū al-'Abbās al-Dīnawarī (d. 340/951) was originally from Iraq where he frequented many of the *mashā'ikh* of Baghdad, among them Ibn al-'Aṭā' and Ruwaym. He later came to Nishapur and then went to Samarqand and died there. *Ṭabaqāt al-sūfīya,* 475-78.

28. This saying is mentioned in *al-Risālat al-qushayrīya* with the addition: "[they call] turning back to the world 'arrival'(*wuṣūl*), baseness of character 'fervour' (*ṣawla*); avarice 'steadfastness' (*jallāda*)." *al-Risālat al-qushayrīya,* 413.

29. Abū Bakr al-Rāzī, Muḥammad ibn 'Abdallāh ibn 'Abd al-'Azīz ibn Shādhān (d. 376/986) was one of the most frequently used direct sources of Sulamī. Abū Bakr al-Rāzī was a well known traveler and collector of the sayings and stories of the Sufis. He came to Nishapur in 340/950 and was well received by the community there. He associated with the *fuqarā'* and frequented their meetings. *Ṭabaqāt al-ṣūfīya,* introduction 18-19.

30. I have translated *qadr al-nafs* as 'the true merit of the ego-self,' based upon the context of the saying, which is that vanity blinds one to the true nature of the ego-self, i.e. blinding it to its baseness.

31. Literally, this means while not *putting himself* in a position wherein one has need of him.

32. Ḥātim al-Aṣamm from Balkh (d. 230/844) was among the earliest *mashā'ikh* of Khurasan. He associated with Shaqīq ibn Ibrāhīm [al-Balkhī] and was the teacher of Aḥmad ibn al-Ḥaḍrawayah. *Ṭabaqāt al-ṣūfīya,* 91-97.

33. The verb here is RF'A, in the passive, which means to be taken up. This has a two-fold meaning: 1) it is accepted by God; and 2) it is removed from the 'earthly realm of existence' and thus disappears from one's regard. Both meanings are implied here. This citation was cited in *Risālat al-malāmatīya,* 110.

34. Dhahabī, *Siyar a'lām al-nubalā',* vol. 14, 547-548.

35. Abū Bakr Muḥammad ibn Aḥmad al-Farrā' (d. 370/980) was one of the great mashā'ikh of Nishapur. He associated with Abū 'Alī al-Thaqafī (d. 328/940) and Ibn Munāzil (d. 331/943) [both disciples of Ḥamdūn al-Qaṣṣār (d. 271/884). *Ṭabaqāt al-ṣūfīya* 507-8. Aḥmad al-Farrā' was one of Sulamī's direct sources for his narrations on the teachings of the Malāmatīya. In *Risālat al-malāmatīya* he narrates 46 citations from him.

36. Abū Bakr al-Shāshī al-Ḥakīm (d. 360/971) was the *shaykh* of the Shāfi'īya of his time in Nishapur, he was unique in his knowledge of jurisprudence, Qur'ānic commentary, and Arabic. Sulamī was his student and narrated hadith from him. Ibn Sharība cites al-Shāshī among the teachers of Sulamī. *Ṭabaqāt al-ṣūfīya,* introduction 23.

37. 'Abdallāh ibn Munāzil, among the most illustrious *mashā'ikh* of Nishapur (d. 328/943), was a major disciple of Ḥamdūn al-Qaṣṣār. *Ṭabaqāt al-ṣūfīya,* 366-69. Al-Qushayrī referred to Ibn Munāzil as "Shaykh of the Malāmatīya, unique in his time." *Risālat al-qushayrīya,* 435. Sulamī's father had known Ibn Munāzil; see Introduction, note 7.

38. Abū Sulayman al-Dārānī (d. 215/830) was among the earliest and best-known *mashā'ikh* of Syria. *Ṭabaqāt al-ṣūfīya,* 75-82.

39. Knowing that self-directed action must always be a result of ego-oriented choice, the Malāmatīya stressed the insufficiency of the aspirant in attaining any state whatsoever through self-directed action. This statement on the part of Sulamī is an essential expression of this attitude of *malāma.* We also have here the basis of the foundational requirement of aspiration, *tark al-tadbīr* (the renunciation of self-directed action). Reminiscent of Sulamī's statement here is the saying of Abū Ḥafṣ who, when he was asked about the means by which the *faqīr* drew near his Lord, said, "The *faqīr* has nothing with which to draw near his Lord but his *faqr.*" *al-Risālat al-qushayarīya,* 274.

40. Abū al-Qāsim Ja'far ibn Muḥammad al-Rāzī. Sulamī narrates of him, " There was no one during his time that was more knowledgeable of this Path than he. He was the master of my teacher Abū al-Qāsim al-Rāzī." Al-Sulamī, *Ṭārīkh al-ṣūfīya,* cited by Abū Nu'aym, *Ṭārīkh Baghdād* vol. 4, 361. (Cited by Ibn Sharība. *Ṭabaqāt al-ṣūfīya,* introduction 21.)

41. Yaḥya ibn Mu'ādh (d. 258/871) was an early teacher of Khurasan. He died in Nishapur. *Ṭabaqāt al-ṣūfīya,* 107-14.

42. Hamdūn al-Qaṣṣār (d. 271/884), was the *Shaykh* of the Malāmatīya of Nishapur. See Introduction, note 55.

43. Khayr al-Nassāj (d. 322/933) was originally from Rayy but he settled in Baghdad. He associated with al-Nūrī, al-Junayd, and Ibn 'Aṭā'. *Ṭabaqāt al-ṣūfīya,* 322-25.

44. Abū 'Alī al-Rūdhbārī (d. 322/933) was from Baghdad, then settled in Egypt. He became the *Shaykh* of Egypt and died there. *Ṭabaqāt al-ṣūfīya,* 354-60.

45. In *al-Luma' fī al-taṣawwuf,* ed. Nicholson, this narrative was reported as: "Because they are a people who gain not in acquiring [possessions] since God is their need, nor does need (*fāqa*) harm them since God is their sustenance." 48.

46. Abū al-'Abbās ibn 'Aṭā' al-Ādamī (d. 309/921) was among the *mashā'ikh* of the Sufis of Baghdad. He associated with Ibrāhīm al-Māristānī and al-Junayd. Abū Sa'īd al-Kharrāz held him in high esteem. *Ṭabaqāt al-ṣūfīya,* 265-72.

47. Abū Ya'qūb al-Nahrajūrī (d. 330/941) from Iraq. He associated with al-Junayd and 'Amar ibn 'Uthmān al-Makkī. He spent the end of his life in Makka. He was highly esteemed by Abū 'Uthmān al-Maghribī who said, "I have not seen among our *mashā'ikh* anyone with more light than al-Nahrajūrī." *Ṭabaqāt al-ṣūfīya,* 378-81.

48. Bishr al-Ḥārith (d. 220/835) was from Merv in Iraq. He lived and died in Baghdad and frequented Fudayl ibn ʻAyyāḍ. *Ṭabaqāt al-ṣūfīya,* 39-47.

49. Yūsuf ibn al-Ḥusayn al-Rāzī (d. 304/916) was the *Shaykh* of al-Rayy and the mountains of Iraq in his time. He was unique in his path for his denouncement of seeking rank, forsaking of affectation, and the practice of sincerity. He associated with Dhū al-Nūn al-Misrī, Abū Turāb al-Nakhshabī, and he accompanied Abū Sa'īd al-Kharrāz on some of his journeys. *Ṭabaqāt al-ṣūfīya,* 185-91.

50. *Munāwalatan,* refers to the practice of giving a student a manuscript along with the authority to transmit it. This was not a common practice in the early days (M. M. Azami, *Studies in Hadith Methodology and Literature* (Indianapolis: American Trust Publications, 1977) 20. Also see Muḥammad Z. Ṣiddīqī, Hadith Literature, *Its Origin, Development, and Special Features,* ed. Abdal Hakim Murad (Cambridge: The Islamic Texts Society, 1993) 86.

51. Al-Sarī al-Saqaṭī (d. 251/865) was the uncle and teacher of al-Junayd. He associated with Ma'rūf al-Karkhī. Al-Sarī al-Saqaṭī was the first person in Baghdad to speak of the inner meanings of divine unity (*tawḥīd*) and the realization of spiritual states. He is the *Imām* of the Sufis of Baghdad and their *mashā'ikh* of his day. *Ṭabaqāt al-ṣūfīya,* 48-55.

52. Shaqīq al-Balkhī (d. 194/809) was among the first and most renown of the *mashā'ikh* of Khurasan. Sulamī believes he was the first to speak of the science of spiritual states in the region of Khurasan. He was the master of Ḥātim al-Aṣamm. He associated with Ibrāhīm Adham and took his path from him. *Ṭabaqāt al-ṣūfīya,* 61-66.

53. Abū Ḥafṣ of Nishapur (d. 270/883) was known as one of the *mashā'ikh* of the Malāmatīya of Nishapur. He was the teacher of Abū 'Uthmān al-Ḥīrī (*Ṭabaqāt al-ṣūfīya,* 115-22). See Introduction, Note 44.

54. One's dues are the obligations that a person may feel others owe them, whether it is in the guise of people's attitudes towards them or what one feels is owed them on account of their standing or station. This tenet is well represented in all the early works on Sufism. A well-known example of this attitude, as well as an example of the dialogue that tended to take place between the Malāmatīya and the Sufis of Iraq is the following story. In this story Abū Ḥafṣ was asked by the Sufi teachers of Baghdad about *futūwah,* or spiritual chivalry. He replied, "You speak [first]! For you are known for your eloquence." To this al-Junayd replied, "*Futūwah* is renunciation of self-regard and disavowal of secondary causes." Abū Ḥafṣ remarked that al-Junayd had spoken well but that for him, "*Futūwah* was acting justly towards others, while not demanding that others act justly towards you." *Ṭabaqāt al-ṣūfīya,* 118. In *Kashf al-Maḥjūb* one finds the saying, "The *faqīr* is not someone whose hand is empty of provisions, but rather a *faqīr* is someone who is empty of desire." *"Laysa al-faqīr man khalā min al-zād, innamā al-faqīr man khalā min al-murād." Kashf al-maḥjūb,* 25.

55. Ruwaym ibn Aḥmad ibn Yazīd (d. 303/915) was from Baghdad and among the most illustrious of the *mashā'ikh* of Baghdad. *Ṭabaqāt al-ṣūfīya,* 180-84.

56. Muḥammad ibn al-Faḍl al-Balkhī and al-Samarqandī are one person . See note 10, *Zalal.*

57. Muḥammad ibn Abī al-Ward (d. 263/876) was among the greatest and most illustrious of the masters of Iraq. He was among the associates of al-Junayd. *Ṭabaqāt al-ṣūfīya,* 249-53.

58. For misplaced text from B see from folio 28/b line 10, [*lā yabtalī* ...] to folio 30/a line 4, [*al-'adb bi masāwī ah-nās*].

59. Maḥfūḍ ibn Maḥmūd (d. 304/916) of Nishapur was among the disciples of Abū Ḥafṣ; and after the death of Abū Ḥafṣ he remained with Abū 'Uthmān the rest of his life. He was one of the most scrupulous of *mashā'ikh* and the most constant of them in the precepts of their path. He had also associated with Ḥamdūn al-Qaṣṣār, Salim al-Bārūsī and 'Alī al-Naṣrābādhī as well as others among the *mashā'ikh. Ṭabaqāt al-ṣūfīya,* 273-74.

60. Abū Bakr Muḥammad ibn Ḥāmid al-Tirmidhī was one of the most illustrious *mashā'ikh* of Khurasan. He associated with Aḥmad ibn Ḥaḍrawayah. *Ṭabaqāt al-ṣūfīya,* 280-83.

61. Abū al-Ḥasan al-Būshanjī (d. 340/951) was one of the followers of *futūwah* in Khurasan. He met Abū 'Uthmān, and in Iraq he associated with Ibn 'Atā', while in Syria Abū 'Amr al-Dimashqī. *Ṭabaqāt al-ṣūfīya,* 458-61.

62. For misplaced text from B see from folio 28/b line 10, [*wa yakūnu al-khalq...*] to folio 30/a line 4, [*al-ikhawān wa al-murāfiqīn...*].

63. Abū Turāb al-Nakhshabī, see *Spiritual Stations*, note 19.

64. Narrated by Ibn Ḥanbal, vol. 2, 248, 376, 427, 414, and 443; *Sunan Abū Dawūd*, vol. 4, 350 (*ḥadīth* 4090); *Ibn Māja*, vol. 2, 1397, (ḥadīth 4174, 4175). In the sources indexed in Wensinck, the last clause is given as, "I shall throw him in the Fire" or into Gehenna". (cited by Maḥmūd Muṣṭafā Ḥalāwī in his edition of *Minhāj al-'ābidīn* by Abū Ḥamīd al-Ghazālī (Beirut: Mu'assasa al-Risāla, 1989) 380.

65. Sahl ibn 'Abdallāh, see *Spiritual Stations*, note 17.

66. Al-Sulamī, *Sulūk al-'ārifīn* in *Tis'at kutub*, 391-408.

67. Each of the four manuscripts used to establish the translation of this phrase have slight textual variants. I have based my translation on the earliest manuscript (Baku) as the least problematic and that which accords best with the subject matter of this section. Key to understanding my translation here is the use of *rifq* to mean 'sustenance'. See note 6 for the text of *Tadhallul al-fuqarā'*.

68. The misarranged section from B ends here from folio 28/b line 10 [*wa yakūnu al-khalq...ā*].

69. A situation in which he is assured that he is not imposing on the one hand while being confident of the permissible nature of the sustenance on the other.

70. These sessions refer to the gatherings in which devotional and love poetry is recited with the intention of deepening the state of the listener, and opening his or her heart to the inner aspects of striving for God. There has been much debate over the status of such gatherings. This disagreement may occur between Sufis and more exoterically oriented Islamic scholars who accuse the Sufis of innovation, but the views of the Sufis themselves have differed from one another since the earliest times. Sulamī wrote a treatise devoted to the subject entitled: *Kitāb al-samā'*, ed. 'Alī 'Aqalih 'Arsān, *Journal al-Tawrāth al-'Arabī*. Kuwait, 1985, vol. 1, 80-94. The unedited work, *Kitāb maḥāsin al-taṣawwuf*, manuscript 1027 *qaf*, fol. 197a-212b, Bibliothèque Nationale, Rabat, The Kingdom of Morocco, also by Sulamī deals to a large extent with the issue of *samā'* and for whom and when attendance of such sessions is permissible or reprehensible. In *Ghalaṭāt al-sūfīya*, Sulamī concisely presents his view on *samā'*, a view that to a large extent, has been followed by Sulamī's predecessors among the teachers of Sufism. He writes:

> [Among the Sufis] a group has mistakenly assumed that *taṣawwuf* is making utterances (*qawl*), ecstatic dancing (*raqṣ*), participation in sessions of listening to the

> melodic recitation of poetry and making pretentious claims and exaggerated expenditures on gatherings. [They have come to this conclusion] because they saw some of the worthy elders enjoying sessions of *samāʿ* from time to time. Such as these are mistaken for they do not know that every heart is polluted with something of the mundane. [Therefore] *samāʿ* is ill advised (*makrūḥ)* for any frivolous heedless ego-self (*nafs*); or moreover, it is not permissible (*harām*). The latter opinion is the most authoritative. Junayd—May the God be pleased with him—said to someone who has asked him about *samāʿ*. "When you see a disciple attracted to *samāʿ*, know that there remains in him (*fī nafsihi*) something of frivolity,"

Al-Sulamī, *Uṣūl al-malāmatīya wa ghalaṭāt al-ṣūfīya*, ed. ʿAbd al-Fattāḥ Aḥmad al-Fāwī Maḥmūd (Cairo: Maṭbaʿ al-Irshād, 1975) 174.

71. Completed with the Praise of God, and His Most Excellent help. May God bless His Prophet and Servant, our Master Muḥammad. May He bless his family and companions. Upon them be salutations of abounding peace! Ibn Yūsuf Manuscript 187/b.

Faqr is a fabric, the warp of which is contentment (*qanāʿa*) [with God], and the weft of which is humble submission (*al-tawāḍuʿ*).

A *faqīr* will have never totally complied with the obligations of *faqr* until he has renounced what is due him.

The root of enmity lies in three things: coveting possessions, coveting deference, and desire for the approval of others.

BIBLIOGRAPHY

The Message of the Holy *Qur'ān*. Translated and explained by Muḥammad Asad. Gibralter: Dar al-Andalus, 1984.

Abdelkader, A. H. *The Life, Personality and Writings of al-Junayd*. Gibb Memorial Fund 14, London: Luzac, 1962.

Addas, C. *Ibn 'Arabī ou La quête du Soufre Rouge*. Paris: Gallimard, 1989.

Algar, Hamid. *The Path of God's Bondsman from Origin to Return*. A Sufi Compendium by Najm al-Dīn Rāzī. Trans. and intro. Delmar, New York: Caravan Books, 1982.

———. "Malāmatīya-in Iran and the Eastern Lands." *EI* 2nd ed. Leiden: E. J. Brill, 1954. VI. 224-225.

———. "Reflections of Ibn 'Arabī in Early Naqshbandi Tradition." *Journal of Ibn 'Arabī Society* vol. 10 (1991): 45-66.

———. "Elements de Provenance Malāmatī dans la Tradition Primitive Naqshbandī." *Des actes du colloque sur les Melâmlis et les Bayrâmis* organizé à Istambul (4-6 juin 1987) par l'Institut Français d'Études Anatoliennes. 1-22.

Arberry, A. J. *Muslim Saints and Mystics: Episodes from the Tadhkirat al-Awliya' (Memorial of the Saints) by Farid al-Din Attar*. London, 1979.

———. "Al-Sulamī." SEI. Leiden: E. J. Brill, 1953. 551.

———. *Sufism: An Account of the Mystics of Islam*. London: Unwin, 1979.

Awn, Peter J. "Sufism—Malāmatīya." *Encyclopedia of Religion*. Ed. Mircea Eliade. New York: Macmillan1987. vol. 14, 104-122.

Azami, Muḥammad M. *Studies in Hadith Methodology and Literature*. Indianapolis: American Trust Publications, 1977.

Baldick, J. *Mystical Islam, An Introduction to Sufism*. New York: University of New York Press, 1989.

Baldick, J. *Imaginary Muslims, Uwaysi Sufis of Central Asia, The*. New York: University of New York Press, 1993.

Ben Stapa, Zakaria. "A Brief Survey and Analytical Discussion on the Origins and the Nature of Sufism." *Hamdard Islamicus* 12 (1989): 75-91.

Bosworth, Edmund. *The Ghaznavids, Their Empire in Afghanistan and Eastern Iran 994:1040*. Edinburgh: University of Edinburgh Press, 1963.

———. "The Early Ghaznavids." *The Cambridge History of Iran*. Ed. R. N. Frye. Cambridge: Cambridge University Press, 1975. vol. 4, 162-197.

———. "Karrāmiyya." *EI* 2nd ed. Leiden: E. J. Brill, 1954. vol. 6, 667-669.

———. "The Rise of the Karāmiyya in Khurasan." *The Muslim World* 50 (1960): 23-14.

———. "An Early Persian Ṣūfī Shaykh, Abī Ṣa'īd of Mayhanah." *Logos Islamikos, Studia Islamica in Honorem Georgii Michaelis Wickens*. Edited by Roger M. Savory and Dionisius A. Agius. Toronto: Pontifical Institute of Mediaeval Studies, 1984. 79-96.

———. "The Ṭāharids and the Ṣaffārids." *The Cambridge History of Iran*. Ed. R. N. Frye. Cambridge: Cambridge University Press, 1975. vol. 4, 90-135.

Böwering, G. "The Qur'ān Commentary of al-Sulamī." *Islamic studies presented to Charles J. Adams*. Edited by Wael B. Hallaq and Donald P. Little. Leiden: E. J. Brill, 1991. 41-56.

Brown, John P. *The Darvishes, or Oriental Spiritualism*. London: Frank Cass, 1968; first edition, 1868.

Bukhārī, Muḥammad ibn Ismā'īl. *al-Jāmī 'al-Ṣaḥīḥ*. Cairo, 1309 A.H.

Burckhardt, Titus. *An Introduction to Sufi Doctrine*. Translated by D. M. Matheson. Lahore: Sh. Muḥammad Ashraf, 1959.

Chabbi, Jacqueline. "Remarques sur le développement historique des mouvements ascétiques et mystiques au Khurasan." *Studia Islamica* 46 (1977): 5-72.

———. "Réflexions Sur le Soufisme Iranien Primitif." *Journal Asiatique* 266 (1978): 37-55.

Chittick, William C. *The Sufi Path of Love: The Spiritual teachings of Rumi*. Albany: State University of New York Press, 1983.

———. *The Sufi Path of Knowledge*. Albany: State University of New York Press, 1989.

———. "Ibn 'Arabī and His School." *Islamic Spirituality: Manifestations*. Edited by Seyyed Hossein Nasr. New York: Crossroads, 1991. 49-79.

Chodkiewicz, Michel. *An Ocean Without Shore. Ibn 'Arabi, The Book, and the Law*. Translated by David Streight. New York: University of New York Press, 1993.

———. *Le Sceau des saints, Prophétie et sainteté dans la doctrine d'Ibn 'Arabī*. Paris: Gallimard, 1986.

———. Awhad al-Din Balyānī, *Épître Sur L'Unicité Absolue.* (intro. and trans.) Paris: Duex Oceḳan, 1982.

———. Review of "Sulamī: La Lucidité implacable, Épître des hommes du blâme." (intro. and trans. Roger Deladrière), Studia Islamica 76 (1992): 193-195.

Cornell, Rkia E. *Early Sufi Women, Dhikr an-niswa al-muta'ābbidāt aṣ-ṣūfiyyāt.* (intro. and trans.) Louisville: Vons Vitae, 1999.

Danner, Victor. *Ibn 'Aṭā'allah's Sūfī Aphorisms, (Kitāb al-ḥikam).* Translated with an introduction and notes. Leiden: E. J. Brill, 1973.

———. "The Early Development of Sufism." In *Islamic Spirituality: Foundations.* Edited by Seyyed Hossein Nasr. New York: Crossroads, 1987. 239-264.

———. "The Shādhilliyyah and North African Sufism." In *Islamic Spirituality: Manifestations.* Edited by Seyyed Hossein Nasr. New York: Crossroads, 1991. 26-48.

De Jong, F. "Malāmatīya-In the Central Islamic Lands." *EI* 2nd ed. Leiden: E. J. Brill, 1954. vol. 6, 223-224.

Deladrière, R. *La Lucidité Implacable,* (intro. and trans.) *Épître des Hommes du Blâme,* by Abū 'Abd al-Raḥmān al-Sulamī. Paris: Arléa, 1991.

———. "Les premiers Malāmatiyya: les Gardiens du Secret." *Des actes du colloque sur les Melâmis et les Bayrâmis* organizé à Istambul (4-6 juin 1987) par l'Institut Français d'Études Anatoliennes. 1-25.

Dermengham, E. *Vies des Saints Musulmans.* (Edition Definitive). Paris, 1983

Dhahabī, Muḥammad ibn Aḥmad, al-. *Siyar a'lām al-nubalā'.* Edited by S. al-Arnā'ūṭ. Beirut: Mu'assasat al-Risāla, 1412/1992.

Encyclopedia of Islam, The. Edited by M Houtsma . Leiden: E. J. Brill, 1927. 2nd Edited by J. H. Kramers, H. A. R. Gibb *et al.* Leiden: E. J. Brill, 1954.

Ernst, Carl W. *Words of Ecstasy in Sufism.* Albany: State University of New York Press, 1985.

Ghazālī, Abū Ḥāmid Muḥammad ibn Muḥammad, al-. *Iḥyā' 'ulūm al-dīn.* Cairo, 1347 A. H.

———. *al-Munqidh min al-ḍalāl wa al-mūṣil ilā dhi al-'izzat wa-al-jalāl.* Arabic edition, translated into French by Farid Jabre. Beirut: Librairie Orientale, 1959.

Gibb, Hamilton A. R. *Studies on the Civilization of Islam.* Edited by Stanford J. Shaw and William R. Polk. Princeton, New Jersey: Princeton University Press, 1962.

Glassé, C. *Concise Encyclopaedia of Islam, The*. San Francisco: Harper Row, 1989.

Graham, Terry. "Abū Sa'īd ibn Abī al-Khayr and the School of Khurasan." *Classical Persian Sufism: from its Origins to Rumi*. Edited by Leonard Lewisohn. London, New York: Khaniqahi Nimatullahi Publications, 1993, 83-135.

Gril, Denis. "Le terme du voyage." *Les Illuminations de La Mecque: The Meccan illuminations, selected texts*. Edited by Michel Chodkiewicz. Paris: Sindibad, 1988.

———. "Adab and Revelation, or One of the Foundations of the Hermeneutics of Ibn 'Arabī." *Muhyiddin Ibn 'Arabī: A Commemorative Volume*. Edited by Stephen Hirtenstein and Michael Tierman. Rockport: Element, 1993. 228-263.

Hājjī Khalīfa. *Kashf aẓ-ẓunūn 'alā asāmī al-kutub wa al-funūn*. Beirut, nd.

Hākim al-Nishabūrī, al-. *al-Mustadrak 'alā al-ṣaḥiḥayn*. Beirut: Dār al-Kutub al-'Ilmīya, nd.

Hartmann, R. "As-Sulamī's Risālat al-Malāmatīya." *Der Islam* 8, (1918): 157-203.

Hodgson, Marshall G. S. *The Venture of Islam*. Chicago, London: The University of Chicago Press, 1974.

Holbrook, Victoria Rowe. "Ibn 'Arabi and Ottoman Dervish Traditions: The Melāmī Supra-Order," Part one. *Journal of the Muhyiddin Ibn 'Arabi Society* 9 (1991): 18-35.

———. "Ibn 'Arabi and Ottoman Dervish Traditions: The Melāmī Supra-Order", Part two. *Journal of the Muhyiddin Ibn 'Arabi Society* 12 (1992): 15-33.

Hujwīrī, 'Ali ibn 'Uthmān al-. *The "Kashf al-maḥjūb" The Oldest Persian Treatise on Sufism by al-Hujwiri*. Translated by Reynold A. Nicholson. Gibb Memorial Series, no. 17. 1911. Reprint. London, 1976.

Ibn 'Abbād, al-Rundī. *Sharḥ al-ḥikam*. Cairo, 1289 AH.

———. *Letters on the Sūfī Path*. (*Rasā'il al-ṣughrā*) intro. and trans. John Renard. New York: Paulist Press (1986).

Ibn 'Arabī, Muḥyi al-Dīn. *al-Futūḥāt al-makkīya*. Cairo, 1329 A.H.

———. *Risālat al-anwār*. In *Rasā'il Ibn 'Arabī*. Hyderabad: Maṭba'at Jam'īyat Dār'rat al-Ma'ārif al-'Uthmānīya, 1361/1948; reprint Beirut: Dār Iḥyā' al-Turāth al-'Arabī, nd.

———. *Kitāb al-tajalliyāt*. In *Rasā'il Ibn 'Arabī*. Hyderabad, 1361/1948; reprint Beirut: Dār Iḥyā', Vol. II, treatise 23, 1-53.

———. *Le Livre de L'Extinction dans La Contemplation*. Translated by Michel Vâlsan. Paris: Les Editions de l'Oeuvre, 1984.

Ibn 'Aṭā Allāh al-Iskandarī, Taj al-Din, Aḥmad. *Laṭāif al-minan fī manāqib Abī al-'Abbās al-Mursī wa shaykhihi Abī al-Ḥasan al-Shādhlī*. Edited by Khālid 'Abd al-Raḥmān al-'Ak. Damascus: Dār al-Bashā'ir, 1992.

———.. *La Sagesse Des Maîtres Soufis*. Translated and presented by Eric Geoffroy. Paris: Bernard Grasset, 1998.

———. *Kitab al-tanwīr fī 'isqāt al-tadbīr*. Cairo, 1281 A.H.

———. *Ibn 'Aṭā Allāh de Alejandriḳa: Sobre el abandono de su mismo*. Trans. *Kitab al-tanwīr* by Gonzâlez, Juan José. Madrid: Lirbos Hiperión, 1994.

———. *Ṣūfī Aphorisms, (Kitāb al-ḥikam)*. Trans. Victor Danner. Leiden: E. J. Brill, 1973.

Ibn Ḥanbal, Aḥmad ibn Muḥammad. *al-Musnad*. Cairo, 1313 A.H.

———. *Kitāb al-Zuhd*. Beirut, 1403/1983.

Ibn al-Jawzī. *Talbīs Iblīs*. Cairo, 1352 A.H.

Ibn Mājah, Abū 'Abd Allāh Muḥammad ibn Yazīd al-Qazwīynī. *Sunnan ibn Mājah*. Cairo, 1952.

Ibn al-Mulaqqin, Sirāj al-Dīn Abū Ḥafṣ 'Umar ibn 'Alī. *Ṭabaqāt al-awlīyā'*. Edited by Nūr al-Dīn Sharība. Cairo: Dār al-Ma'rifa, 1973.

Imber, C.H. "Malāmatīya-In Ottoman Turkey." *EI* 2nd ed. Leiden: E. J. Brill, 1954. vol. 6. 225-228.

Inalcik, Halil. *The Ottoman Empire, The Classical Age 1300-1600*. Translated by Norman Itzkowitz and Colin Imber. London: Weidenfeld and Nicolson, 1973.

Iṣbahānī, Abū Nu'aym, al-. *Ḥilyat al-awliyā' wa-ṭabaqāt al-aṣfīyā'*. Cairo, 1351-7/1932-8.

Jāmī, 'Abd al-Raḥmān al-. *Nafahāt al-uns*, ed. M. Tawhidipur. Tehran, 1918.

Kalābādhī, Abū Bakr Muḥammad, al-. *Ta'arruf li-madhhab ahl al-taṣawwuf*. Cairo, 1980.

Karamustafa, Ahmet T. *God's Unruly Friends: Dervish Groups in the Islamic Later Middle Period 1200-1550*. Salt Lake City: University of Utah Press, 1994.

———. *Sufism: The Formative Period*, Edinburgh: Edinburgh University Press, 2007.

Kharkūshī, 'Abd al-Malik ibn Muḥammad, *Kitāb tahdhīb al-asrār fī uṣūl al-taṣawwuf*, ed. Imām Seyyid Muḥammad 'Alī, Beirut: Dār al-Kutub al-'Ilmīya, 2006.

Kharrāz, Abū Sa'īd, al-. *Kitāb al-Ṣidq*. Cairo: Dar al-Kutub al-Ḥadītha, 1975.

Lings, Martin. *A Sufi Saint of the Twentieth Century*. Cambridge: The Islamic Text Society, 1993; third edition.

Laoust, Henri. "La Classification des sectes dans le *Farq* d'al- Baghdadī" *Revue des Études Islamiques* 29 (1961): 19-59.

Makdisi, George. "Hanbalite Islam." *Studies in Islam*. Edited by Merlin Swartz. New York, Oxford: Oxford University Press, 1981. 216-274.

Makkī, Abū Ṭālib, al-. *Qūt al-qulūb fī mu'āmalāt al-maḥbūb wa-waṣf ṭarīqa al-murīd ilā maqām al-tawḥīd*. Cairo, 1310 A.H.

Malamud, Margaret. "Sufi Organisations and Structure of Authority in Medieval Nishapur." *International Journal of Middle East Studies* 26: (1994): 427-442.

Massignon, Louis, *The Passion of Hallāj, Mystic and Martyr of Islam*, trans. Herbert Mason, Princeton: Princeton University Press, 1982.

Meier, Fritz. "Khurāsan and the End of Classical Sufism" in *Essays on Islamic Piety and Mysticism*. Ed. and trans. John O'Kane, Leiden: Brill, (1999) 189-219.

Molé, M. *Les Mystiques musulman*. Paris: Presses Universitaires de France, 1965.

———. Autour du Daré Mansour: "L'apprentissage Mystique de Bahā al-Din Naqshband," *Revue des Étude Islamique* 27 (1959): 35-66.

Muḥāsibī, al-Ḥarith, al-. *Kitāb al-Ri'āya li-ḥuqāq Allāh*. Edited by 'Abd al-Ḥalīm Maḥmūd. Cairo, 1967.

———. *Kitāb al-tawahhum*, ed. A. J. Arberry. Cairo, 1937.

Muslim, Ibn al-Ḥajjāj al-Qushayrī al-Naysābūrī. *Ṣaḥīḥ muslim*. Beirut: Dar Iḥyā' al-Tawrāth al-'Arabī, 1956.

Nasr, Seyyed Hossien. "Sufism and Spirituality in Persian". In *Islamic Spirituality: Manifestations*. Edited by Seyyed Hossein Nasr, New York: Crossroads. 1991. 206-222.

———. "Spiritual Chivalry." *Islamic Spirituality: Manifestations*. Edited by Seyyed Hossein Nasr. New York: Crossroads, 1991. 304-318.

Nabhānī, Yūsuf ibn Ismā'īl, al-. *Jāmi' karāmāt al-awliyā'*. Edited by 'Iwaḍ, Ibrāhīm ibn Aṭwa. Cairo, 1394 A.H.

Nicholson, R.A. *Studies in Islamic Mysticism*. Cambridge: Cambridge University Press, 1921. 2nd ed. 1967.

Nizami, K. A. "The Naqshbandiyyah Order." *Islamic Spirituality: Manifestations*. Edited by Seyyed Hossein Nasr. New York: Crossroads, 1991. 162-193.

Nurbaksh, Javad. *Spiritual Poverty in Sufism*. London: Khaniqahi-Nimatullahi Publications, 1984.

Norris, H. T. *Islam in the Balkans: Religion and Society between Europe and the Arab World*. University of South Carolina Press, 1993.

Nwyia, Paul S. J. *Ibn 'Abbād De Ronda*. Beirut, 1956.

———. *Ibn 'Aṭā' Allah et la Naissance de la Confrérie Chādhilite*. Beirut: Imprimerie Catholique, 1986.

———. *Ibn 'Abbād de Ronda (1332-1390)*. Beirut: Imprimerie Catholique, 1956.

Popovic, A. and Veinstein, G. *Les Ordres Mystiques Dans L'Islam: Cheminements et situation actuelle*. Paris: Edition de l'École des Hautes Études en Science Sociale, 1990.

Qushayrī, Abū al-Qāsim, al-. *al-Risāla fī 'ilm al-taṣawwuf*. Edited by Ma'rūf Zarīq and 'Alī 'Abd al-Ḥamīd Bilṭajī. Beirut: Dār al-Khayr, 1993.

———. *Sharḥ asmā' Allāh al-ḥusnā*. Beirut, 1986.

Renard, John. "Al-Jihad al-Akbar: Notes on a Theme in Islamic Spirituality." *The Muslim World* 78, nos. 3-4 (1988): 225-242.

Sarrāj, Abū Naṣr al-. *Kitāb al-luma' fī al-taṣawwuf*. Edited by R. A. Nicholson. London: Luzac, 1963.

Siddiqi, Muhammad Z. *Hadīth Literature: Its Origin, Development and Special Features*. Edited by Abdal Hakim Murad. Cambridge: The Islamic Text Society, 1993.

Seale, Morris S. "The Ethics of Malāmatīya Sufism and the Sermon of the Mount." *Moslem World* 58 (1968): 12-23.

Sezgin, F. *Geschichte des arabischen Schrifttums*. Leiden, 1967-.

Sh'arānī, 'Abd al-Wahhāb ibn Aḥmad ibn 'Alī al-Anṣārī, al-. *Ṭabaqāt al-kubarā*. Cairo: Muṣṭafā al-Bābī al-Ḥalabī, 1954.

Schimmel, Annemarie. *Mystical Dimensions of Islam*. Chapel Hill: The University of North Carolina Press, 1975.

———. "Sufism and Spiritual Life in Turkey." *Islamic Spirituality: Manifestations*. Edited by Seyyed Hossein Nasr. New York: Crossroads, 1991). 223-232.

Subkī, Tāj al-Dīn, al-. *Ṭabaqāt al-Shāfi'īya al-Kubrā*. Cairo, 1324 A.H.

Sulamī, Abū 'Abd al-Raḥmān, al-. *Risālat al-malāmatīya*. Ed. and intro. Abū al'Alā al-'Afifi. Cairo: Dār Iḥyā' al-Kutub al'Arabīya, 1945.

Sulamī, Abū 'Abd al-Raḥmān, al-. *Ṭabaqāt al-ṣufīya*. Ed. Nūr al-Din Sharība. Cairo: Maktaba al-Khānajī, 1969.

———. *Darjāt al-Ṣādiqīn*. Ed. Süleymān Ateş in *Tis'at kutub li-Abī 'Abd al-Raḥmān Muḥammad b. al-Ḥusayn b. Mūsā al-Sulamī*. Ankara: University of Ankara, 1981.

———. *Kitāb al-'arba'īn fī al-taṣawwuf*. With *Takhrīj al-'arba'īn al-sulamīya fī al-taṣawwuf*, by Muḥammad ibn 'Abd al-Raḥmān ibn Muḥammad al-Sakhāwī. Beirut, 1988.

———. *Kitāb al-futuwwa. Traité de chevalerie soufie*. Translated by F. Skali. Paris: Albin Michel, 1989.

———. "*Kitāb al-Samā'*." Edited by 'Alī 'Aqalih 'Arsān. *Journal al-Tawrāth al'Arabī*. Kuwait, 1985. vol. 1, 80-94.

———. *Kitāb ādāb al-Ṣuḥba*. Edited by M. J. Kister. Jerusalem, 1954.

———. *Jawāmi' ādāb al-Ṣufiyya and 'Uyūb al-nafs wa-mudawātuhu*. Edited by E. Kohlberg. Jerusalem, 1976.

———. *Manāhij al-'ārifīn*. Ed. E. Kohlberg. Jerusalem, 1979.

———. *Manāhij al-'ārifīn*. Ed. Süleymān Ateş in *Tis'at kutub*.

———. *Darajāt al-mu'āmalāt*. Ed. Süleymān Ateş in *Tis'at kutub*.

———. *Jawāmi' ādāb al-Ṣūfiyya*. Ed. Süleymān Ateş in *Tis'at kutub*.

———. *al-Muqaddima fī al-taṣawwuf*. Ed. Süleymān Ateş in *Tis'at kutub*.

———. *Bayān aḥwal al-Ṣūfiyya* Ed. Süleymān Ateş in *Tis'at kutub*.

———. *Mas'alat darajāt al-Ṣādiqīn*. Ed. Süleymān Ateş in *Tis'at kutub*.

———. *Sulūk al-'ārifīn*. Ed. Süleymān Ateş in *Tis'at kutub*.

———. *Bayān zilal al-fuqarā'*. Ed. Süleymān Ateş in *Tis'at kutub*.

———. *al-Muqadimma fī al-taṣawwuf*. Edited by Ḥusayn Amīn. Baghdad, 1984.

———. *Majmū a-i āṣrār-i Abū 'Abd al-Raḥmān Sulamī*, ed. Naṣr Allāh Pūrjavādī, Tehran: Markaz-i Nashr-i Dānishgāhī, 1369-1430/1980-2009, 3 vols. (vol. 3 ed. Naṣr Allāh Pūrjavādī, and Mohammad Soori).

Sviri, Sara. "Ḥakīm Tirmidhī and the Malāmatī Movement." In *Classical Persian Sufism: from its Origins to Rumi*. Edited by Leonard Lewisohn. London, New York: Khaniqahi Nimatullahi Publications, 1993, 583-613.

Tadīlī, A. *Al-Tashawwuf ilā rijāl al-taṣawwuf.* Ed. by A. Tawfiq. Rabat, 1984.

Thibon, Jean-Jaques. "Le Saint et Son Milieu ou Comment Lire les Sources Hagiographiques," ed. Rachida Chih Denis Gril. Institute Français d'archéologie orientale, cahier des annales islamologiques 19, 2000. 13-31.

Tirmidhī, Abū 'Isā Muḥammad ibn 'Isā ibn Sawrah al-. *al-Sunan al-Tirmidhī*. Beirut: Dār al-Fikr, nd.

Tirmidhī, Muḥammad, ibn 'Alī al-Ḥakīm. *The Concept of Sainthood in Early Islamic Mysticism: Two Works by Al-Ḥakīm Al-Tirmidhī*, trans. John O'Kane and Bernd Radtke, London: Routledge Curzon: 1996.

———. *Thalātha muṣannafāt li al-Ḥakīm al-Tirmidhī: Kitāb sīrat al-awliyā', Jawāb masā'il allatī sa'alahu ahl Sarakhs 'anhā, Jawāb kitāb min al-Rayy*, ed. Bernd Radtke, Beirut: 1992.

Tosun Bayrak al-Jerrahi al-Halveti. *Inspirations on the Path of Blame: Shaikh Badruddin of Simawna.* Vermont: Threshhold books, 1993.

Trimingham, J. Spencer. *The Sufi Orders in Islam.* Oxford: Clarendon Press, 1971.

BIOGRAPHY

Kenneth L. Honerkamp was born in California on July 26, 1947. He completed his early studies in philosophy in 1969, in the same year traveled to the Northwest Frontier Province of Pakistan where he studied Pasthu, Arabic grammar and Islamic law within the *madrasa*s of that region. In Pakistan he had his first encounter with Sufis and studied with them there. In 1979 he traveled to Morocco to continue his studies at the Qaraouiyyine University. This university is part of the traditional education system of Morocco in which the traditional Islamic sciences are taught by the foremost scholars in these fields. In 1981 he received his B.A. in Arabic Literature from the Qaraouiyyine with a critical edition of the *Munabbiha* by Abu Amr al-Dani, on the sciences of the *Qur'ān*. He is also a graduate of the University of Aix-en-Provence, France where he completed his Ph. D. in 1999 after having earned a Master's degree in religion from the University of Georgia at Athens in 1995.

From 1981 to 1993 he taught at the Faculté de Langue Arabe and continued his studies privately with traditional Islamic scholars of Morocco. From 1995 to 1999 he was the program coordinator of the Arabic Language Institute of Fes (ALIF). He presently holds the position of associate professor of Arabic and Islamic Studies at the University of Georgia. He has been there since 1999. He continues to be involved with Arabic manuscripts, particularly in the study and editing of collections of letters of spiritual guidance that passed between teacher and disciple. His analysis and critical edition of *The Greater Collection of the Letters of Ibn 'Abbād of Ronda* (d. 1390/1472) was published in Beirut in 2005. He is presently working on a translation of those letters for Fons Vitae.

INDEX OF PROPER NAMES

(The names in this index appear as in the texts.)

A, ‘A

F

H, Ḥ

I, 'I

J

K, KH

INDEX OF QUR'ĀNIC VERSES AND HADITH

INDEX OF HADITH AND ĀTHĀR

INDEX OF ARABIC WORDS